OFF THE BEATEN PATH™ SERIES

Mississippi

SECOND EDITION

by Marlo Carter Kirkpatrick

The Globe Pequot Press

Old Saybrook, Connecticut

Cover and text design by Laura Augustine
Cover photo by Mark Segal/Index Stock
Maps created by Equator Graphics © The Globe Pequot Press
Illustrations by Julie Lynch

Library of Congress Cataloging-in-Publication Data

Kirkpatrick, Marlo Carter.
      Mississippi : off the beaten path / Marlo Carter Kirkpatrick. — 2nd ed.
        p. cm. —(Off the beaten path series)
      Includes index.
      ISBN 0-7627-0407-1
      1. Mississippi—Guidebooks. I. Title. II. Series.
F339.3.K57   1999
917.6204'63—dc21   98-53480
                                        CIP

Manufactured in the United States of America
Second Edition/First Printing

Contents

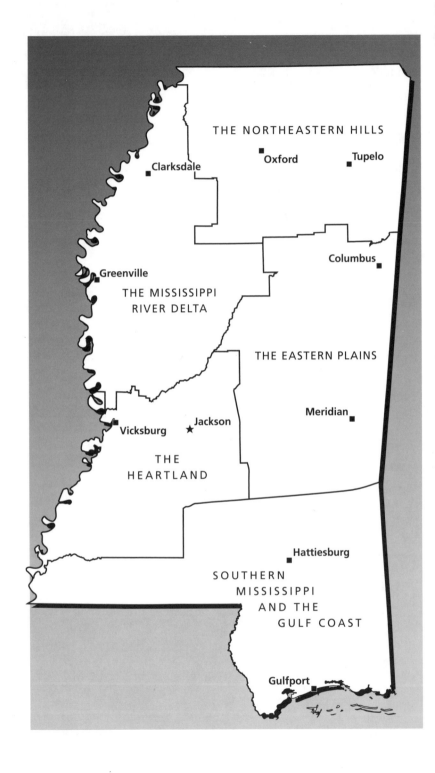

Acknowledgments

This book couldn't have been written without the insight, contributions, and enthusiastic cooperation of friends and colleagues throughout Mississippi. A heartfelt thanks is due to all of the Chamber and CVB directors who responded to my inquiries, scores of restaurant and bed-and-breakfast owners who were so accommodating, and countless local residents who petted my dog and pointed me in the right direction.

A special thanks goes to the many friends and relatives who listened patiently as I recounted my adventures off the beaten path, and to Stephen Kirkpatrick, my favorite traveling companion.

Introduction

The geography that makes up the state of Mississippi is easily defined. Rolling northern hills and wide eastern plains. The flat River Delta and the breezy Gulf Coast.

But the real essence of the state is harder to put into words, for Mississippi is not merely a landscape, but a state of mind.

Mississippi is nicknamed the "Hospitality State," and it's true that most of the people you'll meet here don't have to know your name to lend you a hand or stop and chat for a while. In fact, Mississippians seem to feel compelled to explain themselves, to make sure you leave with an enlightened view of this place they call home.

After all, perceptions of Mississippi are usually based on outdated stereotypes of "boss hog" sheriffs lying in wait for unfortunate travelers, sharecroppers dwelling in shacks without benefit of indoor plumbing, and rednecks running about the countryside clad in white sheets. Native Mississippians tend to view every out-of-state visitor as a personal crusade—they may not be able to change the whole world's opinion, but give them half a chance and by golly, they'll change yours.

Even left to your own devices, you'll soon discover the stereotypes are just that. Far from a haven for rednecks and racists, Mississippi is made up of bustling cities and quaint town squares, breathtaking natural wonders, and a rich culture like no other.

In fact, Mississippi has produced more writers, musicians, and poets per square mile than any other state. Mississippians are fond of saying, "We may not be able to read, but we sure can write." Works by William Faulkner, Eudora Welty, Richard Wright, and John Grisham would certainly seem to back up that claim. Mississippi is the birthplace of country music, the blues, and Elvis, the King of Rock 'n' Roll. Almost everything you hear on the radio has its roots in Mississippi.

And yet the state remains outside the limelight. Other than the casinos that line the Mississippi River and Mississippi Sound, the state really doesn't have any "manufactured" attractions. Things here are genuine and authentic, preserved rather than re-created. And once you've had your fill of the amusement parks and souvenir stands that make one place seem just like the last place or the next place, you'll find Mississippi a welcome change. The turnstiles and ticket takers give way to welcome mats and warmhearted people. Smoggy skylines are replaced by sweeping river views. "Hospitality" is a smile, a gesture, a friendly word—not the place they take you when you've been mugged.

Mississippi: Off the Beaten Path will guide you through the state's diverse geography and its uncommon culture. You'll explore towns tucked away in the rolling hills and travel alongside the "Father of Waters," the mighty Mississippi River that gave the state its name. You'll experience the sometimes harsh realities of life in the delta and the carefree frivolity of life on the beach. You'll converse with ladies in hoop skirts and walk on battlefields where the fate of the nation was determined.

You'll stop in odd little towns with odd little names like So-So, Why Not, Hot Coffee, Panther Burn, and D'Lo—short for a town once deemed "too damn low." There's even a microscopic community named "It" (there's not much there, but you'll know It when you see It). You'll develop an appreciation for natural phenomena, like kudzu and Spanish moss, and an appetite for grits and catfish. Who knows, you may even hear yourself saying "y'all."

But no matter where your Mississippi adventures take you, one thing is certain. You'll experience a land, a people, and a culture like no other.

And perhaps best of all, you won't have to wait in line, make reservations, or know the right people. In many cases you won't even have to buy a ticket.

All you have to do is find it.

Mississippi at a Glance

Transportation

Rules of the Road

Speed Limit: The speed limit on Mississippi interstate highways is 65 miles per hour unless otherwise posted.

Mandatory Seat-Belt Law: Operator and front-seat passengers in any motor vehicle designed to carry ten or fewer passengers are required to wear seat belts. People traveling with children under the age of two are required to restrain the child in an approved child-passenger restraint device or system. Violation of this law will result in a fine of not more than $25.

Natchez Trace Parkway: The speed limit on the Natchez Trace Parkway is 50 miles per hour and is strictly enforced. Hauling and commercial trucking are not allowed. Charter buses may receive special permits by contacting the Natchez Trace Parkway headquarters at (601) 680–4025.

The *only* gas station on the parkway is located at Jeff Busby Park, milepost 193.1.

Be alert for animals wandering onto the parkway.

Commercial Airline Service

Delta, American, Northwest, and Southwest Airlines, as well as a number of airlink carriers, provide service into and within Mississippi. Commercial airports are located in Columbus, Greenville, Gulfport, Hattiesburg, Jackson, Meridian, and Tupelo.

Train Service

Amtrak Services:

Batesville	Jackson
Brookhaven	Laurel
Canton	Meridian
Durant	McComb
Grenada	Picayune
Hattiesburg	Winona
Hazelhurst	

Riverboat Cruises

The ***Delta Queen Steamboat Company*** of New Orleans runs overnight paddlewheel cruises up and down the Mississippi River. Cruises vary in length and theme, include stops in several Mississippi river towns, and are scheduled year-round. For more information, call (800) 543–1949.

Climate

Mississippi experiences a mild, yet noticeable change of seasons. Temperatures are moderate in the spring, fall, and winter; summer highs may be uncomfortable for travelers unaccustomed to the southern heat.

January's average low is 45-50 degrees. Spring and autumn temperatures fall anywhere from the low 60s to mid 70s. From June through September, temperatures reach the upper 90s with very high humidity.

INTRODUCTION

Accepted dress year-round is casual and comfortable.

State Symbols

Flower: Magnolia

Bird: Mockingbird

Motto: Virtute et armis (By valor and arms)

Nicknames: Magnolia State, Hospitality State

For More Information

For more information on Mississippi attractions and events statewide, contact the Mississippi Division of Tourism Development at (800) WARMEST.

For information on specific towns and cities, contact the tourism organizations listed below.

Mississippi Convention and Visitors Bureaus/Tourism Offices

Aberdeen Visitors Bureau
(601) 369–9440 or (800) 634–3538

Rankin First (Brandon and Rankin County area)
(601) 825–2268

Clarksdale-Coahoma County Chamber and Industrial Foundation and Tourism Commission
(601) 627–7337 or (800) 626–3764

Columbus–Lowndes County Convention and Visitors Bureau
(601) 329–1191 or (800) 327–2686

Washington County Convention and Visitors Bureau (Greenville area)
(601) 334–2711

Grenada Tourism Commission
(601) 226–2571 or (800) 373–2571

Hancock County Tourism Bureau (Bay St. Louis area)
(228) 463–9222

Canton Convention and Visitors Bureau
(601) 859–1307 or (800) 844–3369

Cleveland Chamber of Commerce/Tourism
(601) 843–2712

Corinth Area Tourism Promotion
(601) 287–5269 or (800) 748–9048

Greenwood Convention and Visitors Bureau
(601) 453–9197 or (800) 748–9064

Mississippi Gulf Coast Convention and Visitors Bureau
(228) 896–6699 or (888) 467–4853

Hattiesburg Convention and Visitors Bureau
(601) 268–3220 or (800) 63–TOURS

DeSoto Council (Hernando area)
(601) 429–4414

Tishomingo County Tourism Council (Iuka area)
(601) 423–0051 or (800) 386–4373

Kosciusko-Attala Chamber
(601) 289–2981

Lauderdale County Tourism Bureau (Meridian area)
(601) 482–8001 or (888) TOURS–20

Ocean Springs Chamber of Commerce
(228) 875–4424

Jackson County Area Chamber of Commerce (Pascagoula area)
(228) 762–3391

Hazelhurst Chamber of Commerce
(601) 894–3752

Holly Springs Chamber of Commerce
(601) 252–2943

Metro Jackson Convention and Visitors Bureau
(601) 960–1891 or (800) 354–7695

Jones County Chamber of Commerce (Laurel area)
(601) 428–0574

Natchez Convention and Visitors Bureau
(601) 446–6345 or (800) 647–6724

Oxford Tourism Council
(601) 234–4680 or (800) 880–6967

INTRODUCTION

Port Gibson/Claiborne County Chamber of Commerce
(601) 437–4351

Ridgeland Tourism Commission
(601) 956–1225

Tate County Economic Development
Foundation/Tourism (Senatobia area)
(601) 562–8715

Southaven-Horn Lake Area Tourism Council
(601) 342–6114

Starkville Visitors and Convention Council
(601) 323–3322 or (800) 649–TOUR

Tunica Convention and Visitors Bureau
(601) 363–3800 or (888) 4–TUNICA

Tupelo Convention and Visitors Bureau
(601) 841–6521 or (800) 533–0611

Vicksburg Convention and Visitors Bureau
(601) 636–9421 or (800) 221–3536

Yazoo County Convention and Visitors Bureau
(601) 746–1815 or (800) 381–0662

Mississippi Welcome Centers

Conveniently located on major interstates and highways entering the state, Mississippi's welcome centers offer free in-state hotel, motel, bed and breakfast, and campground reservation service.

Welcome center travel counselors will also provide free maps, brochures, and other travel information. Each welcome center features telephones, RV waste disposal facilities, and twenty-four-hour restrooms and weather information.

Welcome center hours are 8:00 A.M.–7:00 P.M. June 1 to Labor Day and 8:00 A.M.–5:00 P.M. the rest of the year. Welcome centers are well-marked, with signs posted on major routes into Mississippi.

The prices and rates listed in this guidebook were confirmed at press time. We recommend, however, that you call establishments before traveling to obtain current information.

The Northeastern Hills

The Northeastern Hill country stretches from the edge of the Mississippi Delta to the foothills of the Appalachian Mountains. Traveling east to west, the land gradually becomes more and more hilly, more and more remote, until civilization becomes nothing more than a distant memory. Rich in history, heritage, and scenic beauty, this is the land that inspired both the complex genius of William Faulkner and the raw emotion that permeates the music of Elvis Presley.

This region includes portions of both I–55 and the Natchez Trace Parkway. Both routes take visitors on a north-to-south journey through the area, but the adventures encountered along each path couldn't be more different. From the modern cities that line I–55 to time-capsule towns along the Tennessee and Tombigbee Rivers, the Northeastern Hills offer a new and different adventure just over the next crest.

The I–55 Corridor

The towns and cities that line I–55 share the fast-paced, modern personality of Memphis, Tennessee, often referred to as "the largest city in north Mississippi." Even the smaller cities along I–55 boast a sophistication that comes from living just barely off a very well-beaten path. Of course, whizzing past the exits at 65 miles per hour is not the best way to soak up the local ambience. Take a short detour from the impersonal asphalt, and you'll find a wealth of unsung treasures mere minutes from the fast lane.

Begin by following I–55 South out of Memphis into **DeSoto County,** named for Hernando de Soto, the Spanish conquistador who became Mississippi's first "tourist" in 1541 and discovered the mighty

Trivia
"Mississippi" is Choctaw for "Father of Waters," referring to the mighty river for which the state is named. The earliest known written version of the name was the French "Michi Sepe."

1

The Northeastern Hills

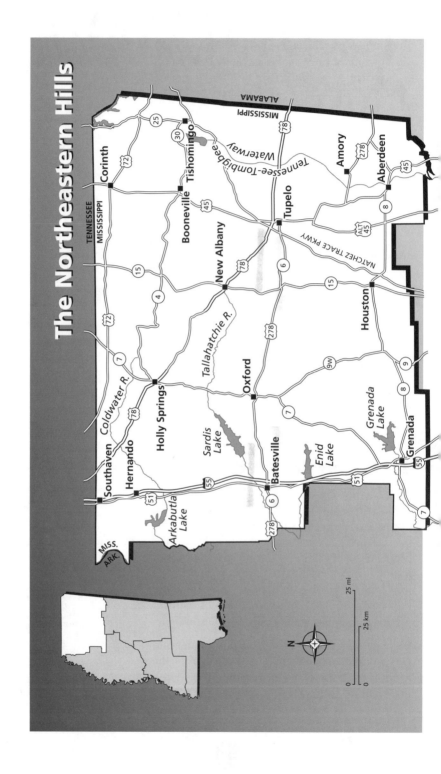

river for which the state is named. As you travel DeSoto County, you'll spot frequent markers along a route dubbed the *Hernando de Soto Memorial Trail.* As de Soto's exact path has long been lost to history, this scenic route is designed to showcase the area's attractions and doesn't attempt to follow in the famous explorer's footsteps.

Pick up the de Soto Trail just south of Memphis near *Horn Lake* and the *Elvis Presley Ranch and Honeymoon Cottage.* This private residence is not open for tours, but fans can drive by to view the cottage where the "King of Rock 'n Roll" brought his young bride Priscilla in 1967. It's located at the corner of Goodman Road (Mississippi Highway 302) and Mississippi Highway 301.

Gulliver would feel right at home at *Brussel's Bonsai Nursery.* The largest nursery of its kind in the United States, Brussel's showcases the oriental art form of "bonsai," the cultivation of miniature trees. Several members of Brussel's staff have studied this ancient art form under Japanese masters and are happy to provide visitors a glimpse into the painstaking world of bonsai. The nursery offers hundreds of specimens, accessories, and tools for sale and features elaborate display gardens filled with tiny trees decades and sometimes more than a century old. You'll find Brussel's just east of Olive Branch off Goodman Road (Mississippi Highway 302). For more information or a mail-order catalog, call (800) 582–2593.

Mississippi's Playing Your Song

*M*ention Mississippi music, and most people think of the blues or Elvis Presley. But the songs don't stop there. Whether you tune in to a country, pop, rhythm and blues, or classical station, you're virtually guaranteed to hear a voice from Mississippi.

Mississippians who've made their voices heard include Brandy, Jimmy Buffet, Bo Diddley, Pete Fountain, Mickey Gilley, W. C. Handy, Faith Hill, B. B. King, Elvis Presley, Leontyne Price, Charlie Pride, LeAnn Rimes, Fingers Taylor, Son Thomas, Ike Turner, Conway Twitty, Muddy Waters, and Tammy Wynette.

Another famous Mississippian doesn't sing himself, but came up with a groundbreaking idea that forever changed the world of music. He's Bob Pittman, founder and President of MTV.

North Mississippi is best known for Elvis Presley lore, but it is also home to another rock-and-roll legend. The *Jerry Lee Lewis Ranch*—marked by distinctive security gates emblazoned with pianos and the words "The Killer"—is just south of Horn Lake in Nesbit. As famous for his multiple marriages and tumultuous personal life as for hit songs like "Great Balls of Fire," Lewis was the subject of a feature film starring Dennis Quaid. The ranch is open for tours Monday–Friday 10:00 A.M.–3:00 P.M. The tour includes a look at Lewis's piano-shaped swimming pool, complete with black and white "keys." Admission is $10.00 for adults and $5.00 for children. Call (601) 429–1290 for directions.

Next, head south of Nesbit and follow the signs to downtown Hernando, where the focal point is the *DeSoto County Courthouse.* Inside, the story of Hernando de Soto, from his voyage to America through his death and burial in the Mississippi River, is depicted in sweeping oil murals painted in the courthouse gallery. Visitors are invited to view the paintings Monday through Friday during normal business hours. The courthouse was once a hot spot for "quickie" marriages, earning quaint little Hernando the nickname "Las Vegas of the Mid South." Marriage laws were once much more relaxed in Mississippi, and Hernando became a magnet for lovebirds from Memphis who just couldn't stand the three-day waiting period required in Tennessee.

Trivia

Arkabutla native James Earl Jones is famous for his resonating voice. Jones can be heard daily reminding news junkies, "This is CNN," but he's best known as the voice of the dreaded Darth Vader in the Star Wars *trilogy.*

The unspoiled beauty that Hernando de Soto first gazed upon centuries ago is found again in a panoramic view of the Mississippi Delta, the South's richest farmland. This legendary land has its dramatic beginning on Delta View Road, 10 miles northwest of Hernando. The mood and mystery of the Delta come together on a steep bluff where the land drops off sharply, then stretches flat and fertile as far as the eye can see.

Take a trip through America's more recent past at *Country Charm,* an antiques shop and museum complex located on a farm 8 miles west of Hernando in *Eudora.* Owner Beth Farnell opened an antiques shop in an old cabin on the property, then expanded her operation one cabin at a time. Country Charm now features twelve separate buildings, each furnished in primitive, early-American antiques. Visitors may tour a re-created general store, sewing room, laundry room, toolhouse, smokehouse, schoolhouse, and barn. Country Charm is open 12:00 noon–4:00 P.M. Friday–Sunday and just about anytime Ms. Farnell is home. Admission is $3.00 for adults and free for children under twelve. To get to Country Charm from I–55, take

Country Charm Shop and Museum

the Hernando exit and travel 9 miles west on Mississippi Highway 304, then look for the small sign.

Area restaurants serving up a tasty sample of DeSoto County specialties include the *Chatterbox,* famous for their delicious desserts, and *Pap's,* known for their fresh Mississippi catfish. As both are described as "way out in God's country," diners would be wise to ask for directions before departing for dinner. Overnight visitors will enjoy a stay at the *Sassafras Inn,* a bed and breakfast offering three guest rooms, an indoor swimming pool, a sauna, and all the sassafras tea you can drink. This comfortable, modern home is located on U.S. Highway 51 off Commerce Street in Hernando. Rates begin at $65. Call (800) 882–1897 for reservations.

If you skipped dinner in DeSoto County, you'll get another chance 15 miles down I–55 South in *Como.* This tiny town's biggest claim to fame is the *Como Steakhouse,* a beef-lover's delight housed in the old town post office on Main Street. You can watch as the cook prepares your juicy steak over an open grill in the dining room, or you can cook your own and take $1.00 off the tab, which is usually less than $20.00. The Como Steakhouse fires up the grill Tuesday–Saturday 5:00–10:30 P.M.

From Como it's just 5 miles south to *Sardis,* another quiet little town where "action" is for the most part limited to skiing and swimming at *Sardis Lake.* There is the *Heflin House Museum,* constructed in 1858 and now operated as a historical museum by the Heflin House Heritage Association. The house is open for tours the third Saturday of every month from 2:00-4:00 P.M.

If you're traveling in the fall, you may want to continue along I–55 South as far as **Grenada** for the **National Fox Hunt Chase and Futurity.** Held the last weekend of October through the first weekend of November, this annual adventure brings as many as 500 hunters, complete with horses and hounds, to Graysport Landing on Grenada Lake. The Chase includes horse shows as well as the traditional fox hunt, with all events free to the public. Tally ho!

Be sure to stop by the **Grenada Lake Visitors Center,** which features a large observation deck overlooking the 38,000-acre reservoir, the largest lake in Mississippi. A twenty-minute multimedia presentation chronicles the construction of the Grenada Dam, and exhibits describe local history and wildlife.

Fishermen and -women will want to make a stop at the **Pro Lures and Minnetonka Moccasins Outlet** (Highway 8 West) before hitting the lake in search of crappie, bass, catfish, or brean. From Grenada head back north on I–55 a short distance until you reach Highway 7, then head northeast toward the Central Crests.

'Til Death Do Us Part

*T*he city now known as Grenada was established in 1836 by the union of the towns of Pittsburgh and Tullahoma. While the two communities were actually joined in a marriage ceremony—complete with an officiating minister—it was not a case of love at first sight.

Originally settled in the early 1830s, the towns were separated only by a surveyor's line, known today as Line Street. Neither town would concede one inch to the other. Each operated its own ferry across the Yalobusha River, a mere mile apart. When Pittsburgh established the area's first newspaper, Tullahoma enticed the cash-strapped editor to move it to their city by paying off his mortgage. Pittsburgh, however, still claimed the area's only post office—until, that is, the residents of Tullahoma stole it, actually moving the building and its contents across the city line in the dark of night.

Eventually both sides wearied of the rivalry, and in 1836, agreed to consolidate. The union would take the form of a wedding ceremony, followed by a community barbecue.

The ceremony was performed on July 4, 1836, but before the barbecue got cold, arguments broke out over which name the new town would be known by. A wise wedding guest suggested starting over with a new name. Grenada was chosen in honor of Granada, Spain, the citizens shared a reconciliatory toast, and the town has enjoyed an atmosphere of matrimonial bliss ever since.

The Central Crests

The gently rolling hills to the east of the interstate seem far removed from the hustle and bustle of urban life. This is Faulkner country, a timeless realm of Civil War battlefields, well-tended historic homes, and picturesque town squares. Most of the more than 500 Civil War battles waged on Mississippi soil were fought in this area, making the few antebellum towns that survived the Union torch all the more impressive. With a rich legacy of history, heritage, and literature, this peaceful area of gently rolling hills is widely regarded as a center for American southern culture.

That said, who could be more of a cultural icon than Elvis Presley? For serious Elvis fans, **Mike McGregor's Leather and Jewelry Shop** is a must-see. Owner Mike McGregor was once the leather craftsman for the King. Visitors to his shop can purchase replicas of Elvis's famous belts and jewelry (ostentatious would be an understatement) and hear stories from the King's glory days. You'll find the shop on Highway 7 just past Water Valley.

Continue on Highway 7 North into **Oxford,** a postcard-pretty college town and literary center listed in the books *The 100 Best Small Towns in America* and *The 100 Best Small Art Towns in America* and called a "thriving New South arts mecca" by USA Today. Oxford's folksy town square, graceful antebellum homes, tree-shaded boulevards, and quintessential southern college campus have been immortalized in more pages than the city has residents.

Begin a literary tour of Oxford with a trip down Highway 6 West and a look at the big yellow Victorian on the left. It's the part-time **home of John Grisham,** former Mississippi state legislator and best-selling author of *The Firm, The Client, A Time to Kill, The Chamber, The Rainmaker,* and other legal thrillers. The estate includes a full-sized baseball diamond upon which Grisham once coached a local Little League team.

Aberdeen
Spring Pilgrimage,
April, (601) 369–4864
Blue Bluff River Festival,
October, (601) 369–9440
Corinth
Slugburger Festival,
July, (601) 287–1550
Grenada
Grenada Lake's "Thunder on Water" Safeboating Festival, June,
(800) 373–2571
Holly Springs
Spring Pilgrimage,
April, (601) 252–2943
Kudzu Festival,
July, (601) 252–2943
Oxford
Double Decker Arts Festival, April,
(800) 758–9177
Ripley
First Monday Trade Day,
Weekend prior to the first Monday of each month,
(601) 837–4051
Tupelo
Gumtree Festival, May,
(800) 533–0611
Oleput, June,
(800) 267–3104
Water Valley
Water Valley Watermelon Carnival, August,
(601) 473–1122

The dust jackets don't stop with Grisham. Willie Morris, Barry Hannah, and Larry Brown have all felt their genius stirred by Oxford's landmarks and landscapes, but it was Nobel prizewinner William Faulkner who first put Oxford on the literary map.

Even if you haven't thought of Faulkner since high school English class, a trip to Oxford will have you searching for your old paperbacks. Faulkner modeled the mythical Yoknapatawpha County, the setting for his tales of glory and decadence in the South, after Oxford and Lafayette County. As a child, Faulkner lived in a small cottage at the corner of South Eleventh and Buchanan Streets, but **Rowan Oak,** Faulkner's antebellum home at the bend of Old Taylor Road, is the place where his genius came to life. The house remains much as Faulkner left it, with his black manual typewriter on display in the study and the outline of his novel, *A Fable,* scrawled on the wall. Rowan Oak is open for tours 10:00 A.M.–12:00 noon and 2:00–4:00 P.M. Tuesday–Saturday; 2:00–4:00 P.M. on Sunday. Even when the house isn't open, the tree-shaded grounds and adjacent Bailey's Woods are the perfect place to enjoy a quiet afternoon stroll.

Trivia

Mississippians are fond of saying, "We may not be able to read, but we sure can write." Works by Mississippi natives John Grisham, William Faulkner, Tennessee Williams, Eudora Welty, Willie Morris, Thomas Harris, Shelby Foote, Margaret Walker Alexander, and Beth Henley would certainly seem to justify that claim.

During his lifetime, Faulkner was regarded as a bit of a character around town. He served briefly as the University of Mississippi's postmaster and was reportedly the worst postmaster in the school's history. Faulkner himself generally agreed with this assessment, explaining that he "didn't care to be at the beck and call of any fool who could afford a postage stamp." Rowan Oak is owned by the **University of Mississippi,** where Faulkner was briefly enrolled as a lackluster student. The university's **J. D. Williams Library** displays Faulkner's 1949 Nobel prize, first edition prints of his books, and early handwritten manuscripts. The inscription on the library's wall, "I decline to accept the end of man. I believe that man will not merely endure, he will prevail," was pulled from Faulkner's Nobel prize acceptance speech. Faulkner is buried in nearby **St. Peter's Cemetery** at the corner of Jefferson Avenue and North Sixteenth Street. Faithful readers and aspiring writers leave dog-eared paperbacks— and the occasional bottle of bourbon—on the author's grave.

Oxford's rich literary heritage is showcased in two annual conferences, the **Faulkner and Yoknapatawpha Conference** and the **Oxford Conference for the Book.** Both events attract aspiring writers and renowned authors from around the world; past speakers have included John Grisham and Stephen King. Call the Institute for Continuing Studies at (601) 232–7282 for conference speakers and dates.

Much of the activity in Oxford is focused on the **town square,** (known simply as "The Square"), which is home to a number of restaurants and specialty and antiques shops as well as the imposing **Lafayette County Courthouse.** Join the locals for breakfast at **Smitty's,** a folksy diner overlooking the square that was once a favorite Faulkner haunt. Other excellent dining choices located on or near The Square include **City Grocery** (152 Courthouse Square), the **Henry Cafe and Jubilee Lounge** (1006 Jackson Avenue East*)* and **Proud Larry's** (211 S. Lamar), which is also the best place in Oxford for live music.

A stroll around The Square isn't complete without a visit to **Square Books** (160 Courthouse Square), a favorite hangout of Oxford's many famous and aspiring writers and widely regarded as one of the South's premier bookstores. **The Southside Gallery** (1116 Van Buren Avenue) brings the international art scene to Oxford with exhibits by noted painters, photographers, and folk artists. You'll also want to browse in the **J. E. Neilson Company Department Store** (119 Courthouse Square), the oldest continuously operating department store in the South.

Anywhere you go in Oxford, you're bound to run into a student or two. The city fathers chose the name "Oxford" in 1837 in hopes of improving their chances of landing Mississippi's first public university. Their efforts were successful; **the University of Mississippi,** known affectionately as **"Ole Miss,"** was founded in Oxford in 1848.

Perhaps the University's most famous feature is the parklike retreat known simply as **The Grove.** Normally a peaceful spot for strolling, counting tulips, or relaxing in the shade, The Grove is packed with tailgaters on football weekends, most of whom put out their best silver and finest table linens in honor of the pregame festivities. And if you attend a **Southeastern Conference football game** at Ole Miss, *don't* come in blue jeans. Football is serious business in Oxford, with a student dress code that demands blue blazers and ties for gentlemen and skirts and high heels for ladies. Attire has relaxed a little since the 1950s and 1960s, when women often sported full-length furs for ninety-degree September kickoffs.

The University has closed its doors only once—when the entire male faculty and student body marched away to fight in the Civil War. The wounded from the fierce battles of Corinth and Shiloh were treated in the university's buildings, and legend has it that spiteful Union troops rode their horses through the university's most hallowed halls. A handful of the university's original buildings survived the 1864 torching of Oxford, including the **Lyceum,** a white-columned Greek Revival structure that houses the administrative offices and serves as the campus focal point and university logo. Also of interest is 1889 **Ventress Hall,** where stained glass windows honor the University Greys, a company of faculty and students who were wiped out in the Battle of Gettysburg.

The **Barnard Observatory** was built to house a magnificent telescope ordered with great excitement by the university science department but never delivered due to the outbreak of the war. Today the observatory houses the **Center for the Study of Southern Culture,** a teaching and research center dedicated to the study of the South. Researchers at the center produced the highly acclaimed *Encyclopedia of Southern Culture,* an eight-and-a-half-pound tribute to everything Southern.

The University of Mississippi Blues Archive is the only research facility in the country dedicated to the study of the blues. The archive includes the personal collection of blues legend and Mississippi native B. B. King.

A (Religious) Conversion on the 10-Yard Line

*I*t's been said that in the South, football is a religion, and Saturday is the day of worship. Northern and mideastern cities can have their basketball; in the South, college football reigns supreme.

Of course, casual spectators may question whether Heaven really cares about the outcome of a football game. For these naysayers, devout Mississippians have but one reply—November 19, 1983.

On that fateful day, the University of Mississippi Rebels and the Mississippi State University Bulldogs met for the annual intrastate bloodletting known as the Egg Bowl. State dominated the first half, but Ole Miss rallied in the second, battling to a precarious 24 to 23 lead in the fourth quarter. Not to be

denied, the Bulldogs drove to the Rebel 10-yard line, and with seconds remaining, lined up to kick the game-winning field goal.

The kick was up . . . it had the distance . . . it split the uprights . . . and then, miraculously, a strong gust of wind blew the winning kick back outside the goal posts.

The ball fell harmlessly back to earth. MSU kicker Artie Cosby stared in disbelief. The Ole Miss team began a wild celebration that lasted into the night. Fans on both sides fell to their knees.

Headlines the next day screamed "Divine Intervention!" and the 1983 Egg Bowl—and its supernaturally influenced kick—made history and highlight reels for years to come.

Call (601) 232–7753 for an appointment to view the artifacts and photographs or listen to any of the more than 10,000 soulful recordings.

University Museums usually promotes its Greek and Roman antiquities, but the average person would probably tell you the *real* attraction there is the **Amazing, Ingenious, and Grotesque Display.** Housed in its own "cabinet of curiosity," this Ripleyesque collection includes a wreath made entirely of human hair, an unidentified "critter" fashioned into a purse, and a pair of fleas dressed as a bride and groom and posing for wedding photos under a magnifying glass. The University Museum also houses an extensive collection of paintings by former Oxford resident Theora Hamblett. Hamblett launched her artistic career at the age of fifty-five, painting scenes from her childhood, dreams, and religious visions. You'll find the museum on the edge of campus at the corner of Fifth Street and University Avenue.

If you stay overnight in Oxford, try one of the town's bed-and-breakfast inns. Listed on the National Register of Historic Places, the newly renovated **Barksdale-Isom House** was constructed entirely of native timber hand-worked by Indian and slave labor. The house was built by Dr. Thomas D. Isom, who gave Oxford its name. The University of Mississippi was chartered in the home's dining room in 1848. The Barksdale-Isom House is located at 1003 Jefferson Street. Call (601) 236–5600 for reservations. Delightful, moderately priced accommodations are also available at **Puddin Place** (601–234–1250) and the **Oliver Britt House** (601–234–8043), both conveniently located near the University and the town square. Rates at the inns begin at around $120.

Take Mississippi Highway 7 North from Oxford to **Holly Springs.** This pretty little town is home to some sixty **antebellum homes and churches,** spared destruction because the ladies of Holly Springs devoted themselves to distracting the Union soldiers sent to torch the town. In this charming setting of white-columned homes and colorful gardens, hoop skirts seem almost mandatory, but the only time they're considered appropriate street attire is during the annual *Spring Pilgrimage.*

The original Holly Springs Pilgrimage allowed visitors to tour twenty-three homes for a quarter. Today, the pilgrimage offers tours of seven homes, which rotate from year to year, guaranteeing repeat visitors new tours each spring. Approximately 5,000 pilgrims visit Holly Springs during the three-day event, usually held the third weekend in April. For next spring's dates and ticket prices, call the **Holly Springs Chamber of Commerce** at (601) 252–2943.

Located at 154 South Memphis Street, the Chamber also offers a **Green Line Tour Map,** a $1.00, self-guided driving tour map that includes sixty historic homes, churches, and landmarks. Of particular interest is **Walter Place,** which served as quarters for Julia Grant while her husband Ulysses occupied the town. When Holly Springs was raided by Confederates under the command of General Earl Van Dorn, the troops were forbidden to enter Walter Place as long as Mrs. Grant was quartered inside. In return for this display of chivalry, Grant placed a safeguard on the house preventing any invasion by Union troops for the remainder of the war, unwittingly establishing Walter Place as a safe haven for Confederate soldiers and spies.

Also of interest is **Hamilton Place,** where the mistress of the house hosted parties, teas, and concerts for the Union troops, hoping to take their minds off their torches. One Union general particularly enthralled with her musical gifts told her, "You and your piano can take credit for saving Holly Springs." You'll also want to drive by **Airliewood,** where General Grant established headquarters and his restless troops shot every picket off the iron fence; **Montrose,** the lushly landscaped headquarters of the Holly Springs Garden Club; and **Wakefield,** home of a brazen belle who actually went so far as to *marry* a Union soldier, a scandal still discussed in Holly Springs today.

History buffs will also want to stop by the **Marshall County Historical**

Catfish, Hush Puppies, and Magic Markers

I was a student at the University of Mississippi when I discovered the wonderful combination of cholesterol and artwork known as Taylor Grocery.

The old-timey grocery store was the center of commerce in Taylor, a one-street town just south of Oxford. There was no hostess, just a friendly woman who split her time between ringing up pickled eggs and beer at the register and waiting on a handful of rickety tables tucked into a graffiti-plastered corner in the back.

The menu was simple. Catfish, catfish, and just for variety, catfish. Plates heaping with the kind of genuine, deep-fried indulgence that actually does your heart good every once in a while. But while the food was delicious, the best part of dinner at Taylor was adding my own clever little maxims to the graffiti-covered walls, tables, and ceiling.

Sadly, Taylor Grocery has, at least for the time being, closed its doors to hungry diners and aspiring poets and artists. But if the store ever reopens and you have the chance to visit, check the walls for words of wisdom from U.S. Senator Thad Cochran, actress Lauren Hutton, singer Jimmy Buffet, and last but not least, aspiring author Marlo Carter.

Graceland Too

*E*ven if you're not an Elvis Presley admirer, you'll find Graceland Too, home of the self-proclaimed "Number One Elvis Fan," to be a memorable stop. Paul McLeod and his son, Elvis Aron Presley McLeod, have transformed their home into a virtual shrine to the King of Rock 'n' Roll.

Father and son have amassed a huge collection of Elvis memorabilia, including records, concert tickets, and flowers from Elvis' grave. Most impressive is the Graceland Too archive, a vast collection of more than 20,000 newspaper clippings and articles related to Elvis. Father and son also take turns manning a fleet of VCRs and television sets, recording any reference to the King. Graceland Too is located at 200 East Gholson Avenue in Holly Springs. If you call ahead (601–252–7954), Paul McLeod will probably tell you their operating hours are anytime you want to stop by and pay the $5.00 admission.

Museum, three floors and twenty-two viewing rooms filled to the rafters with artifacts and displays. The $3.00 admission fee buys a look at Chickasaw Indian artifacts, vintage clothing, Civil War relics, antique toys, and a display detailing events from the 1878 yellow fever epidemic, which took more lives in Holly Springs than the Civil War. Notable artifacts include a condolence card from Mrs. Jefferson Davis to a Mississippi war widow and an 1869 income tax return listing a total tax liability of $27.95. The museum is located at 220 East College Street.

Nearby **Hillcrest Cemetery** (South Market Street) is the final resting place of several yellow fever victims and of Hiram Revels, the country's first black United States senator. Thirteen Confederate generals and a number of Civil War soldiers are also buried at Hillcrest.

A Holly Springs attraction of a different sort is the **Kate Freeman Clark Museum,** a collection of more than 1,000 paintings by a single Holly Springs native. Clark's paintings were shown in Chicago, Boston, Philadelphia, and New York, but she refused to sell even one, perhaps because her mother told her it would be "like selling a child." Instead, Clark willed the entire collection to the town of Holly Springs, including sketches, still lifes, landscapes, even a colorful bird painted on a real leaf. The museum is open by appointment for a charge of $2.00. Call (601) 252–4211.

If all that sightseeing leaves you hungry, stop by **Phillips Grocery** (541 East Van Dorn Avenue), where the burgers were named among the nation's best by *USA Today*. Located next door to the old railroad depot, Phillips was originally opened as a saloon in 1882 by Oliver Quiggins, a former Confederate soldier. The establishment did a thriving business

Airliewood

serving the constant flow of train passengers, many of whom arrived in Holly Springs from the North. The colorful Quiggins delighted in ordering his "Yankee" customers to take off their hats, explaining in no uncertain terms, "I've always been a southern gentleman and I used to shoot you during the war, so you'll take off your hat if you expect service in my place."

If you're in this area on the Saturday or Sunday prior to the first Monday of the month, take Mississippi Highway 4 out of Holly Springs into *Ripley,* then follow Mississippi Highway 15 South to the *First Monday Trade Day.* Best described as "fifty acres of economic chaos," this colorful monthly flea market attracts as many as 1,500 vendors and 30,000 shoppers. A Ripley tradition since 1893, First Monday vendors peddle everything from antiques to food to livestock. For vendor reservations, call (800) 4–RIPLEY. For other information, call (601) 837–4051.

From Ripley, take Highway 15 North to U.S. Highway 72 East and the history-rich town of *Corinth.* The city's location at the junction of two railroads made Corinth a strategic prize in the Civil War. More than 300,000 soldiers and 200 generals occupied the city between 1861 and 1865. Generals William T. Sherman and Ulysses S. Grant both spent time in the Corinth area, and the 1862 siege of Corinth broke the record for the largest concentration of troops in the western hemisphere. Julia Grant, the General's wife, was also a wartime visitor. According to local historians, Mrs. Grant, accompanied by her own slave, set up quarters in a local plantation house. When she left she stripped the place clean, taking even the doors and window glass with her.

By the spring of 1862, Union troops were entrenched so close to Corinth they could hear the rattle of supply trains and the beat of Confederate drums inside the fortified city. Vastly outnumbered, Confederate General P. G. T. Beauregard decided to retreat to nearby Tupelo. The evacuation was conducted with the utmost secrecy. Dummy cannons guarded the line, campfires burned, and buglers serenaded the deserted works. When Union troops cautiously entered the city at daybreak, they discovered only a deserted town.

The Battle of Corinth took place in October of 1862, when the Confederates attempted to retake the town in what was to become the bloodiest battle in Mississippi history. Hand-to-hand fighting engulfed the city, and the Confederates were driven out of Corinth. *Battery Robinette,* a small, well-marked park, is the most accessible of the Civil War sites in Corinth. The site of the Battle of Corinth includes the *Corinth National Cemetery,* the final resting place for Union soldiers killed in some twenty battles in Mississippi and Tennessee.

It's difficult to take a drive through any part of Corinth without crossing the ring of *earthworks* that encircled the city during the war. These hastily constructed ridges of earth formed a protective buffer for the weary soldiers to sleep behind. While the earthworks are found all over town—even running through the occasional front lawn—the larger, more intact sites require a short hike through the woods off Shiloh Road. The 4-foot-high mounds don't look especially impressive until you consider they were constructed by hungry, tired soldiers working in the dark with handheld shovels the size of garden trowels.

Many of the more remote sites haven't changed in the 130-plus years since the war. If a soldier from 1862 woke up today in the wooded area off Shiloh Road, he'd still know exactly where he was. A 26-mile hiking-and-biking trail through the area is expected to be marked and mapped by early 1999. A self-guided historical tour brochure and map to the earthworks and other historic sites is available from the *Corinth Alliance,* 810 Tate Street, (601) 287–5269, and at the *Civil War Interpretive Center,* located on the grounds of the historic *Curlee House,* at the corner of Bunch and Jackson Streets.

Built in 1857, the Curlee House served as headquarters for Confederate Generals Braxton Bragg and Earl Van Dorn and for Union General Henry Halleck. Today the house is owned by the city and is open for public tours 9:00 A.M. to 4:00 P.M. Monday–Saturday and 1:00–4:00 P.M. Sunday.

The Corinth Civil War Interpretive Center on the grounds runs a fifteen-

Roscoe Turner and Gilmore

One of Corinth's most colorful residents was the high-flying Roscoe Turner, an early stunt pilot famous not only for his daring aerial maneuvers, but for his copilot—a pet lion dubbed Gilmore.

Both Turner and Gilmore received national recognition—Turner was the first (and so far, the only) Corinth native to appear on the cover of Time *magazine, and Gilmore, now handsomely stuffed, occupies a spot in the Air and Space Museum in Washington, D.C.*

minute video on Corinth and the War and sells Civil War prints and other memorabilia.

At the opposite end of Bunch Street at the Kilpatrick Street intersection, you'll find the **Fish Pond House.** Although it's not open to the public, the Fish Pond House's most interesting architectural feature is easily viewed from the street. The roof is topped by a copper-lined basin used to catch rainwater—the latest marvel in indoor plumbing when the house was built in 1856.

If you have any questions about Corinth history, the volunteers at the **Northeast Mississippi Museum** at Fourth and Washington Streets are sure to have the answers. The museum displays Civil War relics, Indian artifacts, and local memorabilia, but its biggest asset is a friendly staff of volunteers who delight in spinning tales for out-of-town guests. There's no admission fee, but donations are welcome. The only strict requirement is that you must sign the guest register.

Downtown Corinth is a handsome commercial district of Italianate, Colonial Revival, and Art Deco architecture. You'll discover a number of interesting shops in the area, including **Waits Jewelry.** The store was founded by Ernest Waits, a multitalented entrepreneur born in 1870. Mr. Waits's wife still runs the store today and is happy to answer any questions except those regarding her age. The shop's most remarkable feature is not its merchandise, but the hand-painted murals that circle the high ceiling. Mr. Waits himself painted the landscapes, which depict a day from late afternoon until sunrise and the seasons from August to August. According to his wife, Mr. Waits had never painted before he began the elaborate murals and used "places in his mind" as the models for the work.

Downtown is also home to **Borrum's Drug Store** (604 Waldron Street), the oldest continually operated drugstore in Mississippi. Founded in 1869, Borrum's still serves up thick grilled cheese sandwiches and frosty coke floats from a gleaming soda fountain. The drugstore is run by Camille Borrum Mitchell, who was the first female pharmacist in Corinth. Locals gather beneath the deer heads at Borrum's to watch Ole Miss football games and exchange gossip. Visitors may even hear a tale or two about Sheriff Buford Pusser, whose life was chronicled in the

Walking Tall movie series. Pusser was a native of a small town just across the Tennessee state line and was a frequent visitor to Corinth.

With so much Civil War history in the area, it's no wonder that **C&D Jarnagin,** the nation's largest supplier of uniforms to Civil War reenactors, is also located in downtown Corinth. Call (601) 287–4977 for a look at historically accurate reproductions of 1860s soldiers' garb. Finally, no stroll around downtown would be complete without a snack from **Dilworth's Tamales,** a Corinth tradition since 1890.

Corinth hosts several colorful festivals, the most notable of which is the **Slugburger Festival,** which celebrates that unique southern delicacy, the slugburger. Not to be confused with the garden pest of the same name, the slugburger is a part-beef, part-breading concoction made popular during the Depression when families were hungry and meat was scarce. The origin of the name is subject to some local debate, with theories ranging from "slug" as slang for a nickel, the burger's original cost, or another word for "fake," as in fake meat. In spite of its less-than-appetizing name, the slugburger attracts some 15,000 hungry fans to the July festival held in its honor.

Overnight guests to Corinth may choose one of several bed-and-breakfast inns, where rates begin at around $50. Civil War buffs who didn't get their fill in Corinth may want to take a side trip to **Shiloh,** just across the Tennessee state line. Call (901) 689–5275 for more information on the **Shiloh National Military Park.**

For a break from the war altogether, take U.S. Highway 45 south of Corinth, then go 9 miles east on Mississippi Highway 356 to the **Jacinto Courthouse.** Once the political and cultural center of northeast Mississippi, Jacinto was founded in 1836 as the county seat of Old Tishomingo County. In its heyday, Jacinto was home to a boys' boarding school, a busy stagecoach stop, numerous churches, and even more plentiful bars and taverns.

Jacinto was home to two classes of people—those who drank, fought, and committed adultery, and those who went to church, to temperance meetings, and to bed early. Court was the main source of entertainment for both groups, and the two-story brick courthouse—built in 1854 at a whopping cost of $7,199.72—was the town's focal point.

But just as construction on the courthouse was completed, Jacinto's population began to decline. People moved to cities where the railroad created jobs and business opportunities, and the Civil War claimed many of the residents who stayed behind. The final bell tolled for Jacinto in 1870, when one-million-acre Tishomingo County was divided into the present Alcorn, Prentiss, and Tishomingo counties. No longer a seat of government, Jacinto faded into a ghost town.

Today the town is maintained and operated by the Jacinto Foundation. Tour buildings include the courthouse museum, an 1850s doctor's office, and a country store. The courthouse is open daily, except Monday, May–September and on weekends in April, October, November, and December. Official hours are 1:00–5:00 P.M. Tuesday through Friday and 10:00 A.M.–5:00 P.M. Saturday. For more information, call (601) 286–8662.

The Appalachian Foothills

The Appalachian Mountains begin in the extreme northeastern corner of the state, creating a rugged terrain of rocky outcroppings, thick woodlands, and bubbling streams that run cool and clear even in the heat of a Mississippi summer.

The most remarkable feature of the Appalachian Foothills is the complete solitude, deafening quiet, and total lack of urbanization. In this tranquil, unspoiled section of Mississippi, Mother Nature is the main attraction.

From Corinth, take Highway 72 East to Highway 25 North, then follow 25 to *J. P. Coleman State Park.* Bordered by the *Tennessee River* and beautiful *Pickwick Lake,* J. P. Coleman is a popular resort attracting outdoor enthusiasts from northeast Mississippi and nearby Memphis, Tennessee. The area is home to the largest inland marina in the United States and a scenic waterfall frequented by boaters. Call (601) 423–6515 for more information or cabin rental reservations.

From J. P. Coleman it's just a short drive south along Mississippi Highway 25 to *Iuka.* The land around Iuka is woodsy, hilly, and completely unspoiled; it's characterized by a peace and quiet so complete that urban dwellers may find it a bit unnerving. Named for a Chickasaw Indian chief drawn to the area by its healthful mineral springs, Iuka was a popular spa of the 1880s. The water was bottled in the early 1900s and won first place in the 1904 World's Fair. The *Iuka Mineral Springs Park* on Highway 172 East offers travelers a taste of the same sparkling water Chief Iuka discovered centuries ago.

The *Old Tishomingo County Courthouse* (circa 1889) at the corner of Fulton and Quitman Streets houses a collection of Indian relics, Civil War artifacts from the 1862 Battle of Iuka, and other collections related to local history. The museum is open weekdays 8:00 A.M.–5:00 P.M. but closes for lunch 12:00 noon–1:00 P.M. Lunch is also the best time to check out *Ellie's Snack Bar,* which specializes in slugburgers. Ellie's has been in operation in the one-room building at 108 Front Street since the early 1940s.

Iuka's remote location and rocky terrain make it a natural habitat for the bald eagle. Annual *Eagle Tours on the Tennessee River* have a 100 percent sighting rate. Tours are held in January aboard a deluxe cruising boat. Afternoon excursions are $25 per person; evening tours include a prime rib dinner for $45. Fall foliage cruises set sail in late October at the same rates. Call (601) 423–9933 or (800) FUN–HERE for tour dates and reservations.

Head south on Highway 25 about 1 mile outside the Iuka city limit, turn right on County Road 187, and follow the signs to *Woodall Mountain,* the highest point in Mississippi. At an elevation of 806 feet, Woodall Mountain doesn't require crampons or bottled oxygen, but the view is scenic, the landscape is unspoiled, and the tranquil atmosphere is perfect for a quiet picnic.

Return to Highway 25 and head south to *Tishomingo* and *Tishomingo State Park.* The park offers a unique landscape of imposing rock formations and fern-filled crevices found nowhere else in Mississippi. Massive boulders blanketed in moss jut out from the steep hillsides, and colorful wildflowers border winding trails once walked by the Chickasaw Indians. The historic *Natchez Trace Parkway* runs directly through the park.

Visitors may stay overnight in rustic cabins clinging to the boulder-studded hillsides, then explore a 13-mile nature trail that winds along rocky ridges with spectacular views, through shallow canyons, and beside the rushing waters of Bear Creek. Hikers beware—a walk on the *swinging bridge* high above the creek is not for the faint of heart. An 8-mile *float trip* down Bear Creek is offered April–October. Rappelling and disc golf are also popular park attractions. For information and cabin rental reservations, call (601) 438–6914.

From Tishomingo, take Mississippi Highway 30 West to *Booneville* and *The Quilt Gallery.* He's never sewn a stitch himself, but Claude Wilemon has quite a talent for quilt design. Wilemon works with local seamstresses who transform his designs into one-of-a-kind quilts, all of which are displayed in his home and all of which are for sale. The Quilt Gallery is located in Burton, east of Booneville on Mississippi Highway 30. Look for the big stone house on the right and a sign marked QUILT SHOP. The gallery is open 7:00 A.M.–5:00 P.M. Monday–Saturday, and for $1.00 you can also tour the thirteen-room house. Call (601) 728-3302 for an appointment, or just drop in.

From Booneville it's just a short drive south on U.S. Highway 45 to **Baldwyn** and the **Brice's Cross Roads Battlefield.** Located 6 miles west of Baldwyn on Mississippi Highway 370, the former Civil War battlefield is a National Park Service site.

The Battle of Brice's Cross Roads took place in June of 1864, when Confederate General Nathan Bedford Forrest organized his cavalry for an attack on Union General William T. Sherman's supply line. Union forces moved out of Memphis to stop him, and the opposing units met at Brice's Cross Roads. The outnumbered Confederates attacked vigorously and forced the Union troops back. Union forces began a careful withdrawal, but as the troops crossed Tishomingo Creek a supply wagon overturned, panicking the soldiers and turning their orderly retreat into a full-blown rout. More than 1,500 Union soldiers were captured and nearly as many were killed during the wild flight back to Memphis. A soldier described the scene as a horrible melee in which "live and dead mules were mixed up with live and dead men in the mud and water." The remains of a Federal soldier trampled in the retreat were discovered impacted in the creek bed nearly 100 years later.

The Confederate victory was a brilliant success for Forrest, a colorful military genius who based his strategies on the maxims, "Get there first with the most men," and "Shoot at everything blue and keep up the scare."

Today, well-marked trails and interpretive markers guide visitors through the park, which includes Civil War cannons, a monument, and the Bethany Confederate Cemetery. Audio tapes of a driving tour are available at the visitors center, which houses a battlefield diorama and interactive exhibits and screens a video program narrated by noted Civil War historian and author Shelby Foote. The visitors center is open Tuesday–Saturday 9:00 A.M.–5:00 P.M. and Sunday noon–5:00 P.M. Admission to the visitors center is $2.00 for adults and $1.00 for children. For more information, call (601) 365-3969.

From Baldwyn, follow Mississippi Highway 30 West into **New Albany.** More often associated with nearby Oxford, Nobel prize winner William Faulkner was born in New Albany. The house is no longer standing, but a historic marker designates the site.

New Albany's Main Street is home to two unusual restaurants. Patrons at **Barrett's Grocery and Army Surplus** can buy anything from a ham sandwich to a hunting license, a loaf of bread to a pair of army boots. The clientele at Barrett's includes professionals, blue collar workers, tourists, and garden-variety loafers, all of whom enjoy Barrett's tall tales and camaraderie as much as the food and unlimited shopping possibilities. Diners and shoppers alike gather 'round an old wooden counter edged with a brass plaque reading ON THIS SITE IN 1897, NOTHING HAPPENED to discuss the day's events and local comings and goings. You'll find Barrett's behind a washtub full of flowers at 104 West Main Street. Proprietor Erline Barrett is casual about operating hours and will tell you she's open "can to can't."

If it's a good old-fashioned burger you're craving, stroll down the street to **Latham's Hamburger Inn,** located at 106 West Main. Take a seat on a wooden swivel stool rescued from an old trolley car and sample one of Latham's supersecret recipe burgers, a New Albany tradition since 1927. Visitors have been known to request a frozen supply of burgers for the road.

New Albany also offers some interesting sights outside the main part of town. As you approach the intersection of Mississippi 15 North and County Road 82, look for the small, white picket fence next to the railroad tracks. The fence marks the **Grave of the Unknown Frenchman.** In the 1880s, convict labor was used to build the railroads. According to legend, a wrongly accused Frenchman working on the chain gang received word his wife was dying. Desperate to reach her side before it was too late, he made a break for freedom, was shot and killed by a guard, and was buried where he fell.

Rivers and Rails

The cities and towns in the Rivers and Rails section of Mississippi sprang up as shipping hubs along the railroads and the Tennessee and Tombigbee Rivers, a heritage still celebrated there today.

This is an area where festivals revolve around "railroad days" and bands play on the rivers' banks, where museums display old train whistles and elegant old neighborhoods have their roots in the cotton-shipping trade.

Today the focus of commercial shipping is the **Tennessee-Tombigbee Waterway,** a 234-mile transportation route, scenic passage, and recreational area connecting the inland South with the Gulf of Mexico. The Tenn-Tom is a haven for sportsmen, boaters, campers, and other outdoor enthusiasts; the communities along its banks are dotted with boat ramps and campgrounds offering direct access to the water.

But perhaps first and foremost, this area is Elvis Presley's homeland. From New Albany, take U.S. Highway 78 East to **Tupelo,** a modern industrial center and the birthplace of the King of Rock 'n Roll. No matter which route you follow into the city, it's impossible to miss the many directional signs that point visitors toward the **Elvis Presley Birthplace and Museum.** Vernon Presley, Elvis's daddy, borrowed $180 to construct the two-room, shotgun-style house where the King

Worshipping The King

*I*n the summer of 1982, I entered the workforce as a tour guide at Jimmy Velvet's Elvis Presley Museum in Memphis. A personal friend of the King of Rock and Roll, Velvet remodeled an old gas station across the street from Graceland and filled it with a hodgepodge of photos, costumes, jewelry, and furniture, all of which once belonged to Elvis. Fans from around the world paid $3.00 for me to lead them through the "exhibit hall" and snap their photos in front of Elvis' baby blue Lincoln Continental or perched on the edge of his king-sized bed.

The following summer, I graduated to working at Graceland itself, where my job duties included calming guests who claimed to have seen Elvis' ghost lurking on the staircase, providing tissues for fans who still "can't believe he's gone," and shaking hands with Priscilla Presley, who donned dark glasses and hid in the crowd during a top-secret, undercover inspection tour. The hottest selling item in the gift shop? Bags of dirt from Graceland, $3.95 each, complete with a "certificate of authenticity."

But even two summers immersed in Elvis doesn't qualify me as a true fan of the King. "Fan," after all, is short for "fanatic," which is really the only way to describe the hordes of people who travel from around the world to see where Elvis lived and died.

Even today, more than twenty years after his death, fans wait in line for hours to tour the house, the cars, and the airplanes. They invest their hard-earned cash in T-shirts bearing his likeness and dirt from his flower beds. They tattoo his name on their bodies and name their children "Elvis Aron Presley Jones." They are obsessed.

So what was it about the boy from Tupelo that changed people's lives and continues to touch them today? Was it his unforgettable voice? His smoldering eyes? His undulating pelvis? His tragic, early death? Or was it purely and simply charisma?

No one has ever been able to pinpoint the quality that made a poor country boy a King, but one thing is certain. If you could bag that with a certificate of authenticity, it'd be well worth the $3.95 price tag.

of Rock 'n Roll was born. Two years later, the Presleys were evicted when they couldn't scrape together enough money to repay that modest loan.

The flowered linoleum, worn furnishings, and sepia-toned family portrait are a sharp contrast to the flashy cars, sequined jumpsuits, and extravagant lifestyle more often associated with Elvis. The entire structure is only 450 square feet, and the guide seated at the door is quick to mention that Graceland, Elvis's estate in Memphis, holds a sofa longer than this entire house.

When Elvis hit the big time, he returned to his hometown for a benefit concert to raise money for a park for disadvantaged children. The fifteen-acre property purchased for the park included Elvis's first home, and today thousands of tourists take the exit off U.S. Highway 78 to Elvis Presley Boulevard and head for the tiny shotgun shack at the end of the road.

Admission to the birthplace is a mere $1.00. For $4.00 more, visitors may tour a museum located just behind the house. Exhibits include records, clothes, and other Elvis memorabilia donated by a family friend. The Birthplace and Museum are open Monday–Saturday 9:00 A.M.–5:00 P.M. and Sunday 1:00–5:00 P.M.

Die-hard fans of the King should stop by the *Tupelo Convention and Visitors Bureau* on Main Street and pick up a map to other Elvis-related sites. The short driving tour covers approximately 4 blocks and includes Elvis's elementary and junior high schools and *Tupelo Hardware,* where the King of Rock 'n Roll purchased his very first guitar. For more information about Elvis's early life in Tupelo, call the Convention and Visitors Bureau at (800) 533–0611.

The Civil War Battle of Tupelo is remembered in a small park on West Main Street. After the disastrous Union rout at Brice's Cross Roads, General Sherman ordered General A. J. Smith to "Go out and follow (Nathan Bedford) Forrest to the death, if it costs 10,000 lives and breaks the Treasury." Smith drew the Confederate forces under Forrest and General Stephen D. Lee into battle at Tupelo. A misunderstood direction cost the Confederates the battle—an incident that one of Forrest's men described as "making the General so mad he stunk." Smith, however, was short of supplies, and many of his troops were suffering from heat exhaustion. The Union troops hastily retreated, leaving their own wounded behind.

As Generals Lee and Forrest discussed the day's events around the campfire, Lee wondered aloud why the other Confederate generals couldn't match Forrest's success in battle. "Well General," Forrest is said to have replied, "I suppose it's because I'm not handicapped by a West Point education."

The one-acre *Tupelo National Battlefield* features a large memorial honoring both armies, cannons, and an interpretive marker and map. The *Oren Dunn City Museum,* also located on West Main Street, displays relics from the battle, as well as Indian artifacts and NASA exhibits.

For a unique shopping experience and one-of-a-kind gifts, visit *The Main Attraction and Coffee Bar* (214 West Main). Grab a cappuccino from the Elvis Coffee Bar, then browse shelves, walls, and racks packed with vintage clothing, funky clocks, lava lamps, beaded curtains, Moroccan hand drums, and off-the-wall refrigerator magnets. The Main Attraction also offers a spectacular assortment of jewelry, from very inexpensive to high-dollar pieces made with exotic stones. The Main Attraction welcomes adventurous shoppers Monday–Friday, 11:00 A.M.–5:00 P.M. and Saturday 11:00 A.M.–4:00 P.M.

West Main Street intersects with the historic *Natchez Trace Parkway,* a scenic route more than 8,000 years old. Maintained by the U.S. Department of the Interior, the Parkway is headquartered in Tupelo. A *visitors center* on the Trace just north of town offers information for travelers and exhibits related to the parkway's history. Three miles north of the visitors center is a preserved segment of the original Trace, which leads to the *graves of thirteen unknown Confederate soldiers.* Local legend has it they were executed by their own commander, the ill-tempered Braxton Bragg.

Tupelo offers delightful, unusual accommodations at the *Mockingbird Inn Bed and Breakfast,* where each room represents a different destination. Guests may wake up in Africa, Paris, Athens, Venice, Mackinac Island, Sanibel Island, or Bavaria. Although each room offers its own adventures, travelers would be wise to select a "country" toward the building's interior. The inn is located in the heart of town at 305 North Gloster on a very convenient but somewhat noisy corner. Rates at the Mockingbird Inn begin at $65. Call (601) 841–0286 for reservations.

Travel just 20 miles outside bustling, modern Tupelo and you'll find yourself back in rural Mississippi. Follow U.S. Highway 78 East into Itawamba County, where country music legend Tammy Wynette was born, then take Mississippi Highway 363 to the community of *Mantachie.* Located just over the hill and to the left of the Highway 363 turnoff at Church Street and Museum Drive is the *Bonds House and Museum,* a turn-of-the-century farmhouse maintained by the Itawamba Historical Society. The

Bonds House is not open regularly, but visitors can stroll the quiet grounds and peek inside the windows for a look at life on the farm.

Follow Highway 363 as it loops back toward the west. Just before you reach the end of Highway 363 at U.S. Highway 45, look to your left for **Peppertown Pottery.** Owners Titus and Euple Riley use native clay to create a number of decorative items, ranging from primitive face jugs to birdhouses to that decidedly southern necessity, the hush puppy dispenser. Every piece is a one-of-a-kind treasure. Titus and Euple opened the pottery shop in the early 1980s, but their first partnership began when they were married as teenagers in 1945. You'll find the happy couple at work Tuesday–Saturday 8:00 A.M.–4:00 P.M.

From Peppertown, take U.S. Highway 45 to Mississippi Highway 6 and head west 10 miles to **Pontotoc.** This gracious community features a number of lovely old homes and historic sites. The homes aren't open for tours, but driving-tour maps are available at the **Pontotoc County Chamber of Commerce** located at 81 South Main Street. Sites on the tour include antebellum homes, Civil War battlegrounds, and sites related to the Chickasaw Indians.

Pontotoc is also home to **Westmoreland's,** an eclectic collection of turn-of-the-century farm tools, clothing, quilts, and furnishings. The antiques were all collected by Mildred Westmoreland, whose motto is, "It's more than just old junk, it's American history." Housed in Ms. Westmoreland's home on Highway 9 North, the collection is open by appointment. Admission is $5.00. Call Ms. Westmoreland at (601) 489–7673 to arrange a visit.

From Pontotoc, take Mississippi Highway 41 South to U.S. Highway 278 and the railroad town of **Amory.** Named after Harcourt Amory, a shareholder in the railroad company, the town was founded as a train service stop between Memphis and Birmingham. Nearby Aberdeen was first considered as the stopping point, but the residents of that town, concerned about the noisy train whistles and the "riffraff" associated with the railroad, voted against it.

Follow the signs to the **Amory Regional Museum,** located in an old hospital building. Admission is free and a friendly tour guide will be happy to walk you through the many exhibits related to local history. Displays include Indian artifacts, a military room, and railroad memorabilia housed in an old train car. The most fascinating exhibits, however, are those related to the old hospital itself. Formerly the Gilmore Sanitarium, the museum displays medical equipment from the 1800s through the 1960s. A rate card describes the services of Dr. B. C. Tubb, a prominent local physician of the early 1900s who charged $1.00 for an office visit and $2.00 for house calls. An infant-sized iron lung, original scrub room, and instrument sterilizer that still smells of disinfectant may look primitive to the modern visitor, but once represented state-of-the-art medical equipment.

A log cabin restored and moved to the museum grounds offers a glimpse of small-town life in the 1840s. The cabin is furnished in the style of the period and includes a children's sleeping loft reminiscent of the *Little House on the Prairie* TV series. When you sign the guest register, check for an entry from January 1996 that reads, "I was born in this cabin in 1932." The Amory Regional Museum is open Monday–Friday 9:00 A.M.–5:00 P.M. and weekends 1:00–5:00 P.M.

From the museum, go 1 block over to Main Street and head toward downtown Amory and ***Bill's Hamburgers.*** The menu at Bill's includes hamburgers, hamburgers, and just for variety, hamburgers. It's hard to get confused at Bill's—your only choice is with or without onions. The restaurant has changed hands several times, but the menu has remained the same since 1929. Bill's is on Main Street at Vinegar Bend and is open from 7:00 A.M. (yep, those burgers are so good you may want them for breakfast) until 5:30 P.M. Monday through Friday and 7:00 A.M. to 5:00 P.M. Saturday.

The charming river town of ***Aberdeen*** is less than 20 miles south of Amory off Mississippi Highway 25. Located on the banks of the ***Tombigbee River,*** Aberdeen was one of the busiest ports of the nineteenth century. Huge shipments of cotton crowded the city's docks, and for a time Aberdeen was the second-largest city in Mississippi. Wealthy merchants and planters competed in the building of elaborate mansions, purchasing their furnishings in Europe and shipping them up the Tombigbee by steamboat.

Today Aberdeen's main attraction is a collection of elegant old homes showcasing architectural styles from Greek Revival to Victorian to Neoclassical. All told, Aberdeen boasts more than 200 homes and buildings listed on the National Register of Historic Places.

Several of the homes are open every April during the ***Aberdeen Spring Pilgrimage. The Magnolias***, a palatial, 1850 Greek Revival mansion donated to the city by a local resident, is open for tours daily. Call (601) 369–7956 to reach the attendant or contact the ***Aberdeen Visitors Bureau*** at (601) 369–4864 or (800) 634–3538.

Located at 124 West Commerce Street across from City Hall, the visitors bureau also offers a self-guided driving tour brochure and map of Aberdeen titled *A Search for Gold.* The tour takes visitors past several beautiful homes, including an area of magnificent Victorians known as **Silk Stocking Row.**

Weary travelers will enjoy a stay at the **Huckleberry Inn Bed and Breakfast,** located just off Commerce on Hickory Street in the heart of the historic district. During pilgrimage, hopeful visitors line up on the front porch in case there's a last-minute cancellation. The inn doubles as a tea room, with lunch served Tuesday through Friday. Rates begin at $55. Call (601) 369–7294 for reservations. If the Huckleberry is booked, check with the visitors center for information on a handful of equally charming bed-and-breakfast inns just outside Aberdeen.

The **Old Aberdeen Cemetery** is the site of a tale worthy of Ripley's Believe It or Not. It seems Ms. Alice Whitfield was knitting—a popular pastime in 1854—when she died in her rocking chair. According to local legend, Ms. Whitfield was then buried in the rocking chair, knitting and all. The cemetery, located at the corner of Whitfield and Poplar Streets, also includes a number of Civil War–era gravesites.

Antiques buffs should plan a stop at **Petunia's,** a quaint shop doing business in an old cottage at 100 West Canal Street. Petunia's is owned by a Hollywood makeup artist who's also an Aberdeen native; his mother runs the shop for him between visits.

Points of interest just outside Aberdeen include **Cedarwycke** and **Lenoir Plantation,** two working plantations open for tours by appointment. Located on Mississippi Highway 373 near **Hamilton,** Cedarwycke was built in 1852 as the main house of an 815-acre plantation. Many of the original outbuildings remain, including the old kitchen, root cellar, dog kennel, and smokehouse.

The main house features a unique "daughter's stair." In the 1800s, the only entrance and exit to the daughter's quarters was through a stair that opened into the master suite. The daughter's stair was a safety feature designed to protect the young ladies of the home from weary travelers who might stop and ask to stay overnight in the plantation house. The home's current occupants, Sam and Kathy Crawford, added a separate entrance to the room for their own daughter.

It's the lucky visitor who happens by on an afternoon when Sam's mother, Helen Crawford, is visiting. Ms. Crawford lives just down the road, but she also lived in Cedarwycke before passing it on to her son's family. It's she who painstakingly labeled each of the outbuildings, and she can tell you more stories about the plantation and surrounding area than any history book. If you ask her nicely and promise not to repeat it, she may even share the tale of the Bloody Shirt Incident, a centuries-old scandal that's still discussed only in whispers.

Cedarwycke is very much a lived-in home, and visitors are likely to see Kathy's latest yard sale acquisitions as well as antiques on a tour. Kathy stresses that tours of Cedarwycke are available only in the afternoon, "because my children like to sleep late." Call (601) 343–8400 or (601) 343–8402 for an appointment. The $5.00 admission includes the house, grounds, and all the outbuildings.

The **Lenoir Plantation Home** has been occupied by six generations of the Lenoir family, including present owners Whit and Betty Lenoir. Both Union and Confederate troops occupied the plantation during the Civil War. A family portrait hanging over the mantel still bears a bayonet wound inflicted by Union soldiers looking for treasure hidden in the walls.

Original artwork in the house depicts the Aberdeen of the 1800s. One painting captures several members of the Lenoir family at a spring lawn party. The house in the painting, **Meckford,** still stands in Aberdeen today. A handwritten ledger in the library serves as a family record and includes the names of the plantation slaves recorded in an elegant nineteenth-century cursive. A handwritten cookbook on the same shelf includes recipes for making candles and medicines as well as favorite dishes.

Like Cedarwycke, Lenoir Plantation is open by appointment. Admission is $5.00. The plantation is located on Lenoir Loop in tiny **Prairie.** Call (601) 369–4486 for directions and to arrange a visit.

If you're in the area in November, take Mississippi Highway 8 West to **Vardaman** and the **National Sweet Potato Festival.** The week of activities includes sweet potato pie cooking and eating contests, a flea market, the crowning of the Sweet Potato Queen, and the judging of the most attractive washed and waxed bushel of sweet potatoes. Call the Mississippi Division of Tourism at (800) WARMEST for this year's festival dates.

The Natchez Trace Parkway

The **Natchez Trace Parkway** stretches diagonally across Mississippi, cuts a corner through Alabama, then winds to an end in Nashville, Tennessee, following an unspoiled route through lush forests, beside sparkling streams, and into the heart of America's frontier past.

This timeworn scenic path, more than 400 miles long and 8,000 years old, was originally "traced out" by buffalo, then trekked by Indians, and finally trampled into a rough road by trappers, traders, and missionaries. French maps dated as early as 1733 include the Natchez Trace; British maps of the same period refer to it as the "Path to the Choctaw Nation." From 1800–1820 the frontier brimmed with trade and new settlements, and the Natchez Trace was the busiest highway in the southwest.

But by the late 1820s, the speed of steamboats made travel along the Natchez Trace impractical, and the once-busy road dissolved into the brush. In 1909, the Daughters of the American Revolution spearheaded a campaign to mark the Old Trace, and their work culminated in the Natchez Trace Parkway, a national highway maintained by the National Park Service.

Today's highway closely follows the original trail. The uniquely southern penchant for sharing good tales preserved the colorful legends surrounding the Trace, and historic markers along the way detail the path's romantic history. Indian mounds, ghost towns, and nature trails beckon from just off the paved road.

Visitors exploring northeast Mississippi via the Natchez Trace will encounter wildlife, enjoy natural beauty free of commercial traffic, and pass historic sites too numerous to list. A few words of caution for

Little-Known Facts about the Northeastern Hills

- *The oldest book in the United States, an ancient Biblical manuscript, is housed at the University of Mississippi.*

- *On December 7, 1874, the Jesse James Gang held up Corinth's Tishomingo Savings Bank, escaping with $15,000.*

- *Elvis Presley was scheduled to play in Corinth in 1954, but had to cancel due to low ticket sales.*

- *Tupelo was one of only four cities in the United States that celebrated the first official Mother's Day in 1908.*

first-time Trace travelers—stick to the 50-mile-per-hour speed limit, which is constantly monitored and always enforced. And while the Trace is tranquil and uncrowded by day, it can seem a little dark and spooky at night. Small towns and cities are located at frequent intervals just off the parkway, but there are no commercial establishments and only one gas station on the Trace itself. Finally, night travelers should keep an alert watch for deer, which are known to bolt into the road unexpectedly.

Traveling north to south on the Trace through northeast Mississippi, visitors pass many of the attractions mentioned earlier in this chapter. The parkway runs directly through **Tishomingo State Park** (see page 19) located in the extreme northeastern corner of the state. Near mile marker 293.4 are wayside exits for the **Tennessee-Tombigbee Waterway**, a 234-mile scenic passage and recreational area connecting the inland South with the Gulf of Mexico.

The Trace is headquartered in **Tupelo** (see page 22), home of the **Natchez Trace Visitors Center.** A museum located within the visitors center houses artifacts and displays chronicling the history and development of the Old Natchez Trace and the modern parkway. A scenic nature trail located on the property provides a welcome break from the road.

PLACES TO STAY IN THE NORTHEASTERN HILLS

The following is a partial listing of the many hotels, motels, and bed-and-breakfast inns in the area.

ABERDEEN
Huckleberry Inn
(bed and breakfast),
500 South Hickory Street;
(601) 369–7294

Morgan's Country Home
(bed and breakfast),
20147 Adams Road;
(601) 842–5483

Morgan's Hill Top Inn
(bed and breakfast),
20136 Adams Road;
(601) 369–6521

BELMONT
Belmont Hotel and
Bed and Breakfast,
121 Main Street;
(601) 454–7948

CORINTH
The Carriage House
(bed and breakfast),
515 Fourth Street;
(601) 287–4860

Comfort Inn,
2101 Highway 72 West;
(601) 287–4421

Madison Inn
(bed and breakfast),
822 Main Street;
(601) 287–7157

The Generals' Quarters
(bed and breakfast),
924 Fillmore Street;
(601) 286–3325

Ravenswood
(bed and breakfast),
1002 Douglas Street;
(601) 665–0044

Robbins Nest
(bed and breakfast),
1523 Shiloh Road;
(601) 286–3109

Samuel D. Bramlitt House
(bed and breakfast),
1125 Cruise Street;
(601) 286–5370

GRENADA
Comfort Inn,
1610 State Highway 8 West
(Sunset Drive);
(601) 226–1683

Hampton Inn,
1622 State Highway 8 West
(Sunset Drive);
(601) 226–5555

HERNANDO
Days Inn,
Highway 304 off I–55,
exit 280;
(601) 429–0000

Faulkner Inn
(bed and breakfast),
2424 Highway 301 South;
(601) 429–3195

Sassafras Inn
(bed and breakfast),
785 Highway 51 South;
(601) 429–5864

Shadow Hill
(bed and breakfast),
2310 Elm Street;
(601) 449–0800

HOLLY SPRINGS
Fort-Daniel Hall
(bed and breakfast),
184 South Memphis;
(601) 252–6807

Holiday Inn Express,
155 Clarice Drive;
(601) 252–7770

Rutledge Carriage House
(bed and breakfast),
145 West Gholson Avenue;
(601) 252–3842

Somerset Cottage
(bed and breakfast),
310 South Cedar Hills Road;
(601) 252–4513

HORN LAKE
Ramada Inn Limited,
6851 Interstate Boulevard;
(800) 228–2828

Sleep Inn Motel,
708 DeSoto Cove;
(800) 753–3746

**LINCOLN LTD. BED AND
BREAKFAST RESERVATIONS**
Lincoln Ltd. is a full-time
reservation service for bed-
and-breakfast inns
statewide. For reservations
in any area of Mississippi,
call (800) 633–6477 or
(601) 482–5483.

OLIVE BRANCH
Brigadoon Farm Retreat
(bed and breakfast),
350 Highway 305;
(601) 895–3098

OXFORD
Barksdale-Isom House
(bed and breakfast),
1003 Jefferson Street;
(601) 236–5600 or
(800) 236–5696

Best Western Oxford Inn,
1101 Frontage Road;
(601) 234–9500

Comfort Inn,
1808 Jackson Avenue West;
(601) 234–6000

The Oliver Britt House
(bed and breakfast),
512 Van Buren Avenue;
(601) 234–8043

Puddin Place
(bed and breakfast),
1008 University Avenue;
(601) 234–1250

TUPELO
Comfort Inn,
1190 North Gloster Street;
(601) 842–5100

Courtyard by Marriott,
1320 North Gloster Street;
(601) 841–9960

Mockingbird Inn
(bed and breakfast),
305 North Gloster Street;
(601) 841–0286

Rex Plaza Suites,
619 North Gloster Street;
(601) 840–8000

**PLACES TO EAT IN
THE NORTHEASTERN HILLS**

*The following is a partial
listing of the many restaurants in the area.*

AMORY
Bill's Hamburgers,
Main Street;
(601) 256–2085

COMO
Como Steakhouse,
Main Street;
(601) 526–9529

CORINTH
Borrum's Drug & Fountain
(sandwiches, ice cream),
604 Waldron Street;
(601) 286–3361

Cross City Grille
(sandwiches, salads),
307 East Waldron Street;
(601) 287–7282

Margel's (pasta, seafood,
steaks, gourmet pizza),
707 Foote Street;
(601) 286–0000

GRENADA
Beef House (steak),
1206 State Highway 8;
(601) 226–9990

Country Kitchen
(burgers, blue-plate
specials, breakfast),
15 State Highway 8;
(601) 226–0530

Jake 'n Rips
(barbecue, catfish),
1436 State Highway 8;
(601) 227–9955

Salads, Etc.
(salads, soups,
sandwiches),
2077 Highway 51 South;
(601) 226–8001

The Donut Shop
(donuts, breakfast),
1268 Highway 51 North;
(601) 226–3551

Major fast-food chains

HOLLY SPRINGS
Phillips Grocery (burgers),
541 East Van Dorn Avenue;
(601) 252–4671

HOUSTON
Pearson's Discount Drug
Store (soda fountain),
101 East Washington
Street;
(601) 456–2551

NEW ALBANY
Latham's Hamburger Inn,
106 West Main;
(601) 534–5315

OXFORD
City Grocery
(contemporary American),
152 Courthouse Square;
(601) 232–8080

Henry Cafe and Jubilee
Lounge (American),
1006 Jackson Avenue East;
(601) 236–3757

Yocona River Inn
(steak, catfish),
Mississippi Highway 334,
Yocona;
(601) 234–2464

Major fast-food chains

SOUTHAVEN
Major fast-food chains

TUPELO
Finney's Sandwich
& Soda Shop,
1009 West Main;
(601) 842–1746

Jefferson Place
(beef, seafood),
(Ask about Dr. Nash,
the restaurant's
resident ghost),
823 Jefferson Street;
(601) 844–8696

Johnny's Drive Inn
(burgers, sandwiches),
908 East Main;
(601) 842–6748

Major fast-food and casual
dining chains

WATER VALLEY
Nallie's Place (sandwiches),
903 Central Street;
(601) 473–4691

**OTHER ATTRACTIONS
WORTH SEEING IN
THE NORTHEASTERN HILLS**

BATESVILLE
Factory Stores of
Mississippi

HOLLY SPRINGS
Wall Doxey State Park

SARDIS
John W. Kyle State Park

TUPELO
Tombigbee State Park

Trace State Park

MEMPHIS, TN
Beale Street

Graceland
(Elvis Presley Home)

SHILOH, TN
Shiloh National Military
Park

The Eastern Plains

The Eastern Plains span rich black prairies, pastoral cattle farms, sacred Indian homelands, and bustling industrial centers.

Tradition runs deep here, whether it's found in a carefully restored antebellum home, a hallowed Indian mound, or a modern company's success story.

The stops here have more in common than just freshly painted front porches, and it's more than just the sights and scenery that make this region special. The Eastern Plains are blessed with a singular culture centuries in the making and a rich history that's mellowed into legend.

The Golden Triangle

The small cities of Columbus, West Point, and Starkville make up the region known locally as the Golden Triangle. The three cities work together to promote themselves, capitalizing on the rich diversity of activities and attractions available in this small geographic area.

A tour of the Golden Triangle begins in *Columbus,* a pretty little town of antebellum homes and antiques shops near the Mississippi–Alabama line. Entering Columbus from Highway 82 West, take the Main Street exit and make your first stop the *Tennessee Williams Home/Mississippi Welcome Center.* This cheerful, gray and yellow Victorian built in 1878 was the first home of the famous playwright who introduced the world to Blanche DuBois and penned Marlon Brando's most memorable line—"Stelllla!" Inside, a friendly staffer will provide you with maps, a walking- and driving-tour brochure, and tickets to Columbus tour homes. An audio cassette of the driving tour is also available for purchase or rental.

The city's two historic districts showcase one of the greatest diversities of antebellum architecture in the South. Shaded streets are lined with carefully preserved examples of Greek Revival, Italianate, Federal, and Gothic

33

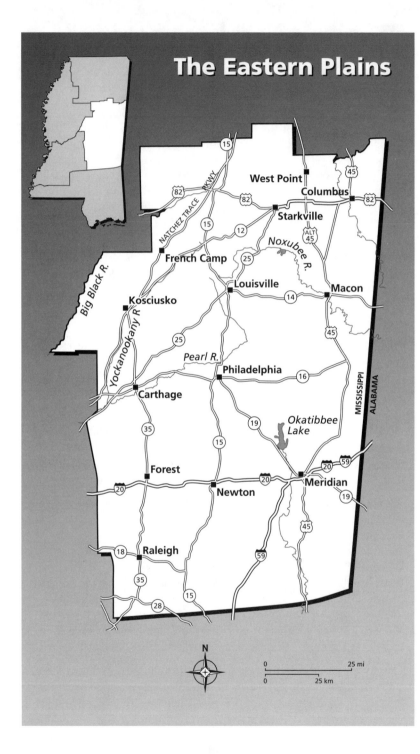

The Eastern Plains

Revival–style mansions and cottages. At least two homes are open for tours any day of the week. Pick up the tour schedule and purchase a $5.00 per-home ticket at the Tennessee Williams Birthplace. Homes are open 10:00 A.M.–4:00 P.M. Monday–Saturday and 2:00–4:00 P.M. Sunday.

Tour homes include *Amzi Love,* built in 1848 and continuously occupied by generations of the Love family ever since; *Highland House,* rebuilt in 1909 after the original home was burned to the ground by a jealous housekeeper; the *Lee Home and Museum,* former residence of Confederate General Stephen D. Lee; and *Temple Heights,* supposedly haunted by an eccentric ghost named Elizabeth. Also on the tour is *Rosewood Manor,* built for a northern-born bride who refused to occupy it, insisting that a ravine near the house would leave her susceptible to "the vapors." Several of the tour homes double as bed-and-breakfast inns. Call (800) 689–3983 or (601) 328–0222 for rates and reservations.

Y'all Come Back Now, Ya Hear?

I've lived in Mississippi for more than ten years now, and the natives still say they can tell I'm "not from around here." My hometown is Memphis, Tennessee—a city, it seems, that's too far north for me to have a truly southern accent.

The much-maligned, equally celebrated, and often-imitated southern drawl is as indigenous to Mississippi as grits and humidity. Visitors may poke fun at the slow, fluid pace of our speech, but can anyone really find the fast-paced, short-clipped, now-now-now! cadence of a Yankee tongue more pleasing than the soothing, melodic, drippin'-with-molasses rhythm of a genuine, southern-fried voice asking for "moah ahs tae, plase?" ("more iced tea, please?")

In the movies, the southern drawl is used as a kind of unflattering shorthand, a lazy way to characterize ignorance, poverty, or redneckism. But we
southerners (even those of us from as far north as Memphis) are actually proud of our melodious, genteel drawl. Down here, slow, sultry, vowel-laden speech is a sign of good breeding, the hallmark that separates the Scarlett O'Haras from the no 'count riffraff.

To us, it's the northern tongue that sounds so foreign. But be warned— one of the gravest sins a visiting northerner can commit is attempting to imitate the southern style of speech. Trust me, you aren't fooling anyone.

Of course, most Yankees are able to enjoy a visit to Mississippi without bringing along a translator. Just listen a little more slowly, and you'll be able to communicate with us just fine. But if you learn only one thing about the southern way of speaking during your visit, make it this: the word "y'all" is short for "you all" and is never, ever singular.

The country estate and bed and breakfast known as **Liberty Hall** has been occupied by descendants of the same family since its construction in 1832. Portraits of the French Huguenot ancestors who built the house still grace its walls. The focal point of the dining room is a series of panels hand painted with French pastoral scenes. When the Civil War broke out, the artist commissioned to paint them returned to his home in South Carolina, leaving a handful of the panels forever unfinished. Rooms are $85; call (601) 328–4110 for reservations.

All of Columbus' tour homes boast their share of history and charm, but the most fascinating home on tour is the magnificent **Waverley Plantation,** appropriate subject matter for everything from *This Old House* to *Unsolved Mysteries.* Waverley was built in 1852 and served as home to the original builder's family until the last descendant died in 1913. For nearly fifty years Waverley sat vacant. Then, in 1962, Robert and Donna Snow fought their way through the overgrown grounds, stepped into the graffiti-plastered foyer, and fell in love. The Snows bought Waverley and began the painstaking process of restoration.

It was a daunting task. Vines had crept in through the broken windows, birds and bats called the cupola home, and every wall was covered with graffiti. The late Donna Snow once remarked that "you weren't anyone unless you had written your name, the date, and who you loved on the wall. I've been privy to every love affair from 1913 to 1962." Remarkably, the vandals and curiosity seekers left the house largely intact. Of the original 718 staircase spindles, only three were missing. Just two panes were broken in the front door glass, and the only damage to two towering, gilded mirrors was a crack inflicted during a Civil War dance.

Room by room, the Snows restored Waverley to its former glory. Today it's hard to believe the opulent mansion was once an abandoned ruin. From the first floor foyer (so spacious it doubles as a ballroom), two curved, freestanding staircases rise to join balconies on the second, third, and fourth floors. Sixteen windows surround the mansion's lofty cupola, 65 feet above the entry.

The Ghost of Waverley Plantation

When Robert and Donna Snow purchased the old Waverley Plantation in the early 1960s, they knew they were buying a piece of history. They didn't know they were also inheriting a former resident.

The Snows had lived in Waverley for about two years when the ghost made her first appearance. Donna Snow heard a child crying, sometimes calling for her "mama." A small indentation began appearing on the upstairs bed, about the size of a child napping. The Snows once sat in the room for an entire afternoon and actually saw the bedclothes straighten themselves when the ghost child "awakened." The little girl has appeared only once, dressed in a ruffled nightgown and standing on the stairway. To this day, her identity remains a mystery.

THE EASTERN PLAINS

MARLO'S FAVORITE ATTRACTIONS IN THE EASTERN PLAINS

Waverley Plantation,
Columbus

Friendship Cemetery,
Columbus

The aroma at the Ole Country Bakery, *Macon*

L. V. Hull's House,
Kosciusko (look for the shoe tree with my name on it)

Neshoba County Fairgrounds
(air-conditioned cabins only), Philadelphia, (601) 656–1742

A whirl on the Dentzel Carousel, *Meridian*

The peanut butter at Weidmann's, *Meridian*

Waverley is located 10 miles north of Columbus and 15 miles east of West Point on Mississippi Highway 50 near the Tombigbee River. The house is open for tours seven days a week from 9:00 A.M.–5:00 P.M. Admission is $7.50.

Twelve antebellum homes are open during the annual **Columbus Spring Pilgrimage.** In addition to the obligatory hoop skirts and blooming gardens, the Columbus extravaganza offers a look at period crafts, with demonstrations ranging from antique doll restoration to lace making to china painting staged in several of the tour houses. Pilgrimage tickets are $15 per three-home tour package. Several antebellum churches that served as Civil War hospitals also open their doors for free tours during pilgrimage week. Call the **Columbus Convention and Visitors Bureau** at (800) 327–2686 for this year's pilgrimage dates.

Columbus was one of a handful of Mississippi cities never occupied by Union troops during the Civil War. In fact, the most significant war-related event in Columbus occurred on April 25, 1866, a year after the war ended. A group of war widows visiting **Odd Fellows Cemetery** decided to decorate not only the graves of their husbands and fathers, but of the Union soldiers buried there as well. A newspaper account of the event read, "We are glad to see that no distinction was made between our own Confederate dead and Federal soldiers who slept their last sleep by them. . . . Confederate and Federal—once enemies, now friends receiving their tribute of respect." The gesture was immortalized in a poem titled, "The Blue and the Gray" (see sidebar, page 40), which was carried in newspapers nationwide. News of the good deed of the ladies of Columbus quickly spread, spurring other communities to follow suit and earning Columbus a reputation as the city "where flowers healed a nation." This simple Decoration Day evolved into America's national Memorial Day, and the cemetery was renamed "Friendship." **Twelve Gables,** the home where the ladies met to plan their Decoration Day, is open for tours during pilgrimage.

Friendship Cemetery is located at the end of South Fourth Street in the South Columbus Historic District behind the Tennessee Williams Birthplace. Fourth Street is interrupted by a small warehouse district; to reach the cemetery, go 1 block over to Fifth Street and head south until Fourth

Street picks up again. From Fifth Street look to your right until you spot a tall wrought-iron fence surrounding the elaborate 1800s monuments.

A stroll through the oldest section of the cemetery reveals exquisite monuments honoring loved ones of the 1800s. A few of the markers are so old their inscriptions haven't merely faded, but have disappeared altogether. Several military graves are marked with swords and Confederate emblems. In the center of the cemetery, the Mississippi state flag, United States flag, and Confederate flag fly over row after row of simple markers honoring the Civil War dead. The Columbus pilgrimage includes a *Candlelight Tour* of Friendship Cemetery, complete with costumed guides who relate true stories about Friendship's "residents." Tickets are $2.00 for adults, $1.00 for children. Tours are conducted 7:00–10:00 P.M.

Located at the edge of the South Historic District on College Street, *Mississippi University for Women* was the first state-supported women's college in the country. Organized in 1884, "the W" campus includes

Friendship Cemetery

twenty-four buildings listed on the National Register of Historic Places. In 1982, "the W" went coed and now bills itself as "Mississippi University for Women . . . And Smart Men, Too."

Downtown Columbus is home to some twenty antiques and gift shops offering one-of-a-kind gifts and collectibles. Many of these specialty shops carry *Jubilations Cheesecakes*, made in Columbus and shipped to cheesecake lovers nationwide.

Columbus is the largest city on the *Tennessee-Tombigbee Waterway.* Parks bordering the Tenn-Tom offer nature trails, boat launches, charter excursions, and Class A campsites. For more information, contact the Tenn-Tom Water-

Little-Known Facts About Mississippi

- *In 1839, the Mississippi Legislature passed one of the first laws in the English-speaking world protecting the property rights of married women.*

- *Mississippi was the first state in the nation with a planned system of junior colleges.*

- *With an estimated population of two million, more whitetail deer make their home in Mississippi than in any other state. Sportsmen bag an average of 275,000 deer in the state every year.*

- *One-fourth of the nation's supercomputing power is housed in Mississippi.*

- *With a population of 2,592,000, Mississippi ranks thirty-first among the fifty states.*

- *Some 78,000 Mississippians joined the Confederate military. By the Civil War's end, 59,000 were dead or wounded.*

- *Mississippi has more certified tree farms than any other state.*

way Development Authority at (601) 328–3286. For camping reservations, contact the U.S. Army Corps of Engineers at (601) 327– 2142.

A 30-mile drive through the countryside south of town leads to a number of rural adventures. From Columbus, take Highway 45 South to Mississippi Highway 388, a pastoral route punctuated by grain silos and populated by disinterested, highly aromatic cows.

Continue east to the ***Bigbee Valley General Store.*** This 150-year-old general store once served as the sole supplier to hundreds of sharecropping families. As the proprietor explains, "They bought everything they needed at this store on credit, then settled up at the end of the year. There was usually nothing left after they paid their bill, but the landowner took care of everything else for them anyway." The post office once operated a branch out of the store, and even though it's long since closed, locals still come in to drop off and pick up their mail. The proprietor simply hands it off to the postman. An ancient typewriter, old shoes, clothes, and a washboard rest in a jumble on a long table, "not for sale but just for folks who like to look at old stuff." Just 5 miles from the Mississippi–Alabama state line, the Bigbee Valley General Store is the perfect spot to enjoy an RC Cola and a moon pie, the official snack of the good ole boys club. The store is open for business and sightseeing Monday–Saturday, except Thursday afternoons.

Back on Highway 45 South, continue into the tiny town of **Brooksville** and follow the comforting aroma of fresh-baked bread to the **Ole Country Bakery.** Tempting cakes, pies, and pastries line the shelves of this old-fashioned bakery operated by the Mennonites, a community similar to the Amish in their dress and lifestyle. A friendly woman clad in a flowered dress and apron and wearing the traditional black cap will take your order for warm baked goods or giant po' boy sandwiches. The bakery is open during breakfast and lunch hours only and is closed Sunday and Monday.

"The Blue and the Gray"

*A*merica's Memorial Day was first celebrated in Columbus in 1866, when a group of war widows decided to decorate not only the graves of their own loved ones, but of the Union soldiers buried in Columbus as well. Their gesture was immortalized in the following poem, originally published in The Atlantic Monthly *in September 1867.*

"The Blue and the Gray"

By the flow of the inland river,

Where the fleets of iron have fled,

Where the blades of grave grass quiver,

Asleep are the ranks of the dead;

Under the sod and the dew,

Waiting the judgment day—

Under the one, the blue,

Under the other, the gray.

From the silence of sorrowful hours

The desolate mourners go,

Lovingly laden with flowers

Alike for the friend and the foe;

Under the sod and the dew,

Waiting the judgment day—

Under the roses, the blue

Under the lilies, the gray.

Sadly, but not with upbraiding,

The generous deed was done;

In the storm of the years that are fading,

No braver battle was won;

Under the sod and the dew,

Waiting the judgment day—

Under the blossoms, the blue,

Under the garlands, the gray.

No more shall the war-cry sever,

Or the winding rivers be red;

They banish our anger forever

When they laurel the graves of our dead;

Under the sod and the dew,

Waiting the judgment day—

Love and tears for the blue,

Tears and love for the gray.

—Frances Miles Finch

Continue on Highway 45 South 9 miles to **Macon.** Take a right onto Mississippi Highway 14 into downtown, turn right on Jefferson Street, then take the first right past the Noxubee County courthouse. The imposing redbrick building on your left is the **Noxubee County Library,** perhaps the only library in the country with bars on the windows and a hanging gallows inside. The library is housed in the old town jail built in 1907. The original iron doors, window bars, and working gallows all remain; the library books are stored in the old cells. Climb the thirteen steps that lead to the gallows if you dare; the librarian promises to "come find you if you scream." Bring your camera—the librarian will loan you a black-and-white striped uniform to slip on while she snaps your photo behind bars. You'll even receive a folder headlined, "Look who's in jail and loves it" in which to display your mug shot. Pretend to be a convict or a bookworm Monday, Tuesday, Thursday, or Friday 8:00 A.M.–6:00 P.M.

From the library, continue on Jefferson Street 2 blocks, then take a left on North Street to **Huntwood Designs.** It's here that artist Diana Jabar creates her distinctive "Yesterday's Ole World Santas," one-of-a-kind Santa Clauses fashioned after Victorian images of Father Christmas. Each 40-inch-tall Santa strikes a different pose, and each Santa face is hand sculpted and hand painted—no two are alike. Bring along a small trinket, toy, or a scrap of cloth from a favorite dress or quilt, and Diana will create a Heritage Santa made just for you. Huntwood Designs is open seasonally and by appointment. Call (601) 726–9866.

Back on Highway 45, you'll spot the **Oak Tree Inn and Restaurant** just south of the turnoff to downtown Macon. The inn was the brainchild of Dr. and Mrs. Guy Blaudeau of Birmingham, Alabama. It seems Dr. Blaudeau visited the Macon area frequently on hunting trips and saw the need for a place for weary outdoorsmen to pass the night and enjoy a good meal. The inn is clean and comfortable, but the real surprise is waiting in **The Sherwood,** the inn's restaurant.

The decor is more early Shoney's than fine dining, with checkered tablecloths and baseball-capped, camouflage-clad diners making up most of the ambience. But open the menu and you'll find an incredible selection of gourmet offerings including veal, steak, seafood, even escargot, accompanied by a fairly good wine list. It's a little taste of the French Quarter, right there in Macon. In fact, Chef Joseph Broussard trained under French chefs in New Orleans and cooked for several renowned eateries, including the New Orleans Country Club, before finding his way to Macon. The Sherwood is open for lunch 11:00 A.M.–2:00 P.M. Monday–Sunday and for dinner

5:30–9:00 P.M. Sunday–Thursday, 5:30–10:00 P.M. Friday and Saturday. Rooms at the Oak Tree Inn begin at $45. Call (601) 726–5835 or (800) 448–6545 for reservations.

"Goin' once . . . Goin' twice . . . Sold!" If you're in the Macon area on a Monday afternoon, stop by the **cattle auction barn** on Highway 45 at the northern edge of town. Even if you don't happen to be traveling with a full-sized cattle trailer, hearing a live auctioneer call for bids on prized livestock is an entertainment experience you won't find just anywhere. Auctions are held every Monday at 1:00 P.M.

Serious outdoorsmen may want to take a side trip to the **Circle M Plantation** south of town. This 6,000-acre hunting preserve is carefully managed to ensure prime whitetail deer, quail, and wild turkey hunting. Overnight accommodations and meeting facilities are available on the property. For more information or to arrange a hunt, call (601) 726-5791.

From Macon, take Highway 45 Alternate North to **West Point,** listed in Norm Crampton's *The 100 Best Small Towns in America.* This point of the Golden Triangle is built around outdoor recreation, with many of its attractions named for nearby Waverley Plantation.

You might not expect to find a championship golf course in a community of 8,000 people, but the **Old Waverly Golf Club** made *Golf Digest's* list of the top 100 courses in America. Designed by Bob Cupp and Jerry Pate, Old Waverly attracts serious players from around the country and hosted the 1999 U.S. Women's Open Championship. Guest green fees are $65 weekdays and $80 weekends. The cart fee is $25. Cottages overlooking the course are available for overnight guests at rates ranging from $65 to $320 per night. Call (601) 494–6463 for reservations.

Avid anglers should plan a stay at **Waverly Waters.** West Point's newest resort offers sport fishing in a seventy-acre lake stocked with largemouth bass, bluegill, and bream. The lake is natural, with an underwater structure of tree tops, stumps, tires, and other fish habitats designed by Bill Dance. The resort also features a professionally designed sporting clay range and jogging and nature trails. Guests stay overnight in the rustic cypress lodge or in one of five cabins. Rates are $350–$400 per night for groups only for the lodge, which sleeps fourteen, and $60 for cabins, which sleep up to four. A full day of fishing is $50, a half-day is $35. Boat rentals are $35 a day or $20 a half-day. Guests must stay overnight to fish. Call (601) 494–1800 for reservations.

THE EASTERN PLAINS

In a town that makes outdoor recreation such a priority, it's only logical that the largest retail outlet for Mossy Oak camouflage wear is found on Main Street. This favorite hunting attire is made in West Point and sold at **Haas Outdoors,** 101 East Main Street.

Lunch or dinner time calls for a trip to **Anthony's** (116 West Main Street), a grocery-store-turned-restaurant that still features the original meat coolers in the back of the main dining room. Lunch at Anthony's is a country-cooked buffet of fried chicken, lima beans, cornbread, and other assorted "Bubba food." Dinner is a more upscale affair, with a menu featuring seafood, steak, and poultry. On "Once in a Blues Moon Night," held the first Saturday of each month, Anthony's brings in a live blues band. Anthony's is open for lunch Sunday–Friday 11:00 A.M.–2:00 P.M. and for dinner Monday–Thursday 5:00–9:30 P.M., Friday and Saturday 'til 10:00 P.M.

MARLO'S FAVORITE ANNUAL EVENTS IN THE EASTERN PLAINS

Columbus

Spring Pilgrimage / Tales From the Crypt,
April, (800) 327–2686

Possumtown Pigfest,
September, (601) 328–4532

Meridian

Jimmie Rodgers Memorial Country Music Festival,
May, (888) 868–7720

Philadelphia

Choctaw Indian Fair,
July, (601) 650–1685

Neshoba County Fair,
August, (601) 656–1742

West Point

Prairie Arts Festival,
September, (601) 494–5121

The population of West Point triples Labor Day weekend when the **Prairie Arts Festival** brings more than 600 vendors and 30,000 festival-goers to downtown. The high point of the festival is a juried art show, but shoppers may also choose from flea market trinkets and fine antiques. Nonshoppers will enjoy four stages of entertainment, food, and children's activities. The Prairie Arts Festival is held the Saturday before Labor Day. The Friday night prior to the Prairie Arts Festival, West Point hosts the **Howlin' Wolf Blues Festival,** a tribute to West Point native and blues legend Chester "Howlin" Wolf Burnet.

From West Point, take U.S. Highway 82 West to **Starkville,** the final point on the Golden Triangle and the home of **Mississippi State University.** Take the downtown exit, turn left on Main Street, then head straight onto the sprawling campus. The state's largest university, MSU is a national leader in agricultural research. If a groundbreaking soybean study doesn't excite you, how about wine-making? A tour of the **A. B. McKay Food and Enology Laboratory** takes wine lovers through the entire process from grapes to glass and concludes with a sampling of Mississippi muscadine wines. Call (601) 325–2440 to schedule a tour and tasting.

Don't leave campus without a hefty ball of Mississippi State's own Edam cheese. Manufactured at the dairy science plant on campus, this smooth, flavorful cheese is sold in one, two, and three-pound balls wrapped in red wax bearing the official university seal. Mississippi State cheese is sold by mail to Edam lovers around the world and in the Cheese Sales Office in the *Herzer Dairy Science Building.* The Herzer building is located on the campus on Stone Boulevard. The cheese shop is open Monday–Friday 8:00 A.M.–5:00 P.M. Tours at the cheese- and ice-cream-making facility are available with notice. Call (601) 325–3228 to schedule a visit.

New to MSU is the *John Grisham Room* in the university's Mitchell Memorial Library, which houses the best-selling author's papers and publications. The room is open Monday–Friday 9:00 A.M.–4:00 P.M.

Contrary to popular belief, there *was* music before MTV. Learn more about the history of the American music industry with a visit to the *Templeton Music Museum and Archives*, a large collection featuring more than 200 music-making machines, 22,000 pieces of sheet music, hundreds of music boxes, and 15,000 recordings, all manufactured or written between 1880 and 1930. The collection is housed in a 1910 Victorian home on Blackjack Road on the MSU campus. Call (601) 325–8301 to see (and hear!) the collection.

While "Bulldog Spirit" may seem to completely dominate the town, Starkville is also home to a number of off-campus attractions. The *C. C. Clark Memorial Coca-Cola Museum* (located at the Northeast Mississippi Bottling Company facility on Highway 12 West) displays more than 2,300 bottles, trays, advertisements, glasses, calendars, toys, and other artifacts celebrating the world's most popular soft drink.

Kids and adults alike will enjoy a visit to *Pinedale Farms*, where the residents include sheep, goats, pigs, rabbits, and chickens, as well as exotic animals like miniature horses, pot belly pigs, emus, and llamas. From Starkville, go west on Highway 82 5 miles past Stark Road. Turn right (north) onto County Lake Road, then immediately right onto Reed Road. Continue 1.5 miles to the Pinedale Farm entrance. Admission is $4.50. Reservations are required, so call (601) 323-9543 to schedule a visit and a picnic.

If you'd like a souvenir of your visit to Starkville, stop by the *Aspen Bay Company* gift shop (1010 Lynn Lane West) for a scented signature candle, visit *Giggleswick* (222 East Main Street) for upscale gifts and home accessories, or pick up a one-of-a-kind work of art at the *Main Street Gallery and Studio* (111 West Main Street).

Overnight guests receive a warm welcome at the *Statehouse Hotel* on Starkville's Main Street. Built in 1925, this charming, completely renovated hotel offers modern comforts in an elegant, old-world setting. Rates begin at $40 for a single and go up to $88 for a suite. Call (800) 722–1903. Starkville is also home to three historic bed-and-breakfast inns. *Carpenter Place,* Oktibbeha County's oldest home (1835), is located 2 miles south of downtown on 140 wooded acres. Rates are $75–$150. Call (601) 323–4669 for reservations. Rates at *The Cedars Bed and Breakfast,* 6 miles south of Starkville, are $45–$65. Accommodations are in an 1836 plantation house on 183 acres. Call (601) 324–7569. *Caragen House* is the only home of Steamboat Gothic Design in Mississippi. Rates at Caragen House are $85 Thursday–Sunday and $100 on Friday and Saturday. Call (888) 857–4053.

The Natchez Trace Parkway

This section of the legendary *Natchez Trace Parkway* includes three major stops and dozens of smaller historic sites marked by the familiar brown and yellow signs. Don't let the European flair of town names like "French Camp" and "Kosciusko" fool you. This leg of the parkway still retains the frontier charm for which the route is famous.

From Starkville, continue on U.S. Highway 82 West approximately 20 miles to Eupora, where Highway 82 intersects the Natchez Trace. Head south on the Trace to mile marker 193.1 and *Jeff Busby Park,* a national park named for Congressman Thomas Jefferson Busby, who introduced the bill calling for the surveying of the Old Natchez Trace and the creation of the modern parkway.

"Starkville City Jail"

In the mid-1960s, Johnny Cash performed a concert at Mississippi State University. Afterward, he went back to his motel and had a few drinks, then decided to go out for smokes.

Maybe it was the few drinks or the intricacies of locating smokes in an unfamiliar town, but Cash wound up parked in a local family's flowerbed. On any other night the family might have been flattered by the country star's unexpected detour, but their daughter

had planned to use the ill-fated flowers in her upcoming wedding and was most distraught to find them flattened.

Cash spent the remainder of his visit to Starkville in the city jail. But far from being humbled by the experience, Cash capitalized on his run-in with the local law, penning a tune called "Starkville City Jail." Cash soon returned to Starkville to sign copies of his new album, bringing with him gifts for the entire Starkville police force.

Jeff Busby features nature trails, campsites, picnic areas, and a panoramic, 20-mile view from the overlook atop Little Mountain, one of the highest points in Mississippi. A well-marked nature trail identifies native plants and describes their use as foods and medicines by early settlers. Be warned—the trail looks deceptively easy, but will definitely leave you winded and ready for a cool drink from the convenience store at the park entrance. If you plan to continue along the Natchez Trace from here, gas up now. The service station at Jeff Busby is the only one located directly on the parkway.

Continue on the parkway 12 miles south of Jeff Busby to **French Camp,** a charming little village established in 1812. Nearly 200 years later, French Camp is still best described as a peaceful settlement on the rural frontier. Attractions just off the Natchez Trace include the **Colonel James Drane Plantation House,** built in 1846, and a **working sorghum mill,** which operates in the fall. The French Camp information center and a gift shop selling syrup and other souvenirs are housed in an 1846 log cabin filled with period artifacts. Open Monday–Friday 8:30 A.M.–2:00 P.M., the **Council House Cafe** serves hearty southern breakfasts and soup-and-sandwich lunches in a rustic, frontier-style setting complete with checkered tablecloths, ladder-back chairs, and tin cups hanging from the fireplace mantel.

A boardwalk leads from the Colonel Drane House to the **French Camp Bed and Breakfast,** a quiet frontier lodge where Daniel Boone would feel right at home. Made from two 100-year-old, hand-hewn log houses, the inn offers a wide back porch overlooking the Natchez Trace Parkway. When the tourists have left for the day and the sun sets slowly over the quiet Natchez Trace, it doesn't require too much imagination to picture a friendly Indian or weary trapper or missionary wandering up the road to become the inn's next guest. The ambience may be rustic, but rest assured the rooms are quite comfortable and modern. Rates begin at $60. Call (601) 547–6835 for reservations.

This tranquil setting is also home to **French Camp Academy,** a boarding school for disadvantaged children. Marked by a sign reading, THE HEAVENS DECLARE THE GLORY OF GOD, the academy's **Rainwater Observatory** houses the largest telescope between Atlanta and Houston. Gaze into the heavens through one of thirteen powerful telescopes, five of which are designed for daytime viewing. Call (601) 547–6865 to schedule a free visit and a look at the stars.

Back on the Trace 20 miles south of French Camp, you'll spot the sign directing you to the **Kosciusko Museum and Information Center.**

Kosciusko began as a community of taverns and inns established to serve travelers on the Old Natchez Trace. Listed in Norm Crampton's *The Best 100 Small Towns in America,* Kosciusko still welcomes visitors today.

Originally known as Redbud Springs, the town's name was changed to the easy-to-remember but impossible-to-spell "Kosciusko" in the late 1830s. The state representative in charge of choosing the name recalled an ancestor's colorful tales about Thaddeus Kosciuszko, a Polish engineer who served on George Washington's staff during the Revolutionary War. Kosciuszko never visited Mississippi, yet the town was named in his honor (minus the "z"), and the most prominent display in the Kosciusko Museum and Information Center is a life-size wax statue of the Polish freedom fighter.

The friendly volunteers at the information center will be happy to tell you more about Kosciusko's history and to provide you with a copy of the *Towers & Turrets* brochure, a **walking and driving tour** showcasing the city's lovely Victorian architecture and numerous historic sites. Use caution exiting the information center—the peace and tranquility of the Natchez Trace gives way to a major highway bypass just off the property, and the sudden increase in traffic can be startling.

To avoid the traffic, take a right onto the bypass from the information center, then turn left at the first light at Jefferson Street. Continue on Jefferson into downtown, then take a right on Huntington Street to the **Kosciusko City Cemetery.** Take the BoBo Street entrance into the cemetery, then continue straight until you come upon a stone woman in Victorian dress in the center of the Kelly family plot.

When Laura Kelly died in 1890, her devastated husband sent her photo and favorite clothing to a renowned sculptor in Italy, asking that the artist immortalize his beautiful wife in stone. The Kellys' house was under construction at the time of Laura's death, and her grieving husband's next instruction was to the builder. Mr. Kelly ordered a third story be added to the house so that he could look out across the cemetery and see the statue of his beloved wife gazing back at him.

Alas, the bereaved husband was rather fickle. By the time the statue arrived in Kosciusko, he had already married Laura's sister. Nevertheless, the **Laura Kelly Statue** was erected in the family plot, prompting the townspeople to speculate what the second Mrs. Kelly must think every time she looked out the window to find her husband's first wife (not to mention her own sister) staring back at her. The **Kelly-Jones Ivy House** still stands at 309 East Jefferson Street, though it's no longer visible from the statue site.

As you return to Huntington Street via BoBo Street, look to your left for a white marker labeled "Mother" and "Father." The names of Mr. and Mrs. W. E. Burdine's nineteen children are inscribed on the marker between their graves. With so many offspring, the prolific Burdines seem to have run out of names toward the end. Child number 17 was christened simply, "Seventeen."

As you leave the cemetery, turn right onto Huntington Street, then take the first right, Allen Street. **L. V. Hull's house** is the ninth on the right, but don't worry about missing it if you forget to count. The tiny house sits behind what is surely the most unusual example of "landscaping" in Mississippi. The yard is packed with carefully positioned artifacts, including several clocks, a handful of hobbyhorses, old television sets, tires, toys, even a bomber jacket. The most common ornaments by far are Mrs. Hull's "shoe trees," with loafers, sneakers, and high-heeled pumps of every size and color displayed on tall stakes protruding from the ground. A few determined azaleas peek out from beneath this odd collection, but there's nary an inch to spare.

Visitors from as far away as Australia have visited Mrs. Hull's yard and toured her similarly decorated and equally packed house. Some call it folk art, others call it junk. Of those who voice the latter opinion, Mrs. Hull asks, "If it's just junk, why do you want to come see it?" Leave one of your own shoes for Mrs. Hull, a friendly woman who welcomes drop-in visitors at just about any hour—even when she doesn't have her teeth in. Be sure to bring along some cash—no visit is complete without a one-of-a-kind souvenir, and virtually every item in the house and yard is for sale.

From Mrs. Hull's house, turn left onto Huntington Street, then continue past the Jefferson Street intersection to the **Mary Ricks Thornton Cultural Center.** Built in 1898, this beautiful Gothic structure once served as a Presbyterian church, then fell into disrepair after years of abandonment and neglect. The building was destined for demolition until Mary Ricks Thornton spearheaded a campaign to save it. It's the lucky visitor who stops by for a tour on a day when Mrs. Thornton is volunteering as a guide. Walking with the help of a cane, Mrs. Thornton leads visitors from room to room, relating the history of the chapel and explaining that she became involved in the restoration because, "I was married in this church in 1930, and I couldn't bear to have it torn down for a parking lot."

After months of fundraising, the Kosciusko-Attala Historical Society purchased the building and restored it for use as a cultural center. Today the building hosts performances, weddings, meetings, and other events and houses **Back Pew Gifts and Antiques** in a former Sunday school classroom. Ornate, stained-glass windows and unusual white-over-wood pews, curved to give every churchgoer a view of the pulpit, are high points on the tour. One of the stained-glass windows is dedicated to Laura Kelly, of statuary fame. The center also features a Delta Gamma room, honoring the three Kosciusko natives and Presbyterian church members who founded the national sorority in 1873. The cultural center and gift shop are open Monday–Saturday 10:00 A.M.–4:00 P.M.

Just before Huntington Street curves to the left, you'll see the **Lucas Hill Bed and Breakfast Inn** on the right. The house was built in 1866 by John Lucas, a prominent businessman who also served as sheriff of Attala County. Today the house is occupied by Lucas's great, great, great-grandson and his family. The guest room at Lucas Hill is comfortably furnished in family antiques and features a large bath with a whirlpool tub and fireplace. The daily room rate is $75. Lucas Hill also houses **Traditions,** a gift shop specializing in heirloom silver, crystal, and linens. For reservations, call (601) 289–7860.

Follow Huntington Street around the curve, then head left on Natchez Street, once a part of the original Natchez Trace, to the 1837 **Hammond-Routt House,** Kosciusko's only year-round tour home. Tickets are available at the ophthalmologist's office next door. Adult tickets are $3.00, children and seniors $2.00. Tours are available Monday–Saturday 8:00 A.M.–4:30 P.M.

Backtrack 2 blocks from the Hammond-Routt House to East Washington Street, then turn left onto the Kosciusko town square and circle around to **Peeler House Antiques.** Peeler House offers a wide selection of English antiques including silver, jewelry, china, porcelain, and furniture, as well as affordably priced gifts. The shop also houses a cheerful cafe perfect for a quick lunch. But the Peeler House's most unusual delight is a full-scale, working carousel set up in a back storage area. Ask Mr. Peeler to crank it up and give you a whirl.

Loop back around the town square, exit past the Chinese restaurant, and you'll see **The Red Bud Inn and Tea Room** straight ahead. Built in 1884, this proud Victorian was the home of Samuel Jackson and his new bride, Lillie. When Samuel was killed in a duel in 1894, his widow began taking in boarders to support herself. A century later, the Red Bud Inn is still welcoming weary travelers. Rates in this elegant mansion begin at $85. Call (601) 289–5086 for reservations. The tea room offers a choice of two luncheon entrees plus dessert for $10 Monday–Friday 11:30 A.M.–1:00 P.M. Dinner is served Saturday evenings 6:30–9:00 P.M.

Oprah Winfrey's first church

Wrap up a tour of Kosciusko with a visit to the area where the town's most famous native, Oprah Winfrey, spent her childhood. While her birthplace is no longer standing, fans can visit the spot where Oprah gave her first public performance; at a church in the Buffalo community, Oprah recited the Easter story. Buffalo Road, now *Oprah Winfrey Road,* makes a loop off Mississippi Highway 12 and passes the church, as well as Oprah's family cemetery and the site of her birthplace.

Reservations and Rails

I f you expect to find Native Americans only "out west," you'll be surprised to stumble upon a bona fide Indian reservation here in the deep South. The legends and traditions of the Mississippi Band of Choctaw Indians dominate the culture in this part of the state, reminding visitors that Mississippi history did not begin on a cotton plantation or a Civil War battlefield.

Further south near Meridian, history is forever intertwined with the railroad. The iron horses brought east Mississippi's first settlers, whose descendants still walk its streets today.

Leave the Natchez Trace Parkway at Kosciusko and take Mississippi Highway 35 South to *Carthage,* then follow Mississippi Highway 488 to *Bryan's Country Store.* Here you'll get your first glimpse of the ancient culture of the Mississippi Band of Choctaw Indians. Bryan's sells more hand-woven Indian baskets than groceries, more colorful, intricate beadwork than convenience store sundries. The baskets come in every shape, size, and color, but in only one price range—expensive. Of course, those interested in a true collector's item won't mind paying a little more for a one-of-a-kind souvenir that embodies the skill and tradition of a centuries-old people. Built in 1929, Bryan's Country Store is open 6:00 A.M.–6:00 P.M. Monday–Saturday.

From Highway 488, take Highway 16 East toward Philadelphia and the *Choctaw Indian Reservation.* If you were expecting the Hollywood version of an Indian village, you're in for a surprise. The Choctaw are savvy businesspeople who've brought industry, commerce, and a comfortable lifestyle to their reservation. The 21,000-acre development is a self-contained city that includes a school, hospital, and a handful of very profitable industries. The Choctaws' newest venture, the 150,000-square-foot *Silver Star Casino,* rises unexpectedly out of the red-dirt prairie just west of Philadelphia on Highway 16, attracting thousands of visitors a day.

The members of the tribe residing on the reservation are descendants of the Choctaws who refused to leave their homeland following the 1830 Treaty of Dancing Rabbit, which ceded the last of the Choctaws' native lands to the United States. Rather than relocate to Indian lands in the west, this small group of proud, determined Choctaws struggled against poverty and segregation to preserve their traditional culture on their native land.

The Choctaws' history before the coming of the "white man" and their subsequent struggles and triumphs are depicted in the *Choctaw Museum of the Southern Indian,* a collection of exhibits and archives relating the tribe's long history in Mississippi, which dates back to the time of Christ. If you're near the reservation in July, stop for the *Choctaw Indian Fair,* a celebration of Native American culture that includes traditional dancing, crafts, stickball games, traditional foods, and entertainment. For this year's Choctaw Indian Fair dates, call the *Philadelphia Chamber of Commerce* at (601) 656–1742.

The land around Philadelphia is sacred to the Choctaws for good reason. According to Indian legend, the entire Choctaw Nation was born at the *Nanih Waiya Historic Site,* an ancient area marked by ceremonial Indian mounds and a sacred cave 20 miles north of Philadelphia off Highway 21. The Choctaws refer to the large mound at the site as the "Mother Mound." During the mass Indian exodus that followed the Treaty of Dancing Rabbit, the Choctaws who remained in Mississippi vowed "never to leave their mother as long as she stood." A flight of steep, wooden stairs leads to the top of the Mother Mound, transporting visitors to an ancient world of myth and legend. Even in the hot stillness of a summer day, it's easy to imagine the ancient Choctaw ceremonies, to hear the beat of drums and smell the smoke of campfires.

The Nanih Waiya site includes a picnic area overlooking a cypress swamp and a park office directly across from the Mother Mound. Ask at the office for directions to the cave mound, marked by legend as the very spot where the first Choctaw Indian entered the world. The cave is partially hidden in a wooded area. It's possible to step inside, but the cave floor is muddy and dark, and spelunking is not encouraged.

In addition to its Indian heritage, the town of **Philadelphia** is famous as the site of one of Mississippi's most unusual gatherings, the **Neshoba County Fair** (see sidebar "Mississippi's Giant House Party").

Like most businesses in Philadelphia, **Peggy's Restaurant** is closed the week of the Neshoba County Fair. But if you're in town any other time of the year, stop by for a home-cooked lunch, served in Peggy Webb's home at the corner of Bay Street and Byrd Avenue. Dining is a casual experience at Peggy's—there's no sign outside, no host to seat you, and no server to take your order. Diners help themselves to an all-you-can-eat buffet groaning with fried chicken, pork chops, chicken 'n dumplings,

Mississippi's Giant House Party

*T*he first thing you'll notice as you approach the Neshoba County fairgrounds are the houses—six hundred whimsical, crayon-colored cabins, most looking as though nothing more than good luck is holding them together. These ramshackle structures have usually been in the same family for generations and have been the subject of divorce disputes and contested wills on more than one occasion. The original cabins on "Founder's Square" are prime pieces of real estate, selling for as much as $50,000 each.

The price tag is only mildly astounding until you realize that for fifty-one weeks out of the year, the cabins are boarded up and the fairgrounds are deserted. That $50,000 is spent to enjoy a mere seven days in August. For that one week, the fairgrounds are jumping with a full-blown midway, harness races, musical acts, and the crowning of a teenage queen. The

Neshoba County Fair is also famous for political stumping, attracting candidates for every office from dogcatcher to President of the United States.

Above all else, the Neshoba County Fair is famous for its hospitality. Many of the cabins have hosted overnight guests since the first Neshoba County Fair more than 100 years ago. Strangers will invite you to join them for lunch or lemonade on the front porch, or even to pass the night in one of the technicolor cabins (be sure to choose one with air-conditioning—a nontraditional indulgence considered a fair faux pas as few as ten years ago). This rare display of universal hospitality has earned the fair the nickname "Mississippi's Giant House Party." For this year's dates, call the Philadelphia Chamber of Commerce at (601) 656–1742. Dress comfortably and bring a handheld fan.

and other southern favorites. The food is wholesome and delicious, but the most memorable feature at Peggy's is the payment policy. Everyone here eats on the honor system. Once you've had your fill, just leave $4.50 in the basket by the front door and be on your way. There's no bill, no receipt, no cash register, just one basket for payment and another for making change. As Peggy explains, it's less work for her, people like to be trusted, and even after years on the honor system, she's never once been stiffed. Peggy serves lunch weekdays from 11:00 A.M.–2:00 P.M. or until the food runs out, which is a definite possibility on fried chicken days.

Firefighters should plan a side trip from Philadelphia to *Louisville* and the *American Heritage "Big Red" Fire Museum.* Coin and stamp collections are common enough, but it's probably safe to say that Bill Taylor is the only person in the South with a personal collection of fire engines—nineteen to be exact. Taylor collects and restores the antique fire trucks and wagons as a hobby and is happy to share his collection with visitors. Louisville is 25 miles north of Philadelphia on Mississippi Highway 15. Call Bill Taylor at (601) 773–3421 for an appointment. If there's no answer, try dropping by the museum on Business 15 just north of Main Street.

From Louisville, take Mississippi Highway 397 South (from Philadelphia, take Highway 16 West to Mississippi Highway 39 North) into rural Kemper County and follow the signs and the gravel road to *Sciple's Water Mill,* the oldest continuously operating water mill in the United States. The original mill was built in 1790 and was owned and operated by four families over the next fifty years. The Sciple family purchased the property around 1840 and has kept it up and running ever since. Today the mill is run by Edward Sciple, who gave up his job as a television repairman to continue the family tradition.

Sciple's Mill sits on a rocky stream surrounded by steep, tree-covered hillsides. Steps made of rock lead to the split-level building where horseshoes hang from the wooden wall and iron cowbells dangle from the rafters. Until the mid-1950s, the mill also ginned cotton and sawed lumber. Today visitors can purchase stone-ground corn, meal, and grits, or just relax down by the old mill stream.

The mill is 10 miles northwest of DeKalb off the Kellis Store Road. Several signs point the way from area highways and byways, but if you need specific directions, call (601) 743–2295 or (601) 743–2754. Sciple's Mill is open Monday–Friday 7:00 A.M.–3:30 P.M. Visitors are welcome to stroll the grounds after hours and on weekends.

From the mill, take Mississippi Highway 39 South to Mississippi

Mississippi Burning

*T*he most infamous chapter in Mississippi history unfolded in 1964, when three civil-rights workers vanished in rural Neshoba County.

James Chaney, Andrew Goodman, and Michael Schwerner disappeared on June 21, 1964, while investigating the burning of a Black church near Philadelphia. Forty-four days later, a still-unidentified informant led the FBI to their bodies, buried in an earthen dam just outside town. All three had been shot. No one was ever charged with the murders.

This dark period in Mississippi history was thrust back into the national limelight in 1988, when Hollywood used the murders as the basis of the movie Mississippi Burning. *Starring Gene Hackman and Willem Dafoe as the FBI agents who "crack the case," this highly fictionalized account of the Chaney, Goodman, Schwerner story was panned by black and white audiences alike.*

Black Mississippians resented the movie's depiction of the FBI as champions of the civil rights cause, pointing out that the FBI entered the case only because two of the victims were white. The black Mississippians, who in reality were the heroes of the story, are portrayed as submissive spectators and are used largely as a backdrop for the FBI action. Likewise, white Mississippians resented the stereotyping of every white southerner as ignorant, bigoted, and limited to a wardrobe of white bedsheets.

But while Mississippi Burning *opened decades-old wounds, it also pointed out the stark contrast between the segregated Mississippi of the 1960s and the progressive Mississippi of today. And while the true story may have been compromised, the film did generate renewed interest and a new appreciation for the work of Chaney, Goodman, and Schwerner, whose deaths helped mobilize and unite all Mississippians, black and white.*

Highway 16 East. You'll pass the tiny towns of DeKalb and Scooba on your way back to U.S. Highway 45 South. Take a left where two-laned Highway 45 broadens to four at **Porterville,** and stop for a snack at **Jack Webb's General Store,** a tidy little establishment that's remained virtually unchanged since the 1930s. Once Jack's wrapped up your freshly sliced hoop cheese and a package of crackers, cross back over U.S. 49 and follow the quiet country road (directly opposite the turnoff to Webb's) 2 miles to the old **Chapel Hill Church.** This century-old chapel is built of native stone and the timbers of an abandoned stagecoach inn. Picnic tables on the quiet grounds are shaded by magnificent old oaks and giant azaleas and populated only by birds and an occasional lizard.

From this quiet rural area, follow U.S. Highway 45 South to **Meridian,** a historic railroad town, bustling industrial center, and the third-largest city in Mississippi.

Meridian's best-known business is **Peavey Electronics,** the world's largest manufacturer of musical amplification equipment. The company began in the early 1960s, when young Hartley Peavey built his first amplifier in the basement of his parents' home, then carried it door-to-door until he found a buyer. When he went to the local bank in search of a start-up loan, the banker told Hartley his daddy would have to co-sign for him. Today, Peavey's amplifiers, guitars, and sound systems are sold in 103 countries around the world and the company employs 2,500 workers—all of whom are paid through an account at the *second* bank Hartley Peavey called on.

President Bush visited Peavey in 1991, calling the company "a true American success story" and "the American dream in action." Major artists, including Brooks and Dunn, Michael Bolton, Eddie Van Halen, Kenny Loggins, and Reba McEntire, enthusiastically endorse Peavey equipment as the finest in the world. Top recording artists often visit Meridian to test new equipment—you never know who you might bump into.

The **Peavey Visitors Center and Museum** tells the Peavey story from Hartley Peavey's first amp to the company's present success. The first Peavey patent, awarded in 1964, is displayed next to Hartley Peavey's original drawing of the company logo on a sheet of notebook paper. A photo dated 1957 captures a young Hartley celebrating his win in the school science fair. The basement workshop where Hartley Peavey built his first amplifier is re-created in detail, all the way down to old issues of *Popular Mechanics* magazine. The tour concludes with a look at the latest instruments produced by Peavey Electronics. Visitors are welcome to test their musical skills on Peavey guitars, drums, and keyboards. The late Melia Peavey, Hartley's wife, established the museum as a surprise gift for her husband in honor of the company's twenty-fifth anniversary in 1990. The museum is staffed by retired Peavey employees, who speak of both the company and its founder in terms of reverence. The Peavey Museum is located on Marion Russell Road off the Highway 45 Bypass. Signs point the way to the museum, which is open Monday–Friday 10:00 A.M.–4:00 P.M. and weekends 1:00–4:00 P.M. Closed Thursday.

Take the Highway 45 Bypass back to I–20/59, then take the Twenty-second Avenue exit into Meridian's art deco–style downtown. **Weidmann's Restaurant** (210 Twenty-second Avenue) has been a fixture in downtown Meridian ever since Swiss immigrant Felix Weidmann established a fruit and vegetable stand on this same corner in 1870. As the business grew, Weidmann expanded his offerings and purchased more and more property, until Weidmann's evolved into one of the area's most popular restaurants.

Weidmann's European-style exterior reflects the original owner's Swiss roots. Inside, photos of famous dinner guests from ever-popular entertainer Jimmy Durante to Meridian native and actress Sela Ward cover the walls, along with a collection of beer steins and deer heads. There's a crock of Weidmann's own peanut butter on every table, a welcome change from the same-old-butter-and-crackers found in most eateries. The peanut butter tradition began during World War II, when butter was in short supply, and has been continued by popular demand ever since. Weidmann's specializes in seafood and steaks and dishes up hefty slices of black-bottom pie that shouldn't be missed under any circumstances, including dieting. The restaurant serves breakfast, lunch, and dinner from 7:00 A.M.–9:30 P.M.

From Twenty-second Avenue, turn left on Eighth Street and follow the signs to **Highland Park** (Forty-first Avenue and Nineteenth Street).

Little-Known Facts About the Eastern Plains

- *Columbus was originally christened "Possum Town" in a dubious tribute to early settler Spirus Roach, who bore an unfortunate resemblance to an opossum.*

- *The Tennessee-Tombigbee Waterway and the Great Wall of China are the only man-made objects on earth visible to astronauts in space.*

- *Before putting down roots on the Mississippi State University campus, a sycamore tree planted outside the university's Dorman Hall flew to the moon on an Apollo mission as a sapling.*

- *At its height in the early 1800s, the Mississippi Choctaw nation included 50 villages and more than 25,000 warriors. The word "Choctaw" means "charming voice."*

- *Meridian's Peavey Electronics is the world's largest manufacturer of musical amplification equipment.*

- *Famed hat maker John B. Stetson honed his skills at Dunn's Falls near Meridian. It was here the haberdasher designed his most popular creation, a men's hat known simply as "the Stetson."*

Since 1909, Meridian's children have flocked to the park for a spin on the rare **Dentzel Carousel.** Hand-carved, hand-painted ponies, goats, deer, giraffes, and lions whirl to cheerful circus music, accompanied by the delighted shrieks and high-pitched giggles of children and adults alike. The carousel was built by Gustav Dentzel in 1895. Meridian's city fathers bought the carousel for $2,000 in 1909 and built the present carousel house following a Dentzel blueprint. About twenty Dentzel carousels exist in the United States, but the Highland Park carousel is one of only a handful still populated by the original animals. The carousel spins weekends year-round from 1:00 –5:00 P.M. and is open daily June–July. The price of a ride has gone up from the original nickel to a quarter—a worthwhile investment for the nostalgic pleasure a ride is sure to bring.

Highland Park is also home to the **Jimmie Rodgers Museum,** a tribute to the railroad worker who came to be known as the "Father of Country Music." Born in Meridian in 1897, Rodgers recorded his first song in 1927. "Sleep, Baby, Sleep" sold more than a million copies and earned Rodgers national fame as an entertainer. Tragically, Rodgers was stricken with tuberculosis at the height of his career. In 1933, he recorded his last songs, performing from a cot set up in the studio. He died later that year at age thirty-six. In 1961, Jimmie Rodgers became the first inductee into the newly formed Country Music Hall of Fame.

The Jimmie Rodgers Museum houses memorabilia from Rodgers's short but memorable career. The museum is open Monday–Saturday 10:00 A.M.–4:00 P.M. and Sunday 1:00–5:00 P.M. Admission is $2.00. Held every May, the **Jimmie Rodgers Festival** features performances by top country music stars. For this year's dates and a list of performers, call the Meridian/Lauderdale County Tourism Bureau at (888) 868–7720.

Meridian offers tours of two historic homes, **Merrehope** and the **F. W. Williams House,** both located at 905 Martin Luther King, Jr., Memorial Drive. Both homes are open Monday–Saturday 9:00 A.M.–4:00 P.M. Admission is $5.00 for adults, $3.00 for children, or $8.00 for adults, $5.00 for children for both homes. Be sure to inquire about Eugenia, Merrehope's resident ghost.

From Meridian, take I–59 South 11 miles to the Savoy exit at Enterprise, then follow the signs to **Dunn's Falls.** This crystal-clear, 65-foot waterfall once served as a power source for a gristmill and for the manufacturing of Stetson hats. The historic gristmill, complete with working waterwheel, is open for tours. Dunn's Falls also features a swimming area in the old mill pond, hiking trails, campsites, and picnic areas with grills. Dunn's Falls is open year-round Wednesday–Sunday. Hours are 9:00 A.M.–5:00 P.M. October–April and 11:00 A.M.–7:00 P.M. May–September. Admission is $1.00.

Continue on U.S. Highway 45 South to **Quitman** and another famous swimmin' hole, the **Archusa Creek Water Park. Archusa Springs** was a popular resort of the 1800s built around a "medicinal" sulfur spring. Located near the Civil War–era Texas Hospital, the spring was frequented by recuperating soldiers. The hospital and resort were destroyed by Union troops in 1864. A Texas Hospital memorial marker and Confederate cemetery are located 2 miles south of Quitman on Highway 45. The spring still flows into Archusa Lake today, and analyses reveal the water is still high in sulfur. Nearby Archusa Creek Water Park offers rustic cabin rentals and outdoor recreational activities in a wilderness setting. Call (601) 776–6956 for rates and reservations.

The King and Queen of the Gypsies

*T*he events that brought Kelly Mitchell, the Queen of the Gypsies, to Meridian's **Rose Hill Cemetery** for burial in 1915 are unknown; perhaps she was simply in the area when she died. Whatever the reason, it was in Meridian that the Queen laid in state for twelve days while members of the tribe gathered from around the nation for her funeral. When the hearse headed out to Rose Hill Cemetery, an estimated 5,000 gypsies followed. When Emil Mitchell, the King of the Gypsies, died years later, he was buried next to his wife, along with several members of the tribe.

Today, the royal gypsy graves are visited frequently by transient tribal members, who leave fresh fruit and juices as a sign of respect. Perhaps they even converse with the spirits of the departed gypsy royals—that would explain why the gravesite has the added feature of patio furniture cemented into the plot.

If you visit the gypsy graves at Rose Hill Cemetery (Fortieth Avenue off Eighth Street) yourself, be sure to bring along some fruit and fresh-squeezed juice. You never know when you might run into a member of the family.

*The following is a partial
listing of the many hotels,
motels, and bed-and-breakfast inns in the area.*

COLUMBUS
Amzi Love
(bed and breakfast),
305 Seventh Street South;
(601) 328–5413

Comfort Inn,
1210 Highway 45 North;
(601) 329–2422

Hampton Inn,
2015 Military Road;
(601) 328–6720

Liberty Hall
(bed and breakfast),
Armstrong Road;
(601) 328–4110

*For reservations, informa-
tion, and directions to the
following bed-and-breakfast
inns, call (800) 689–3983 or
(601) 328–0222.*

Backstrom's Country Bed
and Breakfast

Cartney-Hunt House

Fourth Avenue Cottage
and Ninth Street Suite

Rambling Rose

Suite at Annie's Place

FRENCH CAMP
French Camp
Bed and Breakfast Inn,
1 Bluebird Lane;
(601) 547–6835

KOSCIUSKO
Lucas Hill
Bed and Breakfast,
500 North Huntington
Street;
(601) 289–7860

Red Bud Inn
(bed and breakfast),
121 North Wells Street;
(601) 482–5483

**LINCOLN LTD. BED AND
BREAKFAST RESERVATIONS**
Lincoln Ltd. is a full-time
reservation service for
bed-and-breakfast inns
statewide. For reservations
in any area of Mississippi,
call (800) 633–6477 or
(601) 482–5483.

MACON
Oak Tree Inn,
Highway 45
and Highway 14;
(601) 726–5835 or
(800) 448–6545

MERIDIAN
Comfort Inn,
701 Bonita Lake Drive;
(601) 693–1200

Hampton Inn,
103 Highway 11
and Highway 80 at I–20;
(601) 483–3000

PHILADELPHIA
Days Inn,
Highway 19 South;
(601) 650–3590

Old McDonald Hotel,
Main Street;
(601) 656–1944

Silver Star Resort
and Casino,
Highway 16 West;
(601) 650–1234

STARKVILLE
Carpenter Place
(bed and breakfast),
1280 Highway 25 South;
(601) 323–4669

Hampton Inn,
700 Highway 12 East;
(601) 324–1333

Statehouse Hotel,
215 East Main Street;
(601) 323–2000

The Caragen House
(bed and breakfast),
1108 Highway 82 West;
(601) 323–0340 or
(888) 857–4053

The Cedars
(bed and breakfast),
2173 Oktoc Road;
(601) 324–7569

WEST POINT
Days Inn,
1025 Highway 45 North Alt.;
(601) 494–1995

*The following is a partial
listing of the many restaurants in the area.*

BROOKSVILLE
Ole Country Bakery
(pastries, baked goods,
po' boy sandwiches),
Highway 45 South;
(601) 738–5795

COLUMBUS
Major fast-food chains

KOSCIUSKO
Red Bud Inn and Tea Room
(lunch only),
121 North Wells Street;
(601) 482–5483

MACON
The Sherwood
(veal, steak, seafood),
Highway 45 and
Highway 14;
(601) 726–5835

MERIDIAN
Weidmann's Restaurant
(breakfast, lunch specials,
steak, seafood),
210 Twenty-second Avenue;
(601) 693–1751

Major fast-food chains

PHILADELPHIA
Peggy's Restaurant
(country cooking),
Bay Street and Byrd Avenue

Silver Star Resort
and Casino
(5 restaurants),
Highway 16 West;
(800) 922–9988

STARKVILLE
Easy Street (vegetarian),
122 North Jackson;
(601) 324–2834

The Little Dooey (ribs),
100 Fellowship;
(601) 323–6094

Oby's (sandwiches, gumbo,
red beans and rice),
504 Academy Road;
(601) 323–0444

Starkville Cafe
(country cooking),
211 University Drive;
(601) 323–1665

Major fast-food chains

WEST POINT
Anthony's
(country cooking,
steak, seafood),
116 West Main Street;
(601) 494–0316

**OTHER ATTRACTIONS
WORTH SEEING IN
THE EASTERN PLAINS**

COLUMBUS
Lake Lowndes State Park

LOUISVILLE
Legion State Park

MACON
Noxubee National Wildlife
Refuge

MERIDIAN
Meridian Museum of Art

MORTON
Roosevelt State Park

PHILADELPHIA
Silver Star Casino

QUITMAN
Clarkco State Park

The Mississippi River Delta

*A*ccording to writer David Cohen, "the Mississippi Delta begins in the lobby of the Peabody Hotel in Memphis and ends on Catfish Row in Vicksburg." Home to the richest farmland on earth, the Delta is a land and a people shaped by agriculture and ruled by the Mississippi River, a place where cotton was once king and its subjects sang the blues.

Cohen's statement may be geographically accurate, but a real description of the Delta reaches beyond mere geography. The Delta is not just a place, but a mindset. Natives of the area will tell you that you can never *really* understand the Delta culture unless you were born into it, and you'll soon find that's not an exaggeration.

Some people can't bear a moment in this hot, flat land; others would wither up and die if they had to leave it. As you travel the Delta's back roads and get acquainted with its people and with the land itself, you can decide for yourself which group you belong to.

Blues Alley

*Y*our first Delta stop should be **The Hollywood Restaurant** off Highway 61 in tiny **Robinsonville.** Housed in an 1860s plantation commissary, The Hollywood is mentioned in John Grisham's bestselling novel *The Firm* and in Mark Cohn's Grammy-winning song "Walking in Memphis." A native of New York, Cohn frequented The Hollywood whenever he was in the mid-South, often taking the stage to sing with Muriel the piano player. Not only did Cohn write Muriel into the song, he flew her to New York to play at his wedding. The Hollywood is open for dinner Thursday–Saturday, serving up seafood, steaks, frog legs, catfish, and The Hollywood's famous fried dill pickles. The restaurant usually features live entertainment, but for the biggest

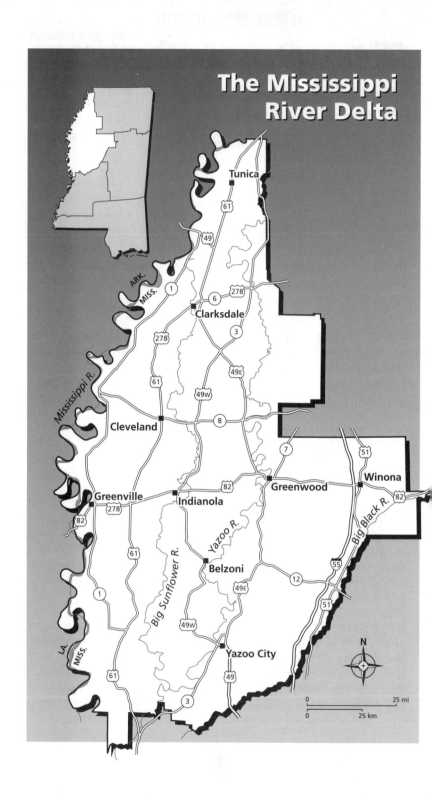

The Mississippi River Delta

Tunica

61

49

ARK.
MISS.

1

6

278

Clarksdale

278

3

61

49E

49W

Mississippi R.

Cleveland

8

7

51

82

Greenwood

Winona

Greenville

278

Indianola

82

Big Black R.

82

61

Belzoni

Big Sunflower R.

Yazoo R.

12

55

49E

1

49W

51

LA.
MISS.

61

Yazoo City

49

N

3

0   25 mi

0   25 km

THE MISSISSIPPI RIVER DELTA

MARLO'S FAVORITE ATTRACTIONS IN THE MISSISSIPPI RIVER DELTA

Rooster Blues Records,
Clarksdale

McCarty Pottery, *Merigold*

Doe's Eat Place, *Greenville*

Cotton in bloom, *as far as the eye can see*

Glenwood Cemetery,
final resting place of the Witch of Yazoo, Yazoo City

Cheese straws from the Mississippi Cheese Straw Factory, *Yazoo City*

Kudzu sculptures,
just outside Yazoo City

Fried catfish with extra hush puppies,
Belzoni

names, scan the crowd—The Hollywood is a favorite of many famous musicians, including the legendary B. B. King.

Once the poorest county in the entire United States, **Tunica** is now a booming tourist resort fueled by the nonstop action of **casino gaming.** But even before the casinos sprang up out of the cotton fields, the **Blue & White Restaurant** was a tourist attraction. The Blue & White has stood at the corner of Highway 61 and Mississippi Highway 4 since 1937. In those days, the Blue & White was a chain of combination service station/restaurant/grocery stores found throughout the mid-South. The old gas pumps are still out front, but today it's the food that pulls in visitors. Elvis Presley was once a frequent patron, and members of the ZZ Top band still stop by for a plate of old-fashioned country cooking whenever they play in Memphis. And country cooking it is. The Blue & White is the best place to get a quick introduction to some southern foods that even a lot of southerners might pass on. After all, it takes a special palate to appreciate turnip greens, country ham, and scrambled pork brains. The Blue & White is open for breakfast, lunch, and dinner.

Playwright Tennessee Williams spent much of his childhood in the Delta and immortalized many of the area's landmarks in his plays. In *The Glass Menagerie,* Amanda Wingfield speaks of a favorite beau who "got in a quarrel with the wild Wainwright boy. They shot it out on the floor of the Moon Lake Casino." The Moon Lake Club was a real place, a casino and dance club near the Mississippi–Arkansas state line that was one of the liveliest Delta night spots of the 1930s. In 1946, Henry Trevino purchased the property, continuing the Moon Lake tradition under the name "Henry's Place" until the 1970s. Today the old casino is a restaurant and bed-and-breakfast inn run by Trevino's descendants. Guests at **Uncle Henry's Place** enjoy gourmet seafood and Creole and Cajun dishes, then retire to rooms in the club's old casino section. Dinner is served Tuesday–Sunday and reservations are required, so call (601) 337–2757 for directions and a seat at the table.

Continue along Highway 61 South through cotton fields and farmland to **Clarksdale.** The soil around Clarksdale is black, rich, and incredibly fertile, and not one square inch goes to waste—where other towns have medians, Clarksdale has cotton. In some sections of the city, cotton is planted right up to the front doors. And in case you were wondering (and who wouldn't?), the cryptic billboard announcing, WELCOME TO CLARKSDALE, HOME OF THE BIG FROG, is part of a campaign inviting large companies to move to the town, where they can be the proverbial "big frog in a small pond."

Cotton and frogs notwithstanding, Clarksdale's biggest claim to fame is as a mecca for fans of the *Mississippi Delta Blues.* The blues is a combination of mournful wails and dryly humorous lyrics that's every bit as much a way of life as a musical form. Born from the chants of slaves who worked the cotton fields in this part of the state decades before the Civil War, the blues is recognized as America's only original music.

Clarksdale was the first stop on the "chitlin' circuit," a route through the Delta traveled by wandering bluesmen in the 1920s and 1930s. Blues legends W. C. Handy, Charlie Patton, Muddy Waters, John Lee Hooker, Robert Johnson, and Howlin' Wolf all called Clarksdale home. Weekends found *Issaquena Avenue* packed with sharecroppers who came to town to shop, socialize, and party in rough-and-tumble nightclubs known as "juke joints."

From these humble beginnings, the blues went on to influence every other form of American music. Polished and transplanted to nightclubs in Chicago, urbanized blues became jazz, and Elvis Presley combined the blues with country music to give the world rock and roll.

The best place to begin a blues tour is the *Delta Blues Museum,* housed in a wing of the *Carnegie Public Library.* In creating the museum, founder Sid Graves said, "I don't want a museum that swims in formaldehyde—I want something vibrant and alive." Vibrant and alive it is. Exhibits include a lifelike wax statue of blues great Muddy Waters and the "Muddywood guitar," a one-of-a-kind instrument commissioned by the ZZ Top band and fashioned of wood from Muddy Waters's cabin. But more engaging than the displays are the blues tunes that ring through the museum, offering a history lesson, cultural experience, and audio tour of the Delta in every note. The museum gift shop sells books, magazines, photos, and, of course, recordings of America's only original music. Pick up a tape or CD for the road; you'll find the blues a perfect accompaniment for the rest of your journey through the Delta.

Attracting fans from around the world, the Delta Blues Museum can't really be considered off the beaten path anymore. In one ten-day period, visitors from Australia, Italy, Colombia, Egypt, Russia, Portugal, Thailand, Spain, Syria, Ireland, Iceland, and England all signed the guest register. To add your name to the list, follow the many signs to the library on Delta

THE MISSISSIPPI RIVER DELTA

Avenue. The free museum is open Monday–Saturday 9:00 A.M.–5:00 P.M.

One block south of the library, Sunflower Avenue is home to two important blues stops. **Rooster Blues Records** is the place to go to find out who's playing the blues where on any given night. The atmosphere at Rooster Blues is laid-back and casual, as are its hours of operation. A sign on the front door informs shoppers that the store is OPEN MOST DAYS ABOUT 9 OR 10, OCCASIONALLY AS EARLY AS 7, BUT AS LATE AS 12 OR 1. SOME DAYS OR AFTERNOONS, WE AREN'T HERE AT ALL. Inside you'll notice another sign warning you not to ask about "the crossroads." According to local legend, bluesman Robert Johnson met with the Devil at a Delta crossroads and agreed to sell his soul for the ability to play the blues. As a skeptical Rooster Blues employee asks, "If he really sold his soul to the Devil, do you think he'd come back to town and tell everybody about it?"

In addition to records, tapes, and CDs, Rooster Blues sells a highly informative **Delta Blues map kit.** The $7.50 investment points the way to hundreds of old stores, farms, churches, grave sites, and other places important to the blues. The kit also contains some interesting trivia, pointing out that nearby **Sledge** was the birthplace of country star Charley Pride and that Harold Jenkins, better known as Conway Twitty, grew up in **Friar's Point.** The map kit even includes directions to Parchman Penitentiary, describing it as the "former residence of such blues notables as Bukka White, Son House, and Sonny Boy Williamson. Although accommodations are free, Parchman is not high on our list of vacation destinations."

Just across the street from Rooster Blues, you'll spot a row of shotgun houses backing up to the Sunflower River. A sign on one of these modest buildings identifies it as the **Riverside Hotel.** Originally Clarksdale's Black hospital, the building became a blues landmark when Bessie Smith, the "Empress of the Blues," died there after a car wreck in 1937. The old hospital became a boarding house and hotel in 1944 and has been home to many blues greats over the past fifty years. While any blues enthusiast will enjoy a daytime visit to the Riverside Hotel, the $25 overnight accommodations are modest to say the least and require guests to share common bathroom facilities.

MARLO'S FAVORITE ANNUAL EVENTS IN THE MISSISSIPPI RIVER DELTA

Belzoni

World Catfish Festival,
April, (601) 247–4838 or
(800) 408–4838

Clarksdale

Sunflower River
Blues Festival,
August, (601) 627–6820

Tennessee Williams
Festival,
October, (601) 627–7337

Greenville

Delta Blues Festival,
September, (800) 467–3582

Greenwood

Mississippi International
Balloon Classic,
June, (800) 748–9069

CROP Day (Cotton Row on
Parade),
August, (601) 453–4152

Indianola

B. B. King Homecoming,
June, (601) 887–4454

Any bluesman worth his salt once strolled and played on the stretch of road called Issaquena Avenue, and although it's harder to catch a street performance these days, you may catch an indoor concert at number 317. A guitar painted on the outside wall and a sign proclaiming NO CAMERAS OR RECORDING DEVICES ALLOWED BEYOND THIS POINT hint there's more than hair cutting going on at **Wade Walton's Barbershop.** The shop's interior walls are plastered with photos of famous and not-so-famous blues artists, and Walton's barbering equipment includes a harmonica as well as a comb and scissors. In the old days, Walton might have been happy to break into a blues tune for the patrons sitting in his chair or visitors who just happened by. Sadly, exploitation by people who recorded the songs and sold them for profit has made Walton and other bluesmen more cautious about sharing their gifts. But even if you don't hear a tune, the barbershop is still worth a stop for the stories. Walton was a personal friend of W. C. Handy, Sonny Boy Williamson, John Lee Hooker, and a number of other bluesmen who figure prominently in his stories of the harsher side of life in the Mississippi Delta. As Walton will tell you, "I lived the blues. The way I worked for no pay, choppin' cotton all day, wasn't nothin' but the blues."

A number of the modest dwellings in this area were once home to the famous or semifamous. A marker near the barbershop on Issaquena Avenue points out the spot where W. C. Handy's house once stood.

Robert Johnson's Deal with the Devil

I went down to the crossroad,

fell down on my knees.

Asked the Lord above, "Have mercy,

Save poor Bob, if you please."

The lyrics to Robert Johnson's "Cross Road Blues" may ask for mercy from the Lord, but according to legend, Johnson actually got his talent from the Devil.

As the story goes, Johnson met with the Devil at the crossroads of Highway 61 and Highway 49 on a dark summer night, and agreed to sell his soul for the ability to play the blues.

Most Delta residents scoffed at the notion of the Devil giving music lessons, but Son House, Willie Brown, and other noted bluesmen of the day were amazed by how quickly Johnson learned to play the guitar.

No other resident of Clarksdale has ever claimed to see the Devil hanging around in the area, but standing at a Delta crossroads on a hot, black summer night, it's easy to imagine a dark figure in the dusty road, waiting for the next aspiring musician.

Ike Turner grew up at 304 Washington Street, and Sam Cooke spent his childhood at 2303 Seventh Street.

Muddy Waters's Cabin

But for a look at a real house of the blues, take a short trip out Stovall Road (which begins in Clarksdale as Oakhurst Avenue) to what's left of *Muddy Waters's Cabin* on the old *Stovall Plantation.* The cabin is just off the road on the left, past a line of small houses. Muddy Waters (born McKinley Morganfield) grew up in this humble cabin and worked on the plantation as a young man. In 1941 and 1942, a researcher studying the blues for a project sponsored by the Library of Congress recorded Waters's music in this cabin. Those recordings were later released as *Muddy Waters: Down on Stovall's Plantation.*

Musicians from Eric Clapton to ZZ Top have credited Muddy Waters as a primary influence on their music, and The Rolling Stones even took their name from the lyrics of a Muddy Waters song. Clapton once said, "Muddy took the music of the Delta plantation, transplanted it in a Chicago nightclub, surrounded it with an electric band, and changed the course of popular music forever." ZZ Top's Billy Gibbons took several pieces of wood from Muddy Waters's delapidated cabin and had them fashioned into the "Muddywood guitar." The instrument toured the country during a fund-raising promotion for the Delta Blues Museum where it's now displayed. Visitors are warned not to take their own souvenirs from what's left of the cabin; a small sign posted on the exterior warns, WE WILL LAY A BIG NASTY MOJO ON YOU IF YOU TAKE ANYTHING.

After hearing so much about it, you're probably ready for your own taste of the blues. The staff at Rooster Blues Records can usually direct you to a *juke joint* (also spelled "jook" joint), or you can check the utility poles around town for homemade flyers announcing performances. Don't expect live music during the week; most blues artists hold day jobs and save their music for Friday and Saturday nights. There are juke joints all over the Delta, but arrangements with the artists are often last-minute and never binding. Since most of these establishments don't have telephones, the only sure way to confirm a blues performance is to show up and wait for the music to start.

A word of warning—the best blues are played in juke joints where people warn you not to go. Incidents do happen, but if you don't mess with any-body (or anybody's date), you should be safe. The Rooster Blues map kit recommends a handful of juke joints to tourists, including **Smitty's Red Top Lounge,** the **Crossroads Bar,** the **Blue Diamond Lounge,** the **River Mount Lounge,** and the **Country Blues Lounge,** which touts "clean rest rooms" as a selling point.

If you just can't muster up the nerve to visit a juke joint, tune in to Early Wright's blues and gospel show on **WROX Radio** instead. One of the first African-American dee-jays in the South, Wright has been spinning blues and gospel tunes in Clarksdale since 1947. His show features blues from 6:00–8:00 P.M. and gospel from 8:00–10:00 P.M. Monday–Friday. Visitors are also welcome to stop by the WROX studio on Delta Avenue for an in-person visit, but be warned—unsuspecting guests often find them-selves being interviewed on the air.

Visitors will soon have yet another opportunity to experience the blues. The old Clarksdale railroad depot is currently undergoing renovation and will soon reopen as **Clarksdale Station and Blues Alley**, an enter-tainment complex featuring shopping, dining, and live musical perfor-mances, all with a blues theme.

Just when you think there's nothing in Clarksdale *but* the blues, someone

Canoe the Mississippi

*T*he Mississippi River winds some 2,350 miles from the central United States to the Gulf of Mexico. One of the most scenic and exciting ways to explore the lower Mississippi River, which includes the entire western boundary of the state of Mississippi, is by canoe.

Clarksdale's **Quapaw Canoe Com-pany** *offers wilderness expeditions on the lower Mississippi River, its backwa-ters, tributaries, bayous, oxbow lakes, and flood plains. Adventurers camp on secluded sandbars, come eyeball to eyeball with river wildlife, and navi-gate swirling eddies the size of a city block, all under the leadership of an experienced river guide.*

Float trips are available along any sec-tion of the river between Cairo, Illi-nois, and the Gulf of Mexico. Trips may last anywhere from a single day to several weeks.

A word of warning—clients must be willing to paddle and to endure nature's extremes, not the least of which is extreme heat during the summer months.

For more information or to plan your Mississippi River adventure, contact John Ruskey at Quapaw Canoe Company, (601) 627–4070, or visit the Web site at www.island63.com.

THE MISSISSIPPI RIVER DELTA

"Ode to Billy Joe"

Visitors to rural Talla-hatchie County can drive over the Tallahatchie bridge where the fictional Billy Joe McAllister jumped to his death in Bobby Gentry's sad country ballad, "Ode to Billy Joe."

will invite you to the **Tennessee Williams Festival.** Young Tom Williams attended school in Clarksdale and spent summers visiting his grandfather, who was the pastor of **St. George's Episcopal Church** and lived in the rectory next door. The playwright's mother wrote of finding a scrap of paper upon which Williams had scrawled, "Before I was eight, my life was completely unshadowed by fear. I lived in a small Mississippi town. . . . My sister and I were gloriously happy." Many of Clarksdale's landmarks and citizens reappeared years later in Williams's works.

Held each October, the Tennessee Williams Festival stars Clarksdale's own citizens, who act out short scenes from his plays on their front lawns and front porches. Festivalgoers receive a map telling them which plays will be performed on which lawns at what time. The festival also includes dinner parties at the old Moon Lake Casino (now Uncle Henry's Place), seminars on Williams's work, musical entertainment, and home tours in the grand **historic district** between Clark and Court Streets—quite a contrast to the bluesy side of life. For this year's festival dates, call the **Coahoma County Tourism Commission** at (601) 627–7337.

Williams is not the only writer to grow up in Coahoma County. *Silence of the Lambs* author Thomas Harris spent his childhood in nearby **Rich.** Of course, if Harris's characters, including the infamous "Hannibal the Cannibal," are based on real people, the locals would probably rather not know about it.

Clarksdale also offers several noteworthy restaurants. A Clarksdale staple since 1924, **Abe's Bar-B-Q** is listed as one of the best pork joints in the South in the books *Roadfood* and *Goodfood*. Abe's occupies a modest building at the intersection of Highways 61 and 49. A little farther south on Highway 61, **Chamoun's Resthaven** serves up stuffed grape leaves, kibbie, baklava, and other Lebanese and Mediterranean delicacies you wouldn't expect to find in the Mississippi Delta. Both restaurants are open for lunch and dinner.

Fans who didn't get their fill of blues lore in Clarksdale should take a side trip down Highway 49 South to **Tutwiler.** A marker where the railroad depot once stood commemorates W. C. Handy's "discovery" of the blues—the spot where the "Father of the Blues" heard a man playing guitar and singing a mournful tune about "Goin' where the Southern cross the Dog"—that's a railroad intersection in nearby **Moorhead.** Aleck Miller, better known as Sonny Boy Williamson, is buried near Tutwiler beside the old **Whitfield M. B. Church** under a new marker erected by Trumpet Records. The grave site is easy to spot—it's the one littered with beer cans, whiskey bottles, spare change, and a dozen rusty harmonicas.

Back on Highway 61 South, be careful not to blink. You'll miss **Mound Bayou,** a town founded by freed slaves who once chopped cotton on Jefferson Davis's brother's plantation. The grounds of the **Mound Bayou City Hall** are adorned with statues of famous African-Americans, including Martin Luther King, Jr., Fannie Lou Hamer, and Malcom X, but the city's most notable attraction is the **cemetery** where the town's founders were laid to rest. Too poor to afford markers, their families fashioned their own. The exquisite, hand-hewn angels and poignant inscriptions are far more impressive than anything money could buy.

The entire town of **Merigold** covers a mere 6 blocks but packs a lot of charm into such a small space. This Delta village (population 608) is home to a handful of quaint restaurants and specialty shops, including **McCarty Pottery.** Turn right at the post office on Highway 61, then left on North St. Mary Street to the low cypress building surrounded by bamboo. There's no sign, but as soon as you open the door you'll know you've found the McCarty gallery and tour gardens. Lee and Pup McCarty have been making pottery for as long as anyone in Merigold remembers, but the clay for their first pieces came from a ravine near Oxford pointed out to them by novelist William Faulkner.

The McCarty collection includes dinnerware, vases, wind chimes, and candlesticks, but the McCartys are best known for their family of pottery rabbits. Each inquisitive bunny has a name, and whether you choose Lettuce, Easter, or Baby Bunny, you'll take home one of Mississippi's most popular souvenirs. Obsessed McCarty collectors can be found all over the world. Even Nikita Khrushchev had a collection of McCarty pottery, supposedly received as a gift from Armand Hammer. McCarty Pottery is open 10:00 A.M.–4:00 P.M. Tuesday–Saturday. If at all possible, try to stop by in the morning for a chat with Mr. McCarty before he retires for his afternoon nap.

The Gallery restaurant, 2 blocks from the studio, is also owned by the McCarty family and serves light lunches on dinnerware fashioned by the artists. Nearby **Crawdad's** is a popular spot for dinner, and Merigold's **Agora's, Westerfield's,** and **Steel Magnolias** gift and antiques shops attract shoppers from throughout the Delta.

The next stop on Highway 61 is **Cleveland,** listed in Norm Crampton's *The 100 Best Small Towns in America.* W. C. Handy wrote about Cleveland in his autobiography, describing a pivotal incident at a dance held in the Cleveland Courthouse. When the audience demanded blues tunes, Handy and his orchestra were at a loss. A local trio stepped in and saved the day, performing bawdy, soulful music the likes of which Handy had never heard, but which he would later incorporate into his own songs. "My enlightenment came in Cleveland, Mississippi," Handy wrote years later. "That night, an American composer was born."

Attractions in Cleveland include the small-but-scenic campus of **Delta State University,** a quaint shopping area along historic **Cotton Row,** and a four-star restaurant. Located on Highway 61, **KC's** specializes in both Chinese and New American cuisine and features a wine cellar stocking more than 500 selections from around the world. For less discriminating palates, **Airport Grocery** (Highway 8 West) bills its fare as "out-of-this-world food at a down-to-earth place," and serves up live blues every Friday night.

Located on Highway 8 East between Cleveland and Ruleville, **Dockery Farms,** the biggest and most famous of the old Delta cotton plantations, is included on a long list of places as the possible birthplace of the blues. A barn bearing the plantation name and dates of operation is visible from the highway and is a popular photo opportunity.

On the other side of Cleveland, Highway 8 West intersects Highway 1 at **Rosedale,** a thriving port on the **Mississippi River.** With acres of riverfront and a 75-foot-high observation tower, **Great River Road State Park** offers spectacular views of the mighty Mississippi and enjoys the distinction of being the world's longest park. Be sure to pack a lunch—picnic facilities atop the shelter guarantee a table with a view. Fishing is good at the park's **Perry Martin Lake**, named for an infamous moonshiner of Mississippi's prohibition era. Perry Martin lived on a houseboat on the lake, keeping a watchful eye on the highly productive, highly illegal stills he had hidden in the woods nearby. The trails visitors roam freely today were *never* prowled after dark in Perry Martin's heyday. You won't find any of Martin's potent moonshine at Great River Road, but one of his prized stills is on display.

Continuing on Highway 1 South, the next stop is **Benoit.** Take a left at the four-way stop (yes, there's only one), go about a mile past the residential district, and take the gravel road to the right. That crumbling antebellum mansion rising out of the field is locally referred to as the **Baby Doll House.** The movie *Baby Doll* was filmed on location here in 1956, and though the locals always refer to it as "that movie with Bette Davis," movie anthologies don't list her among the cast. What they do reveal is that Baby Doll was based on a play by Tennessee Williams and was so scandalous it

Going First Class

Jo Ann Ussery's home in Benoit can literally be described as first class— and as coach, cockpit, and cargo hold.

Upon discovering that a retired passenger jet was more affordable than a simple mobile home, Ms. Ussery had one delivered to her lakeside property, made some changes here and there, and now calls the aircraft home.

The remodeled jetliner features a kitchen, three bedrooms, and one and one-half baths. And if the Jacuzzi in the cockpit should ever flood, Ms. Ussery needn't worry. She can always use her couch cushion as a flotation device.

was condemned by the Legion of Decency. For as long as anyone around Benoit can remember, no one has lived in the Baby Doll House—at least not officially. The house is widely regarded as haunted and boasts a shadowy, convoluted past involving an escaped John Wilkes Booth. A nearby mobile home, however, is inhabited by very real residents and the property on which the Baby Doll House stands is posted. Pull up as far as the gate and get a good look at what must once have been a truly fine Delta home.

Cotton Row

This flat, fertile section of the Delta that stretches from Greenville east to Greenwood is virtually devoid of trees, but you won't need spring buds or fall foliage to tell you what season it is.

In the summertime, the heat shimmers so thickly off the highway you can actually catch it on film. Even the most resilient crops look parched without a daily drenching. Those huge, spidery pieces of machinery spanning the fields are pivot irrigation systems, designed to give each precious acre of cotton and soybeans a good soaking.

Fall sees Cotton Row at its peak, when the fields are white with "Delta Gold." When harvesting takes place in early autumn, trucks loaded with the fluffy stuff travel every Delta highway, leftover strands float lazily in the welcome breeze, and out-of-state visitors pull over to swipe a souvenir boll.

In the winter, the Delta seems determined to relive its prehistoric days as a swamp—the rain never seems to stop, the fertile soil turns to mucky gumbo, and flash floods can literally wash away the back roads.

In the spring, the whole process begins anew. And no matter how many years a particular field is worked, the land continues to reveal new treasures with every pass of the plow. The rich black earth sparkles with glass—once part of a window in a sharecropper's shack. Wild daffodils spring up where a long-ago garden once bloomed, and plows turn up shards of ancient Indian pottery, arrowheads, and even an occasional dinosaur bone or human skeleton.

One of these unusual specimens, a female skeleton affectionately known as "Lucy," resides at the **Winterville Indian Mounds State Park and Museum,** 5 miles north of Greenville on Highway 1. The mound builders' metropolis at Winterville includes fifteen earthen structures, one of them a massive, six-story temple mound. The mounds were built one basketful of earth at a time by the women of the tribe, while the men worked the fields and hunted for dinner. A museum on the Winterville property houses Lucy as well as Indian artifacts recovered from all over the Delta. Visit Lucy Wednesday–Saturday 8:00 A.M.–5:00 P.M. and Sunday 1:00–5:00 P.M.; admission is $1.50 for adults and 50 cents for children.

Continue into **Greenville,** the state's largest city on the Mississippi River. Highway 1 intersects with U.S. Highway 82 here, providing an easy way to navigate the city; virtually every point of interest is located a block or two off Highway 82.

Your first stop should be the **River Road Queen Welcome Center,** a replica of a nineteenth-century stern-wheeler that made its debut at the 1984 New Orleans World's Fair, then returned to Greenville to greet visitors arriving in Mississippi from Arkansas. This landlocked stern-wheeler is located at the intersection of Highway 82 West and Reed Road, just past the Highway 82 and Main Street intersection. Stop to admire the miniature cotton patch planted out front, then head inside where a knowledgeable staffer will provide you with brochures and directions to Greenville attractions, hotels, and restaurants.

From the River Road Queen, head back east on Highway 82 to Main Street, which dead-ends at the **Mississippi River levee,** a marvel of engineering longer and taller than the Great Wall of China. Barges headed for the bustling **Port of Greenville** are visible just beyond the **casinos** that line the levee's edge. For a close-up view of the mighty Mississippi, stop at the observation tower at **Warfield Point Park,** nestled inside the levee off Highway 82, 5 miles south of Greenville. The park offers the only public riverbank campsites on the Mississippi between St. Louis and New Orleans.

At the end of Main Street, 1 block east of the levee, you'll spot the **Old Number One Firehouse Museum.** It's not surprising that Greenville would open a museum honoring fire fighting—in the late 1800s, the city burned to the ground not once, not twice, but on three separate occasions. Exhibits include old fire engines, call boxes, and "fire marks"—plaques displayed only on those homes that carried fire insurance. In the old days, if firemen arrived at a burning home and didn't see the appropriate mark, they would head back to the station and leave the house to burn. Open Monday–Saturday 8:00 A.M.–5:00 P.M. and Sunday 1:00–5:00 P.M., the Firehouse Museum is a favorite with kids, who can dress in fire-fighting garb, pull a real fire alarm, and pretend to douse the flames with a working hose.

Grown-ups with a literary bent will find the *Greenville Writers Exhibit* at the William Alexander Percy Memorial Library (341 Main Street) of interest. According to the local chamber of commerce, Greenville boasts more published writers per capita than any other town in the nation. The list of distinguished authors includes Ellen Douglas, Walker Percy, Hodding Carter, and Civil War historian Shelby Foote, who gained national notoriety as a featured commentator in Ken Burns's epic PBS series, *The Civil War*. The Greenville Writers Exhibit includes photographs, original manuscripts, and displays celebrating Greenville's rich literary heritage.

Dinnertime in Greenville calls for a trip to *Doe's Eat Place,* where you'll find the biggest, best steaks in Mississippi, and quite possibly in all of America. With maps to the restaurant distributed in every convenience store and hotel lobby in Greenville, Doe's can't really be considered off the beaten path, but its stubborn refusal to conform to any level of restaurant normalcy is what puts Doe's on everyone's "must see" list.

No Mistaking It

I'd like to say I stumbled upon the No Mistake Plantation by accident, but to find yourself in Satartia, the smallest incorporated town in Mississippi, you really have to be looking for something.

The town lies just off Mississippi Highway 3, 25 miles south of Yazoo City. I had directions to the No Mistake, but as it turned out I didn't need the hand-drawn map after all—the explosion of color was a dead giveaway. The antebellum plantation home was surrounded by daylilies—thousands upon thousands of daylilies, in every hue and shade imaginable.

After lunch in the tea room, the plantation's owner told me about the first mistress of No Mistake, a planter's wife who had raised a single bale of cotton every year, then used her modest earnings to build this scenic masterpiece—one garden at a time. My host concluded the tour by offering me a well-worn garden trowel and an invitation to take a living reminder of the No Mistake home.

The No Mistake Plantation has changed hands since my visit there, and sadly, no longer allows outsiders to explore its kaleidoscopic grounds. But every summer, when those generations-old daylilies burst into bloom in my own backyard, I relive that afternoon at the No Mistake Plantation— one flower at a time.

For starters, Doe's is housed in a dilapidated old store that looks as though it should be condemned, if not by the building commission then at least by the local health department. Patrons enter through the kitchen, where the owner ("Little Doe") will turn to you with a hefty steak in each hand and say, "Aunt Florence will seat you." Aunt Florence will indeed lead you to a rickety table, where a friendly waitress will soon appear with a bowl of anchovies or a sample of Doe's famous hot tamales. While you wait for the main course, you can eavesdrop on the conversations of other diners in the cramped little room, who range from Doe's regulars chatting with the staff to first-time patrons wondering if the rest rooms might actually be outside somewhere.

Be warned—dinner at Doe's could put you in a coma. The smallest steak on the menu weighs in at a whopping two pounds and comes with French-fried potatoes and fresh bread. Two people can split a steak and leave their table absolutely stuffed for about $25. The food is nothing short of delicious, and though the atmosphere seems a little rustic at first, it soon becomes quite comfortable. Doe's is open only for dinner Monday–Saturday.

The restaurant is located on **Nelson Street,** which is also home to some down-and-dirty blues clubs. Although it's true that some of these establishments have a reputation for vice and violence, visitors who stick to the blues and stay out of the street life aren't likely to run into trouble. A particularly popular club is **The Flowing Fountain** at 816 Nelson Street, where the headline act was once a young married couple named Ike and Tina Turner.

For a day-long dose of the blues, follow the crowds to a forty-acre patch in the Delta outside Greenville on the third Saturday in September. Once you've attended the **Delta Blues Festival,** nothing but a live performance will ever do again. The festival brings the biggest names in blues for an all-day blowout—the Woodstock of the blues world. Bring a lawn chair or blanket and an ice chest and be warned—late September in Mississippi is still hot and humid.

Nearby **Stoneville** is home to the largest USDA research facility in the nation. The **Silicon Valley of Agriculture** isn't open for public tours, but an ever-growing lobby display explains how common household items like disposable diapers and aerosol cans were developed through USDA research. Take home a cotton bale of your own (in miniature, of course) from **Little Bales of Cotton,** a downtown Stoneville shop specializing in cotton souvenirs.

If you're staying in Greenville overnight, make reservations at the *Azalea House Bed and Breakfast,* conveniently located on Washington Avenue. Surrounded by more than 100 blooming azaleas, this 1915 home is nothing short of breathtaking in the early spring. Rates begin at $65. Call (601) 335–0507 for reservations.

From Greenville, take U.S. Highway 82 East toward Greenwood, or backtrack to State Highway 1 and pick up a few more attractions farther south.

Located 5 miles off Highway 1 South on Mississippi Highway 12, *LeRoy Percy State Park* is home to the only *hot spring* in Mississippi, but it's not the place for a leisurely soak—the ninety-four-degree water has already been claimed by the local alligator population. You can enjoy a not-*too*-up-close-and-personal visit with the scaly reptiles (rumored to enjoy marshmallows) from a raised boardwalk above their hot artesian water home. A nature trail through the park offers a look at the Delta of old—a steamy jungle of a place overrun by Spanish moss and cypress trees.

You can camp overnight or stay in a cabin at LeRoy Percy, or you can return to Highway 1 and continue south a short distance to *Chatham.* This small community on picturesque *Lake Washington* is home to two bed-and-breakfast inns, *Mount Holly* (601–827–2652) and *Linden-on-the-Lake* (601–839–2181). Rates range from around $85 to $150.

Highway 1 intersects with Highway 61 South at *Rolling Fork,* birthplace

The Birth of the Teddy Bear

*O*ne of the world's most popular toys was born in tiny Onward, Mississippi, as the result of a Presidential pardon.

In 1902, President Theodore Roosevelt participated in a black-bear hunt in the Onward area. The President didn't have much luck, and not wanting him to leave without a trophy, the local guide caught a bear cub and tied it to a tree for the President to shoot.

Roosevelt refused to kill the defenseless animal, claiming it would not be sportsmanlike. A cartoonist with the Washington Post captured this noble gesture on paper, and the story of "Teddy's Bear" quickly spread nationwide.

Soon after, a savvy New York merchant named Morris Michton made toy history by creating a cuddly, lovable toy bear and christening it the "Teddy Bear." Michton went on to found the Ideal Toy Company, starting the entire business with revenues generated by the original Teddy Bear.

of blues great Muddy Waters. A bend in the road near Rolling Fork is home to a growing collection (or herd) of *wire-sculpted dinosaurs* fashioned by a local resident. Continue south past this menagerie to Onward, birthplace of the teddy bear (see sidebar, page 76).

The *Onward Store* on Highway 61 displays photographs from President Roosevelt's famous bear hunt and sells souvenir teddy bears from the spot where this favorite childhood toy originated. The store is open 7:30 A.M.–7:30 P.M. seven days a week.

The highlight of a trip to tiny *Valley Park* is *Buddie Newman's Train Museum.* The railroad once passed through the Newman family property, and young Buddie grew up to the sound of the train whistle. When the railroad company abandoned the line that ran through the property, Buddie bought a section of the track, two train cars, and a caboose and created a miniature railroad museum. If Buddie's home, he'll walk you through the museum, tell you about his forty-year career in the Mississippi state legislature, and even take you for a 1-mile ride on the working train. The museum is behind Buddie's home on Highway 61.

Even if you've ventured as far south as Buddie's, it's just a short backtrack up Highway 61 to the northeastern section of the Delta. Heading north back toward Greenville, you'll pass through tiny towns boasting the most creative names in the state—tongue-twisting monikers like Anguilla, Nitta Yuma, and Panther Burn.

Highway 61 North and U.S. Highway 82 intersect just outside Greenville near *Leland.* As you head east on Highway 82, keep a sharp eye out for talking frogs, fashion-conscious pigs, and perennial roommates Bert and Ernie. This Delta town is home to the *Birthplace of the Frog,* a museum honoring Leland native Jim Henson, the creator of the beloved Muppets®. You'll find original Muppets and Muppet memorabilia at this fanciful exhibit on South Deer Creek Drive. Fans will delight in learning the inspiration behind their favorite Muppets; for example, Kermit the Frog is affectionately named after Henson's boyhood best friend. Hobnob with the stars of *The Muppet Movie* and *The Muppets Take Manhattan* Monday–Friday 10:00 A.M.–4:00 P.M. or seven days a week Memorial Day–Labor Day. Be sure to add your name to the guest register, which already lists Muppet fans from Australia, England, and Japan.

Continue on Highway 82 East to *Indianola,* the birthplace of blues legend B. B. King. King began his musical career singing gospel, but as he explains, "Gospel songs got me encouragement. Blues tunes got me a tip and a beer. Do I really need to say anything else?" Indianola features a park and a street named after its most famous homeboy, who returns to entertain at the **Annual B. B. King Homecoming,** a day-long festival and down-home blues concert held the first weekend in June. Indianola is a far cry from Hollywood, but you will find King's handprints, footprints, and autograph in the sidewalk at the corner of Second and Church Streets.

For a memorable dining experience, don't miss the **Crown Restaurant and Antique Mall,** the birthplace of catfish pâté.

Open for lunch only, the restaurant offers an upscale menu starring Evelyn Roughton's world-famous catfish recipes. You'll have a choice of several entrees, one of which is always an exotic concoction like catfish thermadore, shrimp-stuffed catfish, or black-butter catfish. You'll also be required to sample Evelyn's award-winning catfish pâté, which is manufactured and sold on the site and won Evelyn a Special Achievement Award from the Catfish Farmers of Mississippi. You can buy a tub of the pâté and any of the pie mixes at the restaurant, or take home one of their mail order catalogs—recognized by the *New York Times* as one of the best gourmet food catalogs in the country. Lunch includes dessert, your choice of any or all of the Crown's collection of homemade pies. The total bill for the entire experience, including iced tea, is a mere $8.00.

Evelyn and her husband Tony opened the antiques mall first, then added the restaurant in 1976. Antiquing has since taken something of a backseat to the food, but all of the seventeenth-, eighteenth-, and nineteenth-century English antique furnishings are for sale. If you really liked the table you ate off of or the chair you sat on, you can take it with you. Lunch is served from 11:00 A.M.–2:00 P.M. Monday–Saturday. Visit the Crown at 110 Front Street in downtown Indianola (601–887–4522), or call (800) 833–7731 to order a catalog.

On your way out of Indianola, stop by the **Indianola Pecan House** on the left side of Highway 82 just west of the 82–49 intersection and pick up a snack for the road. The Pecan House offers gourmet nuts, candies, spices, desserts, and dressings (be sure to try the Vidalia onion jelly) and usually has a tableful of samples that's worth a stop in itself. You can also pick up one-of-a-kind Delta souvenirs, ranging from catfish neckties to Civil War sculptures. The Pecan House also does a thriving mail-order business; call (800) 541–6252 for a catalog packed with goodies.

From Indianola, continue along Highway 82 East and follow the signs to **Florewood River Plantation State Park.** The park offers living history interpretations of life on an 1850s cotton plantation. More realistic than the perpetual parties and hoop skirts of *Gone With the Wind,* Florewood focuses on the endless details of daily life and includes costumed docents working in the schoolroom, smokehouse, and blacksmith's shop as well as the gentry residing in the "big house." Admission is $3.50 for adults and $2.50 for children. Florewood is closed on Monday and offers limited tours December–February. Call (601) 455–3821 or (601) 455–3822 for more information.

Just as you come into **Greenwood,** you'll spot signs pointing you toward the **Cottonlandia Museum.** The $2.50 admission buys a look at several rooms of artifacts dating all the way back to the Ice Age. Exhibits include Indian pottery, 10,000-year-old mastodon bones, a swamp diorama, an April 15, 1865, news clipping with the headline, "President Dead," and pieces of the Union gunboat *Star of the West* recovered from the waters near Greenwood. Among the more unusual displays is a room dedicated to the memory of prominent Greenwood citizen Carrie Pillow Avent, whose forte was exotic dancing. With its carefully labeled exhibits and stenciled signs hanging on the wall, a visit to Cottonlandia is a bit like an elementary school field trip.

A museum of a different kind occupies the dining room at archaeologist Bill Hony's house. The **Prayer Museum** is a collection of artifacts

Christmas With Sandy

*E*very December, visitors from around Mississippi travel to Carrollton to celebrate Christmas with Sandy Haley. The strange thing about this holiday tradition? Sandy has been dead for more than thirty years.

Angry because her parents wouldn't let her go out one night, fifteen-year-old Sandy swallowed the poison her father used to combat pests on the family farm. What was meant to be a dramatic gesture instead was fatal. Sandy died on June 24, 1966, and was buried in the Haley family plot across the street from Hickory Grove Baptist Church.

Every Christmas since, Sandy's mother, Mayzell Haley, has decorated her daughter's grave with hundreds of lights, countless figurines, stars, and angels, a fully trimmed Christmas tree, and Santa's sleigh, complete with eight tiny reindeer. The display has its own electric meter, attached to a utility pole installed by Mississippi Power Company just for Sandy's grave. A timer turns the lights on at 4:55 P.M. and off at 11:00 P.M.

Sandy's mother describes the Christmas display as a way of easing sorrow with celebration. Sandy's visitors, many of whom have signed a guest book at the cemetery fence, describe it as "touching," "tragic," and "bizarre."

But while opinions may vary, one thing is certain. Though she's been dead for more than three decades, Sandy Haley will always have company for Christmas.

representing a number of religions including Hinduism, Buddhism, Judaism, and Christianity. Prayer beads, church bells, and antique Bibles are only a sampling of the thousands of religious artifacts that make up this personal collection. For an appointment and directions to Bill Hony's house, call (601) 453–7306.

Greenwood has always seen itself as a genteel town of cultured Delta folk; this concern with propriety and appearances helped make *Lusco's* (722 Carrolton Avenue) one of the most popular dining establishments of the Prohibition era. Restaurateur Charles Lusco built private, partitioned rooms that allowed his guests to imbibe without fear of being observed. Even today, guests at Lusco's enjoy delicious seafood and steaks in private cubicles, summoning discreet waiters with the touch of a buzzer. Of course, the rules concerning alcohol are a little more relaxed today—the restaurant serves beer and wine coolers and allows guests to bring their own wine and liquor. But don't overindulge—remembering which cubicle is yours after a trip to the rest room can require all of your wits. Reservations are recommended; call (601) 453–5365.

Greenwood hosts two popular summer festivals worth braving the heat. June brings the *Mississippi International Balloon Classic,* five days of balloon rides and entertainment highlighted by the mass ascension of nearly 100 colorful hot-air balloons. The August *CROP Day* festival is the best time to tour Greenwood's historic *Cotton Row,* the second-largest cotton exchange in the United States. For this year's festival dates, call the *Greenwood Tourism Council* at (800) 748–9069.

If you're in the area in the spring, continue east of Greenwood on Highway 82 to charming *Carrollton,* where the stately mansions and cozy cottages built by Carroll County's original settlers are open for tours during the *Carrollton Spring Pilgrimage.* Visitors will also discover a collection of antebellum churches (one built with funds raised through a chain letter), a town square that looks more like a movie set than anything from the real world, and what must surely be the last bank in America conducting business without the benefit of computers and fax machines. Drop by Carrollton anytime for a peaceful stroll around the square, or if you simply can't take life at such a relaxed pace, call (601) 237–4752 for this year's pilgrimage dates.

Hunters may want to take a side trip to *Wolfe Creek Outfitters* in nearby Kilmichael. This 6,000-acre hunting preserve is carefully managed for prime whitetail deer and wild turkey hunting. Overnight accommodations and meals are available on the property. For more information or to arrange a hunt, call (601) 262–4411.

Once you've explored the eastern edge of the Delta at Carrollton, backtrack about 25 miles on Highway 82 West to Mississippi Highway 7 South. The **Itta Bena** area is home to not one, but two churchyards rumored to be the *final resting place of blues great Robert Johnson.*

As a rule, bluesmen lived a rough life, often dividing their time between playing the blues, romancing other men's wives, and engaging in "cuttin's" and "shootin's." Johnson was no exception. He was living in Greenwood when he was poisoned by a jealous lover (or a lover's jealous husband, the story isn't clear which) at a local juke joint and died a horrible death—a fitting end, some said, for the man who sold his soul to the Devil for the ability to play the blues. In spite of this wicked pact and his wicked ways, Johnson was buried in a churchyard—or at least, it's believed he was buried in *some* churchyard, *some*where. Conflicting stories place Johnson's grave in either the **Payne Chapel M. B. Churchyard** at **Quito** or the **Mount Zion M. B. Church** just north of **Morgan City.** The Mt. Zion site features an elaborate four-sided marker engraved with the words, "His music struck a chord that continues to resonate. His blues addressed generations he would never know and made poetry of his visions and fears." The bare spot at the top of the monument once displayed Johnson's photo—no doubt stolen by a fan. To get to the Mt. Zion church, take a left at the sign on Highway 7 that says MATTHEW'S BRAKE NATIONAL WILDLIFE REFUGE. Mt. Zion is the white frame church on the left.

Catfish Corridor

The Catfish Corridor reaches from Belzoni through Yazoo City and south to the Delta's end at the kudzu-covered hills near Vicksburg. South of Greenwood, King Cotton's dominance has been challenged by a new crop. Here the green and white fields give way to *catfish farms*—acre after acre of square ponds where Mississippi's newest cash crop thrives. Eighty percent of the world's farm-raised catfish comes from this area of Mississippi.

Continue on State Highway 7 South to **Belzoni** and **Humphreys County,** the **World Catfish Capital.** With more than 120 catfish farms covering more than 36,000 acres, catfish is the number one crop in the county. At 6,000 catfish per acre, the county's fishy residents far outnumber its human population.

The **Catfish Capital Visitors Center** honors the bewhiskered crop with exhibits tracing the industry from pond to plate. The Catfish Capital

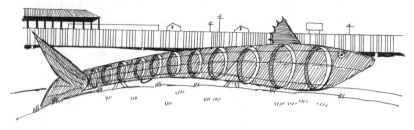

Catfish Fountain at Catfish Capital

can even arrange a catfish farm tour for you; just call (800) 408–4838 and give them a little advance notice. To get to the visitors center, take Highway 7 to U.S. Highway 49, take a left onto Jackson Street, then take the next road to the right. The Catfish Capital is hard to miss—look for the 40-foot catfish fountain out front. If a look at the exhibits leaves you longing for a taste, head up U.S. Highway 49 West about 5 miles to *Isola* and *Peter Bo's* restaurant. Owner Peter Bo will fry up an order of catfish anytime of the day or night, breakfast included.

Things in Belzoni get really, *really* fishy the first Saturday in April, when the entire county turns out for the *World Catfish Festival.* Activities include live entertainment, the crowning of the Catfish Queen, the world's largest fish fry (5,000 pounds, plus hush puppies), and a catfish-eating contest that's not for the squeamish.

For more information on catfish and the World Catfish Capital, visit www.capital2.com/catfish.htm.

Of course, there's more to Belzoni than just catfish. The most famous artist to come from the Delta is the late Ethel Wright Mohamed, whose work hangs in only two places—a Belzoni exhibit known as *Mama's Dream World* and the Smithsonian Institution in Washington, D.C. Dubbed "the Grandma Moses of stitchery," Mrs. Mohamed used intricate needlepoint pictures to tell her stories of life in the Delta. Mrs. Mohamed captured her children, her housekeeper, even the family pets in needle-point, referring to them all as "my funny little people." Other than a few pieces donated to charity and the work displayed in the Smithsonian, all of her creations remain in Belzoni; Mrs. Mohamed never sold a single stitch. Call (601) 247–1433 or (601) 247–4932 to arrange an appointment to tour Mama's Dream World. Chances are good your guide will be the artist's own daughter, herself a feature in the stitchery. Carol Mohamed Ivy also operates Belzoni's sole bed and breakfast, the *Magnolia Inn.* Rates begin at $35; call (601) 247–4932 for reservations.

Before you leave Belzoni, take a break from the road at **Wister Gardens,** a fourteen-acre park on the northern outskirts of town. Be sure to snap a picture of the statue of Johnny Appleseed, presented to Wister Henry, the garden's founder, by the Men's Garden Club of America.

From Belzoni, take Mississippi Highway 12 East to **Lexington** and the **Booker-Thomas Museum.** Fannye Booker founded this small museum behind her home to "show young people how life was in the olden days." Her collection includes old farm tools, household gadgets, water buckets, and wood-burning stoves, but the artifact most indicative of how times have changed is the bell once used to summon Mrs. Booker's own grandmother, who worked as a slave. Mrs. Booker's home and museum are located on Highway 12 just outside of Lexington; look for the house with wagon wheels along the driveway, or call (601) 834–2672 for directions.

Back on Highway 49, catfish ponds continue to dominate the stretch of road south of Belzoni. Most of the ponds are at eye level, but an occasional rise in the road offers a glimpse across surface after shimmering surface. Keep an eye out for the blatant poachers known as cormorants—large black birds that swoop down into the ponds to catch an easy dinner.

The Lady in Red

*O*ne of the strangest mysteries in Mississippi history began on April 24, 1969, when a backhoe digging on the Egypt Plantation unearthed the Lady in Red.

At a depth of just three feet, the backhoe struck a fitted, cast-iron coffin with a glass lid. Inside was the perfectly preserved body of a petite young woman. She was clad in an expensive red velvet dress with a frilly lace collar. Her small hands were encased in white gloves, her dainty feet in stylish black boots. She had been dead for more than a century.

The workers who unearthed the lady described her as "miraculously preserved, with long auburn hair and the beautiful skin of a young woman."

Her body had been preserved in alcohol, an unusual funeral practice of the early 1800s. Based upon the embalming technique and style of her clothing, the Lady in Red died in the late 1830s.

No one ever came forward to claim the lady and no record of her burial was ever found. With no clue as to her identity, the owner of Egypt Plantation had the lady interred at Odd Fellows Cemetery in nearby Lexington, where she remains today. The marker on her grave reads simply, "Lady in Red . . . Found on Egypt Plantation . . . 1835–1969."

After those long, flat roads stretching to the horizon, the hill that signals the entrance to *Yazoo County* looks more like a small mountain. The county bills itself as the spot "where the Delta meets the hills," and indeed, one side of the county touches the flat edge of the Delta while the other rolls gently into the loess bluffs.

For a unique dining, shopping, and conservation experience, stop by the *Hines Broadlake Grocery* on Highway 49 just north of Yazoo City. Daily lunch specials featuring Eva Hines's country cooking bring in hungry farmers from all over the Delta. Every Thursday at Hines is fried pigskin day and Fridays are one giant barbecue. The grocery is located across the road from the Hines's working farm, where Eva and her husband John raise their own cattle and hogs. The grocery half of the business sells their homegrown beef and pork—every last bit of it. You'll find freezers stocked with pigs' feet, tongues, tails, snouts, and other parts city folk have probably never dreamed of ingesting. Eva is usually happy to let first-time guests sample some of the more unusual delicacies, including hog's head cheese, which she describes as "everything that's left."

If you were able to handle the hog's head, you might even be ready to graduate to chitlins (also known as chitterlings), another delicacy whose source of origin is seldom discussed. Pick up an order at the *All My Childrens* (no, that's not a typo) fast food restaurant just a mile or two down the road in *Yazoo City.*

The Witch of Yazoo

*I*n the late 1800s, Yazoo City was home to a self-proclaimed witch, a crazy old woman who lured fishermen to their deaths in her home on the banks of the Yazoo River.

Eventually, a group of vigilantes chased the old woman into a nearby swamp, where she met her death in a pool of quicksand. Just before her "ghastly, pockmarked" head was sucked below the surface, she vowed to return from the grave and burn the entire town on the morning of May 25, 1904. The old woman's body was pulled from the quicksand and buried in Glenwood Cemetery, the plot surrounded by a thick iron chain, each link 15 inches long.

You guessed it. On May 25, 1904, all of downtown Yazoo City was indeed destroyed by fire, and visitors to the old woman's grave found a link missing from the chain.

You'll find the century-old chain and a new marker inscribed, "the Witch of Yazoo" near the center of the cemetery at the intersection of Lintonia and Webster Streets. Visit the witch and give the chain a tug yourself—if you dare.

Little-Known Facts About the Mississippi River Delta

- In 1992, Tunica County boasted 20 hotel rooms. Six years and a dozen Las Vegas–style casinos later, the county is home to more than 6,000.

- Blues artists born in the Mississippi Delta include:

Charlie Patton	Robert Johnson	Muddy Waters
Billy Deaton	B. B. King	Mississippi John Hurt
Skip James	Bukka White	Sonny Boy Williamson
Otis Spann	John Lee Hooker	Son House
James "Son" Thomas	Sam Chatmon	Ike Turner

- The world's first franchised Holiday Inn opened its register in Clarksdale.

- Actor Morgan Freeman of Driving Miss Daisy, Seven, and Kiss the Girls fame grew up in Tallahatchie County and still owns a farm in nearby Charleston.

- The Norris Bookbinding Company of Greenwood is the largest Bible binding plant in the nation.

- More than 80 percent of the world's supply of farm-raised catfish comes from Mississippi.

- The 4-H Club was founded in Holmes County in 1907.

- Twenty-nine ships sunk during the Civil War lie beneath the Yazoo River.

In addition to a Delta side and a Hill side, Yazoo City boasts a dark side. The tale of the **Witch of Yazoo** (see sidebar, page 84) has been kept alive not only by local residents, but by writer Willie Morris, a Yazoo City native who repeated the spooky story in his book of childhood reminiscences, Good Old Boy.

The witch's tale is repeated every spring during the **Discover Yazoo Festival,** which includes fire sales in Yazoo City shops, twilight tours of Glenwood Cemetery, a competitive scavenger hunt, musical entertainment, arts and crafts, and a street dance. Call the **Yazoo County Convention and Visitors Bureau** at (800) 381–0662 for this year's dates.

You'll find the convention and visitors bureau offices in the **Triangle Cultural Center** on Washington Street. Housed in the old Main Street School built in 1905, the redbrick building is an attraction in itself. The Triangle Center houses a **Jerry Clower Exhibit,** honoring the late country comedian and former Yazoo City resident (say "haw!") and the *"Jimmy Carter Slept Here"* display, a roomful of furniture from a local home where the former President once passed the night (rumor has it the china he ate off of is locked away in a safe deposit box). To get to the Triangle Cultural Center, take Highway 49 to Broadway Street, go down the steep hill, then take a right at the first traffic light. The visitors center and exhibit rooms are open Monday–Friday 8:00 A.M.–4:00 P.M.

Be sure to ask the friendly staff for a walking tour guide to the *Yazoo City Historic District.* The homes included aren't open for tour, but a stroll along wisteria-lined streets offers a look at charming examples of Victorian, Queen Anne, Gothic, Italianate, and Greek Revival architecture. Staff at the visitors center can also give you directions to homes of significance you won't find listed in brochures, like the childhood homes of author *Willie Morris* and motivational speaker *Zig Ziglar* and the house where Jimmy Carter spent the night.

Housed in a restored turn-of-the-century mansion, the *Oakes African-American Cultural Center* displays photographs, folk art, sculpture, and other exhibits celebrating African-American history in Yazoo County. The mansion was once the home of Augustus J. Oakes, a prominent Yazoo City resident who founded Oakes Academy, a private school for African-American children, in 1884. Oakes is buried in Glenwood Cemetery.

For a Yazoo City adventure that's not just *off* the beaten path, but way, way *above* it, give *Zoo City Skydivers* a call. For around $200 you can

The Legend of Casey Jones

*S*hortly after midnight on April 30, 1900, the train Cannonball *left Memphis, Tennessee, with Jonathan Luther Casey Jones at the throttle of engine #382. Trying to make up time on his run to Canton, Jones barreled through a stop signal only to spot a freight train stalled on the track ahead. Realizing a crash was inevitable, Jones ordered his fireman to jump clear, but stayed on board himself to try and brake the train. Casey's heroic effort cost him his life.*

The tale of Casey Jones and the ill- fated Cannonball *might have ended that night if not for the musical skills of an engine wiper named Wallace Sanders, who composed "The Ballad of Casey Jones" as a tribute to his friend. The song became a hit, and Casey Jones became a legend.*

As for engine #382, it was repaired and put back in service on the same route. Just three years later, the 382 crashed again, killing the train's fireman and critically injuring its engineer. All told, the doomed 382 took five lives before it was finally retired from service in 1935.

take a morning lesson, then jump out of a perfectly good airplane the same afternoon. You'll even get a video to show all your friends. Brave souls can reach Zoo City Skydivers at (601) 932–4010.

If all that action stimulates your appetite, or if you just need a snack for the road, pick up a tin of **Mississippi Cheese Straws,** baked locally at the **Mississippi Cheese Straw Factory** and sold in shops all over Yazoo City. You'll also find a wide selection of goodies at **Gilbert's Gourmet Gifts,** a specialty foods shop located in the back of the family hardware store. Gilbert's also offers unique souvenirs, including the popular kudzu candle. Further shopping opportunities await at the **Cheshire Cat, Essco's,** and **Cindi's,** but if it's antiques you're looking for, the locals recommend a trip to the nearest pawn shop, explaining that "some people just don't realize what they have."

As you head out of town, you'll notice a profusion of green vines covering everything—*everything*—in sight. This rampant vegetation is **kudzu,** described by writer Lewis Grizzard as "the vine that ate the South." You'll find thriving displays of kudzu all over Mississippi, but the tenacious vine is especially prolific in the area between Yazoo City and Vicksburg. Once hailed as the remedy for the erosion of valuable farmland, kudzu became a nuisance, then an example of nature gone wild, when its growth could not be contained. The stuff grows an average of six inches per day, so fast you can almost watch it spread. The thick vine eagerly swallows up telephone poles, trees, buildings—virtually anything in its path. Don't stand in one place too long!

Wrap up your visit to the Delta by heading east on Mississippi Highway 16, then north up I–55 to **Vaughn,** where you'll spot an exit directing you to the **Casey Jones Railroad Museum State Park.**

The museum of Mississippi railroad memorabilia is housed in an old depot less than a mile from the site of the crash that killed engineer Casey Jones (see sidebar, page 86). The museum is open Monday, Tuesday, Thursday, and Friday from 8:00 A.M.–4:00 P.M. and Wednesday and Saturday from 8:00 A.M.–noon. Admission is $1.00 for adults and 50 cents for children.

An old barn on Possum Bend Road is home to **Harkins Woodworks,** where Greg Harkins makes rocking chairs by hand using techniques passed down from the mid-1800s. Harkins's famous chairs have graced the homes of Presidents Bill Clinton, Ronald Reagan, George Bush, and Jimmy Carter, as well as those of Pope John Paul II, Paul Harvey, Bob Hope, and George Burns. Place your own order on your way through Vaughn, then leave a shipping address and be patient—Harkins spends about thirty hours on each chair, even handpicking the tree he starts with. Harkins has turned down offers to automate and mass produce, preferring to stick with the exquisite craftsmanship that makes each chair a signed, dated, one-of-a-kind work of art. Call (601) 673–8229 or (601) 859–6054 for directions to Harkins's shop.

PLACES TO STAY IN THE MISSISSIPPI RIVER DELTA

The following is a partial listing of the many hotels, motels, and bed-and-breakfast inns in the area.

BELZONI
Magnolia Inn
(bed and breakfast),
304 Hayden Street;
(601) 247–4932

CHATHAM
Linden-on-the-Lake
(bed and breakfast),
Lake Washington Road;
(601) 839–2181

Mount Holly Plantation Inn
(bed and breakfast),
140 Lake Washington
Road East;
(601) 827–2652

CLARKSDALE
Days Inn,
1910 State Street;
(601) 624–4391

Hampton Inn,
710 South State Street;
(601) 627–9292

CLEVELAND
Comfort Inn,
721 North Davis Avenue;
(601) 843–4060

Molly's Bed and Breakfast,
214 South Bolivar Avenue;
(601) 843–9913

GREENVILLE
Azalea House
(bed and breakfast),
548 South Washington
Avenue;
(601) 335–0507

Comfort Inn,
3080 Highway 82 East;
(601) 378–4976

Days Inn,
2500 Highway 82 East;
(601) 335–1999

Hampton Inn,
2701 Highway 82 East;
(601) 334–1818

Miss Lois' Victorian Inn,
331 South Washington
Avenue;
(601) 335–6000

GREENWOOD
Comfort Inn,
401 Highway 82 West;
(601) 453–5974

Days Inn,
335 Highway 82;
(601) 453–4363

Hampton Inn,
635 Highway 82;
(601) 455–5777

INDIANOLA
Comfort Inn,
910 Highway 82 East;
(601) 887–6611

LINCOLN LTD. BED AND BREAKFAST RESERVATIONS
Lincoln Ltd. is a full-time reservation service for bed-and-breakfast inns statewide. For reservations in any area of Mississippi, call (800) 633–6477 or (601) 482–5483.

TUNICA/ROBINSONVILLE
Bally's Saloon and Gambling Hall Hotel,
1450 Bally Boulevard;
(601) 357–1500

Casino Inn,
2440 Commerce Landing;
(601) 363–9996

Circus Circus Casino
and Hotel,
1010 Casino Center Drive;
(601) 357–1111

Fitzgerald's Casino,
711 Lucky Lane;
(601) 363–5825

Grand Casino Tunica,
13615 Old Highway 61
North;
(601) 363–2788

Hampton Inn,
Highway 61 at Highway 304;
(601) 363–6711

Harrah's Tunica Mardi Gras
Casino and Hotel,
1100 Casino Strip
Boulevard;
(601) 363–7777

Holiday Inn Express,
4250 Casino Center Drive;
(601) 363–0030

Hollywood Casino Hotel
and RV Park,
1150 Casino Strip
Boulevard;
(601) 357–7700

Horseshoe Casino
and Hotel,
1021 Casino Center Drive;
(601) 357–5500

Sam's Town Hotel and
Gambling Hall,
1477 Casino Strip
Boulevard;
(601) 363–0711

Uncle Henry's Place
(bed and breakfast),
5860 Moon Lake Road;
(601) 337–2757

YAZOO CITY
Comfort Inn,
1600 Jerry Clower
Boulevard;
(601) 746–6444

**PLACES TO EAT IN THE
MISSISSIPPI RIVER DELTA**

*The following is a partial
listing of the many restaurants in the area.*

CLARKSDALE
Abe's Bar-B-Q,
Highway 61 and Highway 49;
(601) 624–9947

Chamoun's Resthaven
(Lebanese),
419 State Street;
(601) 624–8601

Major fast-food chains

CLEVELAND
Airport Grocery
(casual dining),
Highway 8 West;
(601) 843–4817

KC's (fine dining),
Highway 61;
(601) 843–5301

GREENVILLE
Doe's Eat Place (steak),
Nelson Street;
(601) 334–3315

Major fast-food chains

GREENWOOD
Lusco's (steak, seafood),
722 Carrollton Avenue;
(601) 453–5365

Major fast-food chains

INDIANOLA
The Crown Restaurant
(catfish; lunch only),
110 Front Street;
(601) 887–4522

ISOLA
Peter Bo's (catfish),
Highway 49 West;
(601) 962–7281

ROSEDALE
White Front Cafe
(hot tamales),
Main Street;
(601) 759–3842

TUNICA/ROBINSONVILLE
The Blue and White
Restaurant (country
cooking, breakfast),
Highway 61 and Highway 4;
(601) 363–1371

The Hollywood Cafe
(seafood, steak, catfish,
frog legs),
Highway 61;
(601) 363–1126

Uncle Henry's Place (fine
dining, Cajun, Creole),
5860 Moon Lake Road;
(601) 337–2757

*Tunica area casinos house
dozens of restaurants offering casual dining, fine dining, all-you-can-eat buffets,
and fast foods.*

YAZOO CITY
Hines Broadlake Grocery
(sandwiches, burgers,
country cooking),
Highway 49;
(601) 746–6518

**OTHER ATTRACTIONS WORTH
SEEING IN THE MISSISSIPPI
RIVER DELTA**

DURANT
Holmes County State Park

GREENVILLE
Bayou Caddy's Jubilee
Casino

Las Vegas Casino

The Light House Point
Casino

TUNICA

Bally's Saloon and Gambling Hall Hotel

Bluesville

Circus Circus Casino and Hotel

Fitzgerald's Casino

Grand Casino

Harrah's Tunica Mardi Gras Casino and Hotel

Hollywood Casino Hotel and RV Park

Horseshoe Casino and Hotel

Lady Luck Rhythm and Blues Casino

Sam's Town Hotel and Gambling Hall

Sheraton Casino

The Heartland

The Heartland stretches from Jackson, Mississippi's capital city and geographic center, through several rural communities south of the "big city" limits, then west to the historic towns that line the bluffs of the mighty Mississippi River.

As explorers of this area of the state soon discover, the Heartland manages to be urban and rural, Old South and New, and cosmopolitan yet down-home friendly—all at the same time.

The Jackson Metro Area

Ask out-of-state visitors to name a city in Mississippi and they'll usually pick Jackson, recalled from that often-recited list of state capitals learned in elementary school. But adventures in the Jackson Metro Area aren't limited to the capital city. Many of the region's genuine pleasures lie in the spirited college towns, quaint country villages, and folksy town squares just outside the city limits.

A tour of the Metro Area begins just off I–55 South in *Canton,* where the focal point is the antebellum *Madison County Courthouse.* Hollywood came to Canton in 1995 when the courthouse played a starring role in the movie version of best-selling author John Grisham's first novel, *A Time to Kill.* Hollywood visited again in 1998 for *My Dog Skip,* a feature film based on a book by another noted Mississippi writer, Willie Morris.

Even before Canton hit the silver screen, the *Courthouse Square* was famous as the home of the *Canton Flea Market.* Held twice yearly, this juried economic extravaganza attracts 1,100 vendors from 29 states and thousands of shoppers from around the country. Wares include fine art, paintings, pottery, jewelry, crafts, antiques, and plants displayed around the Courthouse Square, in the old jailhouse, and on the grounds of Grace Episcopal Church, Sacred Heart Catholic Church, and other area churches. Come prepared to fight the traffic and pay a premium price for a good parking spot, and don't forget your flashlight—the best

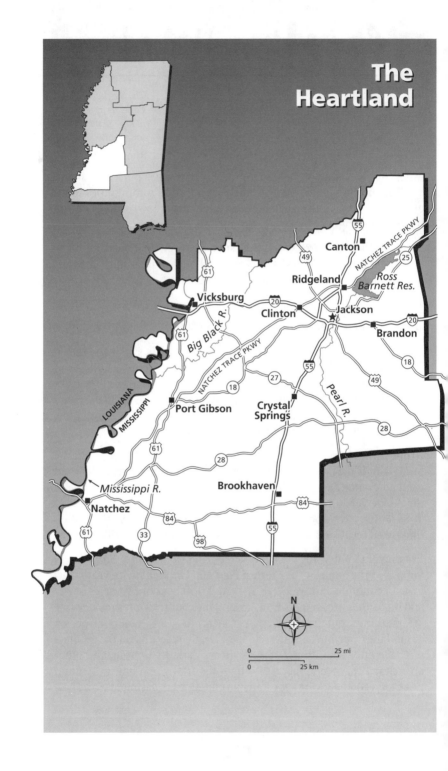

The Heartland

Canton

Ridgeland

Ross Barnett Res.

NATCHEZ TRACE PKWY

Vicksburg

Clinton

Jackson

Brandon

Big Black R.

NATCHEZ TRACE PKWY

Port Gibson

Crystal Springs

Pearl R.

LOUISIANA

MISSISSIPPI

Mississippi R.

Brookhaven

Natchez

N

0   25 mi

0   25 km

deals are made before dawn. The Canton Flea Market is held the second Thursdays of May and October. Call (800) 844–3369 for more information, including details on shuttle bus packages featuring highly coveted and well-worth-it rest room privileges.

From Canton it's just a short drive south past the horse stables on Highway 51 to **Madison,** one of Mississippi's premier residential communities. Madison's tiny downtown district is a favorite haunt of antiques buffs, who are sure to find treasures in the many shops that circle the **Historic Madison Depot Station** on Main Street off Highway 51 (Main Street is also Mississippi Highway 463). For a handcrafted souvenir, stop by **Pickenpaugh Pottery,** also located on Main Street near the depot area. Visitors to Pickenpaugh will usually find a landscaping project in progress that's every bit as unique as the pottery.

From downtown Madison, take a side trip along Mississippi Highway 463 to the **Chapel of the Cross.** The tranquility that envelops this tree-shaded churchyard and antebellum chapel is reason enough for a visit, but if you're in the mood for a mystery, drop by around twilight. You might be lucky enough to bump into the **Bride of Annandale**—the chapel's resident ghost. (See sidebar, page 96.)

Mississippi Highway 463 intersects Mississippi Highway 22 just northeast of **Flora** and the only petrified forest in the eastern United States. The **Mississippi Petrified Forest** was designated a National Natural Landmark by the National Park Service in 1966. According to geologists, the giant trees embedded in the earth here are some thirty-six to thirty-eight million years old. A well-marked trail through the wooded park can be easily explored in half an hour. The path ends in the earth science museum and gift shop, where visitors may purchase sparkling crystals, chunks of petrified wood, fossils, and other geological souvenirs. The Petrified Forest is open 9:00 A.M.–6:00 P.M. April–Labor Day and 9:00 A.M.–5:00 P.M. the remainder of the year. Admission is $4.00 for adults and $3.00 for children.

Chapel of the Cross

Sportsmen planning a trip to the Flora area should call ahead for reservations at **Kearney Park Farms** (601–879–3249), a quail hunting and sporting clays facility offering guided hunts and overnight accommodations.

From Flora it's just a short drive along U.S. Highway 49 South to tiny **Pocahantas.** A small sign points out the POCAHANTAS TRADING DISTRICT, but if you're headed for **Big D's Bar-be-cue,** it's just as easy to follow your nose. Barbecued pork ranks right up there with grits and catfish on the list of Mississippi delicacies, and Big D's is the perfect spot to stop for a sample (don't forget the napkins).

Continue on Highway 49 South from Pocahantas into Jackson, or double back on Mississippi 463, then follow Highway 51 south of Madison to **Ridgeland.**

Ceramics enthusiasts should make time to visit the **Gail Pittman Studio and Outlet** (290 South Perkins, 601–856–5646). Artist Gail Pittman began "playing around" with ceramics at her kitchen table in 1977. Today, the Gail Pittman collection includes more than 140 products ranging from dinnerware to home accessories to wall coverings, available in more than 40 original, colorful patterns. Gail Pittman pieces are prized by fans, collectors, and brides-to-be nationwide and make distinctive gifts.

Other shopping opportunities in Ridgeland include the **Log Village**, a charming area of folksy shops, and the **Antique Mall of the South**, which promises "no crafts or flea market items." Both are located on Highway 51.

The entrance to the northern section of the scenic **Natchez Trace Parkway** is in Ridgeland directly off Highway 51. A short jaunt along the Trace leads to the **Mississippi Crafts Center,** housed in a log cabin complete with rocking chairs on the front porch and a cheerful fire burning inside. The crafts center displays and sells one-of-a-kind masterpieces made by the members of the Craftsmen's Guild of Mississippi, including basketry, pottery, woodwork, and jewelry. The crafts center also stages frequent live demonstrations—visitors may arrive to find artisans whittling, weaving, carving, or quilting on the front porch.

The Madison–Ridgeland stretch of the Natchez Trace Parkway borders the 33,000-acre **Ross Barnett Reservoir.** Continue north along the Trace from Ridgeland and you'll arrive at the **Reservoir Overlook,** a grassy plateau that offers a lovely view of the water and provides the perfect setting for a picnic. The "rez" is a hot spot for power boating, skiing, sailing (watch out for those jet skis!), camping, and fishing.

When the sun goes down, activity moves to the many restaurants and nightclubs that dot the shoreline in the **Main Harbor Marina** area just off Spillway Road. Stop by **Cock of the Walk** for a taste of Mississippi farm-raised catfish served by waiters clad in flamboyant riverboat garb. Dinner is served on tin plates in a casual atmosphere that's perfect for families traveling with kids. But stay alert—you don't want to get hit by the flying cornbread.

Things get even more casual at **The Dock,** a restaurant/bar/marina overlooking the water where the people are friendly, live bands jam past midnight, and the only truly appropriate attire is a bathing suit. The Dock is the place to be on a sunny Sunday afternoon, sipping a cool

Lights, Camera, Action!

*I*n the last decade, Mississippi has become a hot spot for Hollywood.

The Firm, The Client, A Time to Kill, The Chamber (all based on best-selling novels by Mississippi author John Grisham), My Dog Skip, Ghosts of Mississippi, Mississippi Burning, and Mississippi Masala were among the many movies made in Mississippi.

Several of these films were shot in and around Jackson, where celebrity sightings became commonplace. Sandra Bullock, Chris O'Donnell, Alec Baldwin, James Woods, and director Rob Reiner were all spotted in local restaurants. Faye Dunaway had her portrait painted by a Jackson artist, Gene Hackman played golf at a Madison country club, and Keifer Sutherland took a turn on the drums at a local nightspot.

Delighted to meet a genuine "Sister Act," Whoopi Goldberg entertained a group of nuns from St. Dominic Hospital in her rented Madison County home. And I must confess to calling all of my friends from a local gym when Samuel L. Jackson and Matthew McConaughey showed up for a workout.

Not content with just watching, thousands of Mississippians flocked to open casting calls for roles as extras. Several of my friends and business associates vied for parts, and a few actually made it to the silver screen.

As for me, I admit to waiting in line for two hours in hopes of making the cut for A Time to Kill. Alas, the word from Hollywood was, "keep your day job."

drink and watching the boats go by. Ask a local to tell you about the night the deck of The Dock collapsed, tossing hundreds of revelers into the reservoir. Dockburgers are the house specialty here, and beer is usually the beverage of choice. A frozen, pink concoction known as the Dock Rocker is a favorite among the locals, but be warned—only those with a strong tolerance and a designated driver should tackle it.

From the reservoir area, take Spillway Road (which turns into Lake Harbor Drive as it crosses the reservoir back into Ridgeland) to Old Canton Road, then head south into *Jackson.* You'll know you've left Ridgeland and entered Mississippi's capital city when you cross County Line Road, a major thoroughfare lined with retail shops and restaurants. Located at the intersection of I–55 and I–20, Jackson is hardly off the beaten path, but even this busy city nicknamed the "crossroads of the South" offers a few undiscovered treasures.

If you tend to equate "museum" with "stuffy," your first stop should be the *Jim Buck Ross Agriculture and Forestry Museum.* From County Line Road, pick up I–55 South, exit at Lakeland Drive, turn left, then follow the signs to the museum complex. The Ag Museum includes living history re-creations of life on an 1860s farm (watch out for those chickens!) and in a 1920s small town, as well as a 40,000-square-foot exhibition hall featuring talking, snoring (yes, snoring) mannequins so lifelike they've been known to make unsuspecting visitors jump. The museum and grounds are open 9:00 A.M.–5:00 P.M. Monday–Saturday and 1:00–5:00 P.M. Sunday. Admission is $4.00 for adults, $3.00 for seniors, $2.00 for children aged 6 to 18, and 50 cents for children under 6.

The Bride of Annandale

Annandale was a huge Madison County plantation built in the 1840s. The plantation owner's daughter, Helen Johnstone, fell in love with the dashing Henry Vick, and their wedding was planned for May 21, 1859, at the Chapel of the Cross. But mere days before the nuptials, Henry was killed in a duel. He was buried at midnight in the churchyard behind the chapel, and the devastated Helen wore her wedding gown to the funeral. Helen eventually married, but never forgot her first love. The last words uttered from her deathbed were, "He's coming back for me."

Visitors to the Chapel of the Cross often report sightings of a sad woman clad all in white, sitting on a bench near Henry Vick's grave. If you go, don't wait for Helen past twilight. It's illegal to prowl the cemetery after dark, and as a number of unfortunate ghost-hunters can verify, it's a law that's strictly enforced.

THE HEARTLAND

The Ag Museum is also home to the ***Chimneyville Crafts Gallery,*** which displays and sells work by the members of the Craftsmen's Guild of Mississippi.

After a taste of life on the farm, get back on I–55 South and head toward downtown Jackson. Take the Fortification Street exit, head right to North Jefferson Street, then turn left to tour ***The Oaks,*** the oldest house in the capital city. Built in 1846, the house served as General William Tecumseh Sherman's headquarters during the Civil War. Period furnishings include the sofa from a young Abraham Lincoln's Illinois law office.

Back on Fortification Street, you may be surprised to spot a white picket fence smack on the corner of one of Jackson's busiest intersections. The fence surrounds the 1857 ***Manship House,*** home of Jackson's Civil War–era mayor, Charles Henry Manship. In addition to his civic involvement, Manship was an early practitioner of ornamental painting, specializing in the same type of "faux finish" work popular in homes today. Manship transformed the inexpensive lumber used to trim the home's interior into rich wood grains and fine marble. The stenciled floors in the nearby Mississippi Governor's Mansion are also believed to be Manship's work. Both The Oaks and the Manship House are closed on Monday, and the Manship House is also closed on Sunday.

Head just a couple of blocks south of Fortification Street and you'll find yourself in the heart of downtown Jackson. The city was originally laid out following Thomas Jefferson's checkerboard plan, which alternated squares of urban development with squares for public use or "greens." The result is a downtown district in which trees outnumber utility poles, and it's actually possible to hear birds singing above the traffic. Mississippi's version of a "bustling metropolis" is green and smog-free, with high-tech business conducted in buildings that witnessed the Civil War and sociable natives always ready to extend a gracious southern welcome.

MARLO'S FAVORITE ANNUAL EVENTS IN THE HEARTLAND

Canton

Canton Flea Market,
May and October,
(888) 868–7720

Mississippi Championship Hot Air Balloon Festival,
July, (800) 844–3369

Jackson

Dixie National Rodeo,
February, (601) 961–4000

Mal's St. Paddy's Day Parade, March,
(601) 355–7685

Jubilee! JAM,
May, (601) 960–2008

Sky Parade, *Labor Day Weekend, September,*
(601) 982–8088

Mistletoe Marketplace,
November, (601) 948–2357

Natchez

Spring and Fall Pilgrimages, *mid-March to mid-April; month of October,*
(800) 647–6742

Steamboat Jubilee and Best Floozie Contest,
June, (800) 647–6724

Great Mississippi River Balloon Race,
October, (800) 647–6724

Vicksburg

Civil War Re-enactments,
May and July,
(800) 221–3536

From the historic to the ultramodern, attractions in Jackson share a cultural flair. In addition to antebellum *City Hall* and the *"New" Capitol* building (dedicated in 1903), the handful of city blocks that makes up downtown is home to no fewer than a dozen historic buildings and museums, all within easy walking distance.

In the 1860s, Union troops reduced the town to a smoking ruin, earning Jackson the dismal nickname "Chimneyville." More than 130 years later, the handful of antebellum structures that survived the Civil War are still among the city's most impressive. The home of Mississippi's governors since 1842, the proud Greek Revival–style *Governor's Mansion* at 300 East Capitol Street served as a hospital during the war and was the scene of General Sherman's victory dinner following the fall of Vicksburg. When the state legislature recommended destroying the deteriorating mansion in the early 1900s, public outcry saved the building. Rescued by cries of "Will *Mississippi* destroy that which even *Sherman* would not burn?" the mansion was instead renovated to its former glory, opened for public tours, and designated a National Historic Landmark. Free tours are conducted on the half-hour Tuesday–Friday 9:30–11:00 A.M.

Capitol Street dead ends at the *Old Capitol,* a favorite landmark of Mississippians and home of the *State Historical Museum.* This restored architectural marvel houses exhibits chronicling Mississippi history from the days of the Indians to the Civil War through the Civil Rights movement, but the real attraction is the building itself—a magnificent Greek Revival statehouse built in 1833. Much of Mississippi's past is preserved in the corridors of this proud old building. It was here that the Ordinance of Secession was passed in 1861 in a hall "crowded to the point of suffocation with visitors who beckoned the state to secession." Jefferson Davis spoke here on more than one occasion, and the governor was arrested on the staircase at the war's end. There's no admission charge to visit this grand old museum, which is open weekdays 8:00 A.M.–5:00 P.M., Saturday 9:30 A.M.–4:30 P.M., and Sunday 12:30–4:30 P.M.

Housed in the first school for African-American children in Mississippi, the *Smith Robertson Museum and Cultural Center* (528 Bloom Street, 1 block off High Street) celebrates the state's African-American history and heritage. The museum is named for Smith Robertson, a former slave who became a successful businessman, respected community leader, and eventually served as a Jackson alderman. Exhibits document the contributions of African-Americans to education, politics, business, and the arts in Mississippi. Smith Robertson schedules regular folk art demonstrations and workshops and operates a gift shop featuring locally crafted African-American artworks. The museum is open weekdays 9:00 A.M.–5:00 P.M., Saturdays 9:00 A.M.–noon, and Sundays 2:00–5:00 P.M. Admission is $1.00 for adults and 50 cents for children.

Visitors particularly interested in African-American heritage may want to take a side trip to northwest Jackson to see the **former home of Civil Rights activist Medgar Evers**. A field secretary for the NAACP, Evers was shot and killed by a sniper in the driveway of his home in 1963 (see sidebar below). Evers's widow Myrlie donated the house, located at 2332 Margaret Walker Alexander Drive, to Tougaloo College, which is preserving it as a historic and cultural site. Call (601) 977–7839 or (601) 977–7842 to arrange a tour of the property where Medgar Evers lived and died.

The city of Jackson dedicated both the library in Evers's neighborhood and the street on which it stands to his memory. Neighborhood residents raised funds and erected a life-sized, bronze **statue of Evers** in front of the library at 4215 Medgar Evers Boulevard.

Justice for Medgar Evers

*O*n June 12, 1963, Medgar Evers, a field secretary for the NAACP, was shot and killed by a sniper in his own driveway. A white supremacist named Byron De La Beckwith was tried twice for the murder in 1964. Both trials ended in hung juries.

In 1989, the Hinds County District Attorney's office reopened the case when new evidence revealed that the now-defunct state Sovereignty Commission, created in 1956 to preserve segregation, aided Beckwith's defense by screening potential jurors.

Hinds County Assistant District Attorney Bobby DeLaughter prosecuted Beckwith, now seventy years old, for the third time in 1994. Thirty-one years after the murder, Beckwith was found guilty.

The reopening and retrying of the Beckwith case was the subject of the 1996 feature film Ghosts of Mississippi, *which starred Alec Baldwin as Bobby DeLaughter, James Woods as Beckwith, and Whoopi Goldberg as Evers's widow, Myrlie Evers-Williams. Evers's sons, Darrell and Vann, played themselves in the movie; his daughter Reena was played by Yolanda King, daughter of the late Martin Luther King, Jr. The film was shot on location in Jackson.*

Describing the scene in which the guilty verdict is finally returned, Darrell Evers said, "It was like reliving the entire thing. . . . I always wondered if I'd be able to cry in that scene. It was no problem."

Margaret Walker Alexander Drive was named for another famous African-American, the late author of the best-selling novel *Jubilee*, often referred to as the African-American version of *Gone With the Wind*.

Mississippi can't compete with the Napa Valley, but the state is home to a handful of wineries, one of which is located in downtown Jackson. Take South State Street to East Silas Brown Street and sample the vino made at the *Aspen Winery.* The winery offers tours, tastings, and sales of premium wines blended from California and Mississippi grapes. Tours are conducted Tuesday–Friday 11:00 A.M.–6:00 P.M. and Saturday 10:00 A.M.–5:00 P.M. Call (601) 355–WINE for more information.

After you've completed your tour of downtown, cross back to the north side of Fortification Street and drive through the lovely old area known as *Belhaven.* Towering trees, generations-old southern gardens, and an eclectic collection of architectural styles are the hallmarks of this gracious old neighborhood. Slow down when you reach *Pinehurst Street* across from the *Belhaven College* campus—you may catch a glimpse of Pulitzer prize–winning author *Eudora Welty.* Miss Welty grew up in Jackson, and as a child, often roller skated through the marbled halls of the State Capitol Building on her way to the downtown library. She was usually greeted at the door by a frowning librarian, who would send little Eudora back home to put on her petticoat, a lecture on proper library etiquette still ringing in her ears. Today, Eudora Welty's rare public appearances generate crowds of admirers, and the main branch of the Jackson Public Library System is known as the Eudora Welty Library.

Serious art collectors (and not-so-serious art enthusiasts) should visit *Brown's Fine Art and Framing* (630 Fondren Place), the *Southern Breeze Gallery* (Highland Village Shopping Center, Frontage Road), or the *Suite 103 Gallery of Art* (125 S. Congress Street, in the Capitol Towers Building). Each of these upscale galleries showcases work by Mississippi artists, including paintings, pottery, jewelry, and sculpture.

Jackson is home to countless restaurants, with two of the best found in the *Lefleur's Gallery* shopping center off I–55 north of downtown. For big spenders, *Times Change* features a changing menu of upscale entrees that includes beef, seafood, and poultry. The atmosphere is intimate; patrons waiting for a seat at one of seven tables gather around a small bar overlooking the area where Chef Tom Lambing chops, grills, and sautés. Just a few doors down, adventurous diners gather around a *sushi bar* to watch another Tom—Itamai-san Tomio Demura—turn fresh fish into an art form at *Little Tokyo.*

If you're interested in the Jackson nightlife, your next stop is *Hal 'n Mal's.* Operated by brothers Hal and Malcolm White, this downtown restaurant and bar serves up some of the best food and hottest entertainment in Jackson. Malcolm White describes the place as a "ladder club—we get the big acts on their way up, then we get 'em again on their way down."

The colorful White also stages one of Jackson's wackiest annual events, the *Mal's St. Paddy's Day Parade.* Part pub crawl, part Mardi Gras, and 100 percent green, the parade rolls through downtown Jackson on the Saturday closest to St. Patrick's Day. Past parade themes have included "Irish I Was a Movie Star," "Irish I was a Catfish," and "Elvis was Irish." The day-long, free festivities include a fun run, children's parade, and street dance featuring several bands.

Of course, parties in Jackson aren't limited to the holidays. The *Dixie National Rodeo and Livestock Show* storms into the capital city in early February, featuring all the ropin' and ridin' a cowboy could ask for, plus performances by the top stars in country music. Rodeo participants caravan all the way to Jackson in covered wagons and horse-drawn carriages.

Held Labor Day weekend at the Jackson International Airport, *Sky Parade* features hot air balloons, stunt flying, and live entertainment and is famous for stunning military air shows guaranteed to give you goose bumps.

But perhaps the most impressive cultural event hosted by Mississippi is the *International Ballet Competition,* which visits the United States every four years. Jackson is the only U.S. host city for the IBC, which assembles the world's most talented dancers in competition for the gold medal. The 1998 event brought ticket holders from seven foreign countries and thirty-eight states. The IBC returns to Jackson in 2002.

Overnight visitors to Jackson will find luxurious bed and breakfast accommodations in the heart of downtown at the *Millsaps Buie House* (601–352–0221), at the *Old Capitol Bed & Breakfast Inn* (601–956–2133), and in nearby Belhaven at *Fairview* (601–948–3429). Rates begin at about $85.

Just west of Jackson off I–20, the college town of *Clinton* features a historic *"Olde Towne"* district marked by bricked streets, one-of-a-kind bookstores, and antiques and specialty shops. Founded in 1826, Clinton's *Mississippi College* is one of the oldest in the nation and was the first college in the United States to graduate a woman. The *Provine*

Chapel on campus served as a combination hospital and horse stable during the Civil War.

Tiny *Byram,* located just south of Jackson on I–55, made history in Japan when the town's *swinging bridge* was featured on the popular Japanese television program *Bridges of the World.* One of only four suspension bridges left in Mississippi, the 360-foot, graffiti-plastered, wooden plank bridge was built in 1905 by Mississippi engineers who dubbed it the "mini-Brooklyn Bridge." The bridge is open to pedestrian traffic only, offering a pleasant stroll across the Pearl River.

Growing the Distance

In November of 1997, Mississippi-based WorldCom, Inc. and MCI Communications Corp. announced the largest corporate merger in United States history.

The $37 billion purchase of MCI by WorldCom made the new company, MCI WorldCom, the second-largest long-distance provider in the United States, made Clinton home to one of the largest communications companies in the world, and made Bernie Ebbers, the colorful CEO of WorldCom and mastermind behind the acquisition, a household name.

In 1983, Ebbers, a former milkman and junior high basketball coach, met with three investors in a Hattiesburg coffee shop to discuss starting a long-distance company. A waitress is credited with naming the company, scribbling "Long Distance Discount Calling" (later changed to Long Distance Discount Service) on a napkin.

During the first year of operation, the LDDS board met in the Western Sizzler. When Ebbers took over as CEO in 1985, LDDS was operating out of a converted gas station—the telephone

switch was housed in the oil-change bay. According to an early investor, "The only experience Bernie had in operating a long distance company was that he had used the phone."

Apparently, that was all the experience Bernie Ebbers needed.

During the first ten years under his leadership, LDDS stock appreciated an average 57 percent a year. LDDS expanded its service area to include the entire continental United States and more than 250 foreign countries. Motivated sales teams met targets that should have been impossible. In 1995, LDDS changed its name to WorldCom, reflecting its global aspirations in the communications industry. By the time of the MCI merger, WorldCom had become the nation's fourth-largest long-distance provider.

Today, MCI WorldCom serves one-fourth of the long distance market and more than 22 million small-business and retail customers.

All in all, not too bad for a company that began as an idea in a coffee shop.

Farmland and Festivals

ollow the signs from I–55 South to U.S. Highway 49 South, where the cityscape quickly gives way to rural Mississippi. Communities just outside the Metro Area are known for their festivals, which usually honor a favorite local crop, and for their folk art, pieces of which are perceived as cultural masterpieces or dressed-up junk depending on who you ask and how much it costs.

For a fresh taste of life on the farm, stop by ***Spell's Blueberry/Pumpkin Farm*** in ***Richland.*** Depending on the season, you can sample fresh, juicy berries or choose your own version of the Great Pumpkin. A witch frequents the farm around Halloween, to the delight of children who are encouraged to leave the pumpkin patch with the biggest specimen they can roll.

Eskimos and catfish probably have nothing in common except ***Jerry's Catfish House,*** an igloo-shaped restaurant located right on the highway in ***Florence.*** Jerry's claim to fame is an all-you-can-eat deal on Mississippi's favorite bewhiskered treat. If you're into "junking," the ***Magnolia Flea Market*** on Highway 49, 5 miles south of Florence, assembles twenty or so dealers peddling antiques, furniture, collectibles, toys, Oriental rugs, and other assorted stuff. Search for treasures any time from 10:00 A.M.–5:00 P.M. Tuesday–Saturday or 1:00–5:00 P.M. Sunday.

The igloo and flea market are just up the road from the tiny community of ***Star,*** where country music sensation Faith Hill hit her first high note in the church choir. Star is also home to one of nature's oddities. Ask a native for directions to the ***Rockhouse,*** a shallow cave in a wooded hillside. The Rockhouse isn't particularly impressive unless you know the story behind its origin. It seems the sandstone in the area is high in salt; the whitetail deer who live in the woods around Star actually *licked* the cave into existence.

Continuing south on Highway 49, you'll spot signs directing you to the ***Piney Woods Country Life School.*** Founded in 1909, this boarding school for disadvantaged African-American students has attracted national attention for its old-fashioned teaching philosophy and phenomenal success.

The school was founded by Dr. Laurence Jones, who came to Mississippi with nothing but a Bible, $1.65 in change, and a dream of a school where a "head, heart, and hands" education would be available for poor, rural black children. Dr. Jones taught his first classes under a cedar tree and was nearly lynched by a group of men who thought he was preaching against whites. After talking with Dr. Jones, the men were so inspired that they not only put away their rope, but donated $50 to the school. The tree is still standing, marked by a plaque reading, A LOG, A DREAM, A VISION, A RESTLESS URGE, A YOUNG MAN, LAURENCE C. JONES. Nearby is the log cabin that served as Piney Woods' first schoolroom by day and as Dr. Jones's quarters and a sheep shed by night.

Dr. Jones's dream is now a national model that's been featured in numerous publications and on more than one segment of *60 Minutes*. In fact, the school's reputation has gained such respect that in 1995, scores of celebrities from Eddie Murphy to Maya Angelou held a fundraiser in Washington, D.C., to provide inner-city children with scholarships to Piney Woods. Visitors are welcome to tour the fifty-acre campus and the surrounding 1,950 acres of farmland, lakes, and pine woods and to view exhibits chronicling the school's inspiring history.

If you're hungry, continue on Highway 49 South into **Mendenhall** and follow the signs to the **Revolving Tables Restaurant.** The house motto is "Eat 'til it ouches"—a goal made easy by the Revolving Tables' serving style. Diners sit at large round tables and take turns spinning a lazy Susan groaning with chicken 'n dumplings, mashed potatoes and gravy, cornbread, and other southern delicacies prepared by cooks who've never heard the word "cholesterol." Spin the lazy Susan at lunch- or suppertime (as many times as you dare) for about $10.

The catchy country tune "Watermelon Crawl" was surely inspired by a visit to nearby **Mize.** The population of this small **Smith County** community nearly doubles in July, when locals and out-of-towners alike cool off at the Mize **Watermelon Festival.** This day long celebration includes a flea market, seed-spitting contest, greased watermelon races, watermelon-eating contest, and the obligatory crowning of the Watermelon Queen. The Watermelon Festival is held the third Saturday in July unless the month has five Saturdays; then the festival moves to the fourth Saturday. To get your juicy slice, take Highway 49 South to Mississippi Highway 28, then follow the signs a few miles east to Mize.

If you travel west of Highway 49 on Highway 28, you'll find yourself in **Hazelhurst**, the setting for Beth Henley's Pulitzer Prize–winning play *Crimes of the Heart.* The dark comedy was later made into a movie starring Jessica Lange, Sissy Spacek, and Diane Keaton.

Hazelhurst's **Signature Works**, a manufacturer of housewares and paper products, is the nation's largest employer of the blind and visually impaired. The company's grounds feature Mississippi's only **Garden for the Blind**. While beautiful to look at, the garden can also be enjoyed by the visually impaired. All of the plants were chosen for their distinctive aromas or unusual textures. A bubbling fountain provides a melodic backdrop, and fixed pathways are outlined with handrails for easy navigation. The effort to create the garden was spearheaded by Margaret McLemore, a Hazelhurst resident who visited a similar garden while traveling in England. For more information or to enjoy a stroll through the garden, contact Ms. McLemore at (601) 894–2608.

If you're in the Hazelhurst area on the last Saturday in June, head north on I–55 to **Crystal Springs,** home of the annual **Tomato Festival.** The celebration recalls Crystal Springs's history as the "Tomatopolis of the World" with live entertainment, a flea market, children's activities, and, of course, tomatoes. Fried green tomatoes, tomato sandwiches, stuffed tomatoes, salsa—even tomato gravy ladled over hot tomato biscuits. Ketchup, anyone?

From Crystal Springs, continue on I–55 North toward I–20 and the towns and cities that fell in the path of the Civil War assault on Vicksburg. General Ulysses S. Grant's campaign for the "Gibraltar of the Confederacy" left a swath of destruction through this area of the state. But what seemed an unfortunate location in the 1860s is now a business advantage, with the cities and towns that suffered Civil War destruction now welcoming thousands of Yankees and Rebels drawn to the area for its rich Civil War history.

One of many skirmishes took place in **Raymond,** a small community located on Mississippi Highway 18. The Greek Revival **Hinds County Courthouse** and **St. Mark's Episcopal Church,** both located on West Main Street, served as Civil War hospitals; century-old bloodstains still mar the church floors. A driving tour brochure including fourteen historic buildings, many significant to the war, is available from the **Raymond Chamber of Commerce.** Call (601) 857–8942. And if you're looking for an old 45, album, or tape, stop by **Little Big Store,** located in the historic **Raymond Depot Building** at 201 East Main Street. Little Big Store specializes in out-of-print and rare records.

Continue south on Highway 18 approximately 20 miles to **Utica** and the **Museum of the Southern Jewish Experience**. Located on the grounds of the Henry S. Jacobs Camp for Living Judaism, the museum chronicles the history of the Jews in the American South through historical photos and artifacts, a central sanctuary, and changing exhibits. The museum is open daily 10:00 A.M.–5:00 P.M. Admission is $5.00 for adults, $4.00 for students and senior citizens. Call (601) 366–6352 for more information.

From Utica head north to I–20 West and **Edwards,** site of the **Battle of Champion Hill.** The Confederate loss at Champion Hill led to the fall of Vicksburg, which ultimately cost the Confederacy the Civil War. A noted military historian emphasized the importance of the battle to the war's outcome, writing that "the drums of Champion Hill sounded the doom of Richmond." The battle for Champion Hill is reenacted from time to time; call the Mississippi Division of Tourism at (800) WARMEST for the next battle date.

Edwards is also the home of the "world famous" **Cactus Plantation.** Follow the giant billboards (a la "See Rock City") and you absolutely cannot miss this prickly attraction. Sights at the Cactus Plantation include a farmhouse listed on the National Register of Historic Places, lazy Shetland ponies dozing in the sunshine, assorted chickens, and more than 3,000 varieties of colorful cacti, including one particularly interesting specimen dressed in southern gentleman's attire. Known as "the Cactus Colonel," this peculiar creature is displayed under the caption, "My cactus is finger-sticking good." Be sure to visit the "gift shop," a makeshift market displaying everything from Civil War–era wine bottles to flower pots to minié balls. The Cactus Plantation is open Monday–Saturday 9:00 A.M.–5:00 P.M. and Sunday 1:00–5:00 P.M.

If you thought the Cactus Plantation was unusual, take the **Bovina** exit off I–20 to **Earl's Art Gallery.** Earl Simmons lives in the second story of this rambling, crooked, cheerfully gaudy building he constructed from pieces of scrap lumber, metal, and other discarded parts. The first floor houses Earl's shop, a museum of his work and personal artifacts, and a handful of tables he refers to as "the restaurant." As Earl explains it, he started with "naked ground" and made up the floor plan as he went along, resulting in floors, walls, and ceilings that slant at crazy angles and entire rooms that lean to one side. A tour of the premises is reminiscent of a trip through a funhouse. Two dollars buys a tour of the small museum displaying Earl's critically acclaimed folk art—colorful paintings and sculpted chickens, trucks, buses, and cars made of discarded household items and scraps of wood and metal. Where others see trash, Earl sees raw material. If you see anything you like, speak up—most everything in the museum is for sale. To get to Earl's Art Gallery, follow the main road through Bovina, take a left at the stop sign, and keep to the left. Earl's will be on the left. Take special note of the multitude of hand-lettered signs adorning the structure; in addition to advertising the gallery, they help hold up the building.

The River Cities

A tour of the River Cities begins in Vicksburg, home of the Vicksburg National Military Park, and ends in Natchez, where you'll find the highest concentration of antebellum mansions in the United States.

This section of the state features at least one historic bed-and-breakfast mansion, Civil War monument, or well-preserved battlefield in every 10-mile stretch. Reminders of the antebellum South and the War Between the States dominate not only the landscape, but the very mindset of the people here, reminding visitors that soil once fought and died for is never again an ordinary plot of ground.

From Bovina, follow I–20 West toward the Mississippi River, through steep loess bluffs, gently rolling hills, and ever-encroaching kudzu to the Civil War time capsule that is *Vicksburg.*

President Abraham Lincoln called this river city "the key . . . let us get Vicksburg and all that country is ours. The war can never be brought to a close until that key is in our pocket." A victory at Vicksburg would sever Texas, Arkansas, and Louisiana from the Confederacy and give the Union complete control of the Mississippi River. For over a year, Vicksburg seemed impregnable as Union forces made several fruitless attempts by land and water to capture the city.

When direct charges failed, Grant decided to starve the city into submission. For forty-seven days and nights, the Union forces engaged in "the grand sport of tossing giant shells into Vicksburg." Accompanied by their slaves and taking their furniture and possessions, the frightened citizens sought shelter from the constant rain of shells in caves dug into the hillsides. (Six of these shelters remain hidden in the bluffs surrounding Vicksburg, but the caves aren't easily accessible, and the locals advise against any spelunking.)

Soldiers and citizens suffered alike as the siege wore on. The summer heat was terrible, water supplies dwindled, and mule meat became a delicacy. As the long, sweltering days passed, the distance between the lines shrank, until aggressors and defenders were virtually eyeball-to-eyeball. During lulls in the shelling, Union and Confederate soldiers exchanged jokes and stories along with coffee and tobacco, and two brothers from Missouri who were fighting on opposite sides were reunited.

On July 3, with his army and the civilian population starving, General John C. Pemberton met with Grant to discuss the terms of surrender.

When Grant demanded "unconditional surrender," Pemberton replied, "Sir, it is unnecessary that you and I hold any further conversation. We will go to fighting again at once. I can assure you, you will bury many more of your men before you will enter Vicksburg." Grant relented, and on July 4, the Confederate flag over the courthouse was lowered, and the Stars and Stripes flew once again in Vicksburg. It would be more than 100 years before the city again observed the Fourth of July.

"Giddyup, Jeff Davis!"

Throughout the Civil War, General U. S. Grant rode a horse named "Cincinnatis." In his memoirs, however, the northern general owned up to stealing a horse from Confederate President Jefferson Davis's Brierfield plantation near Vicksburg.

What did the Union general christen the stolen mount?

"Jeff Davis," of course.

The final days of siege and battle are replayed endlessly on the green expanses and rolling hills of the *Vicksburg National Military Park,* where 1,800 acres of fortifications and earthworks lined with monuments tell the dramatic story of the defense and fall of the "Gibraltar of the Confederacy." The Confederate and Union lines are identified, and markers trace the progress of the Union soldiers as they pushed uphill under fire in the thick heat of the Mississippi summer. Generals made of stone lead the charge, bronze horses eternally race into battle, and moss-covered cannons guard the city against a final attack.

Nearly all of the twenty-eight states that sent soldiers to Vicksburg erected markers, statues, and monuments in the park, the largest of which is the *Illinois Memorial,* an imposing dome-topped structure inscribed with the names of every Illinois soldier present at Vicksburg. Forty-seven stone steps leading into the monument represent the forty-seven days of siege. Of the thousands of names listed inside, two are of particular interest. Fred Grant, the general's twelve-year-old son, is listed as his aide. Also listed is Albert D. Cashire, who served throughout the Vicksburg campaign. When Cashire was hospitalized years later, he was discovered to be a *she*—an immigrant named Jennie Hodgers, who had masqueraded as a man for nearly half a century.

Also displayed at the Military Park is the **USS Cairo,** a Union ironclad sunk by the Confederacy and raised after 100 years underwater. Remarkably intact artifacts recovered from aboard ship, including a running watch, dishes, photos, and clothing, are displayed in an adjoining museum. The National Military Park is located at 3201 Clay Street; for information on guided tours, tapes, and events, call (601) 636-0583. The Military Park is open seven days a week from 8:00 A.M.–5:00 P.M. Admission is charged by the car.

Visitors often remark that Vicksburg is still fighting the Civil War, and at least twice a year, they're absolutely right. The city's Civil War story is reenacted in May and again in July during the **Vicksburg Civil War Siege Reenactment.** The **Memorial Day Reenactment** includes Union and Confederate tent camps, truce periods during which soldiers barter for coffee and information and attend church services, and bloody assaults on the Confederate lines. Smaller in terms of the number of participants but equally stirring is the **Fourth of July Reenactment,** which concludes when Union troops take control of the city, lower the Confederate flag, and raise the Stars and Stripes over the courthouse—usually to the jeers and taunts of the townspeople, who seem to forget this is not *really* 1863.

The reenactors themselves are a serious bunch, often refusing to acknowledge they're playing a part. Their clothing, campsites, ammunition, even their conversation with spectators is authentic to the 1860s. Many of the reenactors who make the annual trek to Vicksburg travel thousands of miles to participate in the campaign—much as their ancestors did nearly a century and a half ago. And whether they're motivated by sympathy for the conquered or the romance of fighting for a lost cause, the majority of reenactors prefer to fight for the Confederacy—even the Yankees.

Relive the siege any time of year through **The Vanishing Glory,** a thirty-minute, wide-screen production that relies on the eyewitness accounts, letters, and diaries of citizens and soldiers to tell the Vicksburg story. Show times are every hour on the hour from 10:00 A.M.–5:00 P.M. at the theater at 717 Clay Street. Admission is $5.00 for adults and $3.00 for children.

A number of Vicksburg's **antebellum mansions** survived the siege and are open for tours and as bed-and-breakfast inns. Many of the homes played significant roles in the war and still bear the scars of battle. A Union cannonball tore through the front door at **Cedar Grove** and is still embedded in the parlor wall. In addition to bed-and-breakfast accommodations and house tours, Cedar Grove offers romantic dining by candlelight, cocktails in the formal gardens, and sweeping views of the Mississippi River. With rooms available in the mansion, carriage house, and garden cottages, Cedar Grove is the largest bed-and-breakfast in Mississippi. Call (800) 862–1300 for rates and reservations.

A bomb squad was called to **McRaven** in the 1950s to remove a live Civil War shell from a wall. Built in three separate sections, McRaven combines the distinct architectural styles of the Frontier (1797),

Empire (1836), and Greek Revival (1849) periods. The master of McRaven was shot and killed by Union troops in the garden and may be one of several ghosts who reportedly call McRaven home. The house is among Mississippi's most haunted—lights turn on and off by themselves, footsteps echo in empty stairwells, the piano stool moves of its own accord, and the current owner claims the *previous* owner often follows him around the house. When asked if he minds living alone in such a place, this brave fellow smiles and says, "Who's alone?" McRaven welcomes ghost hunters nine months out of the year but is closed December–February.

Balfour House was the home of Civil War diarist Emma Balfour and the setting for the 1862 **Confederate Christmas Ball,** which was interrupted when a courier burst in with news of Union gunboats approaching on the Mississippi River. The ball is reenacted complete with this startling interruption each December; call the **Vicksburg Convention and Visitors Bureau** at (800) 221–3536 or (601) 636–9421 for ticket information and this year's dates.

The **Duff Green Mansion** served as a Civil War hospital, with Confederate soldiers treated in the basement to shield them from the shells and the unfortunate Union wounded quartered on the roof. The mistress of the plantation, Mary Green, gave birth to a son in a cave during the Vicksburg siege and christened him William Siege Green. Overnight guests at **Anchuca** can sleep in the same bed where Jefferson Davis, President of the Confederacy, often passed the night. And if you're traveling with Rover, you'll want to stay at the **Cherry Street Cottage,** where well-behaved pets are welcome.

Several additional homes welcome visitors during the annual **Spring and Fall Pilgrimages.** For a complete list of the many historic tour homes and bed-and-breakfast inns and this year's Vicksburg Pilgrimage dates, stop by the welcome center located near the scenic **Mississippi River Bridge** or call the Vicksburg Convention and Visitors Bureau at (800) 221–3536.

Prominently situated atop a hill on Cherry Street, the 1858 Vicksburg courthouse was a favorite target for Union shells until all of the Federal prisoners in Vicksburg were moved into the courtroom—a ploy credited with saving the building. The **Old Court House** is now one of the state's best historical museums, filled to the rafters with an extensive collection of Civil War letters, soldiers' diaries, period clothing, and other artifacts related to Vicksburg history. Exhibits include the tie worn by Confederate President Jefferson Davis upon his inauguration, a never-surrendered Confederate flag, and a minié ball that supposedly impregnated a local woman when it passed through a soldier's "private parts" before striking her own. Nicknamed "Vicksburg's Attic," the Old Court House is literally packed with artifacts—some items are even suspended from the ceiling. Tours are self guided, but if curator Gordon Cotton is in, ask him to tell you a story or two. Cotton knows more of the local lore and legend than anyone in Mississippi and has an endless repertoire of tales that bring Vicksburg's long-ago history to vivid life.

Several historic homes and the *Vicksburg Garden District* are located on Washington Avenue, which also runs into a quaint area of shops and small museums. The *Biedenharn Museum of Coca-Cola® Memorabilia* is housed in the building where Coca-Cola was first bottled in 1894. The museum chronicles the history of the world's most popular soft drink and serves up "the real thing" in floats from the old-fashioned soda fountain. *Yesterday's Children Antique Doll and Toy Museum* displays more than a thousand playthings, and the *Gray and Blue Naval Museum* houses the world's largest collection of Civil War gunboat models. *The Corner Drug Store* includes a collection of Civil War medical equipment and cure-alls and more than one bullet scarred with the teeth marks of unfortunate patients forced to undergo surgery without the benefit of anesthesia. For a one-of-a-kind Civil War souvenir, stop by *Wilson's Racket Store* and take home an original *Johnny Reb wood carving.* Local artisan Johnny Roland hand carves the soldiers, as well as hunters, Indians, dogs, and cows, so no two are alike. A Confederate soldier will set you back about $100; for $195 you can take home a likeness of General Grant or Robert E. Lee.

Vicksburg's slogan is "History and Much, Much More," and true to its word, the city does offer more than Civil War attractions. The *Great Animal Adventures Children's Museum* (721 China Street) explores the world of veterinary medicine and the contributions animals make to medical research. Housed in stable built in 1888, the museum showcases artifacts collected by Dr. Bill Lindley, a local veterinarian who described medicine as "any substance which, when given to a mouse, produces a scientific paper." Animal Adventures is open 9:00 A.M.–5:00 P.M. Monday–Saturday, 1:30 P.M.–4:30 P.M. Sunday. Admission is $2.00 for adults, $1.50 for children.

Boo the villain, cheer the hero, and throw peanuts at the entire cast of *Gold in the Hills,* a live performance originally staged in 1934 and listed in the *Guinness Book of World Records* as the longest-running old-fashioned melodrama. Call (601) 636–0471 for ticket information and showtimes.

For a more fast-paced adventure, call *Mississippi River Adventures* (601) 683–5443 or (800) 521–4363 for a hydro-jet tour of the Mississippi River. Guides point out the local flora and fauna as well as Civil War sites. Three one-hour tours depart daily from the waterfront at the foot of Clay Street at 10:00 A.M., 2:00 P.M., and 5:00 P.M. Tours are $16 for adults, $8 for children 6 to 12, and free for kids under 6.

For an experience that's not only off the beaten path but more than a little off-the-wall, swing by *Margaret's Grocery, Market, and Bible Class* on Highway 61 a few miles north of the center of Vicksburg. A sign proclaiming ALL IS WELCOME, JEWS AND GENTILES atop a huge tower of red, white, and blue masonry sprinkled with Bible verses and cryptic phrases is the first hint that Margaret's offers more than bread and milk. In fact, the groceries are hard to spot inside, overshadowed by reproductions of the Ark of the Covenant and the Ten Commandments, a glass doorknob referred to as "the all-seeing eye," and other unique artifacts, most of which are decorated with tiny mirrors, costume jewelry, and Mardi Gras beads.

The elaborate archways, pillars, and towers of brick are the work of the nearly ninety-year-old Reverend H. D. Dennis, Margaret's husband. The Reverend promised Margaret if she married him, he'd turn her store into a palace, and he was true to his word. The Lego-like construction project hasn't stopped yet; the Reverend is still adding on to the elaborate structure, which serves as a combination residence, grocery store, and house of worship. "God is the greatest architect," Dennis says. "I'm only his assistant."

The teetering structures stretch more than 100 feet along Highway 61, attracting stares, waves, honks, and more than a few tourists curious enough to venture inside. Margaret and the Reverend welcome visitors, but don't stop unless you have time to listen to one of the Reverend's fiery sermons, which usually includes a dire warning about the "boats," the floating *casinos* that line the river in front of Vicksburg. Margaret herself is also on hand, quick to point out that they don't charge admission, but welcome "free donations." Margaret's Grocery is more than a bit eccentric, but visitors will leave with a warm feeling, assured that "they can do right if they really want to," and knowing the Reverend will pray for their safe journey.

Serious outdoorsmen or nature buffs may consider a side trip to the *Tara Wildlife Management Reserve.* Nestled between Eagle Lake and the Mississippi River some 35 miles north of Vicksburg, this 20,000-acre wildlife habitat offers guided hunts and wildlife photography expeditions. Game includes turkey, deer, duck, squirrel, and rabbit.

Overnight accommodations are available on the property. For more information or to arrange a tour or hunt, contact Tara Wildlife Management Services, Inc. at (601) 279–4261.

If your favorite game isn't in season or you're not the huntin' and fishin' type, continue south on Highway 61 to the all-but-extinct town of **Grand Gulf.** Once one of the busiest ports between New Orleans and St. Louis, Grand Gulf endured a series of disasters that eventually wiped out the town. Grand Gulf stoically survived citywide fires, a yellow fever epidemic, and a devastating tornado before the Mississippi River changed its course, gobbling up fifty-five city blocks in the late 1850s. What little was left of the once-thriving city was burned by the Union army during the Civil War.

Though you'll still find it on the map, Grand Gulf is so small it doesn't even have a zip code. This isolated hamlet's sole claim to fame is its rich nineteenth-century history, preserved in the **Grand Gulf Military Monument Park.** The 400-acre park includes Fort Wade, where heavily armed Confederates repelled Grant's initial landing attempt; the **Grand Gulf Cemetery,** where black Union troops who occupied the town are buried and the headstones offer a synopsis of Grand Gulf's tragic history; well-preserved earthworks built by the Grand Gulf defenders; and several restored buildings moved to the park from other sites in Mississippi, including the Sacred Heart Catholic Church from the ghost town of Rodney. The park museum—named one of the best small museums in the nation by *Reader's Digest*—contains hundreds of Civil War artifacts, including soldiers' letters and diaries, guns, and bloodstained uniforms. An outbuilding houses a collection of carriages and wagons, including a rare Civil War ambulance and a one-man submarine used to smuggle whiskey during Prohibition. The Mississippi River is visible for miles from the park's observation tower, and it's easy to imagine Grant's troops assembling for the attack.

The park also includes nature trails and facilities for tent and RV camping. Admission is charged only for the museum and RV camping. Grand Gulf Military Monument Park is located 10 miles northwest of Port Gibson and U.S. Highway 61 on Grand Gulf Road.

Nearby **Port Gibson** is probably the only town in the South that uses a quote from the much-loathed General Grant as its slogan. In a rare departure from his scorched-earth policy, General Grant declared Port Gibson "too beautiful to burn" and left the town's picturesque collection of homes and churches unscathed. Port Gibson was the first town in Mississippi designated a National Historic District.

Most of the *antebellum homes and churches* that so enchanted the general are located directly on Highway 61 South, which turns into Church Street in Port Gibson. Drive as far as the visitors center located at the south end of the street, where a helpful volunteer will provide you with maps, brochures, and background information on the homes and churches, then leave your car parked at the visitors center and enjoy a walking tour of Church Street.

Port Gibson's most striking structure is the *First Presbyterian Church,* its steeple topped by a 10-foot gold hand pointing heavenward. The church was built in 1859 under the dynamic leadership of the Reverend Zebulon Butler. Butler himself labored with the workers and craftsmen during the church's construction, but he died just before the building was completed. Ironically, the first service held in the new church was his funeral. The original hand atop the steeple was fashioned of wood—to the delight of area woodpeckers, who showed little respect for this holy symbol. The present metal hand topping the church has become Port Gibson's most famous landmark. Notable features inside the church include the original slave gallery and the chandeliers from the steamboat *Robert E. Lee,* each of which features a figure of General Lee on horseback.

Just down the street is *St. Joseph's Catholic Church,* where an eerie trick of the light and stained glass makes the very air inside the church seem blue at any hour of the day. Exquisite panels carved of walnut depict the life of Christ and enhance the solemn atmosphere of reverence that permeates this 1849 house of worship. Church Street is also home to the oldest synagogue in Mississippi, *Temple Gemiluth Chessed.*

Most of the historic homes along Church Street are open for tours only during Port Gibson's annual *Spring Pilgrimage* weekend, but *Oak Square Plantation* (601–437–4350 or 800–729–0240) accommodates visitors and overnight guests year-round. Call for rates and reservations. For this year's pilgrimage dates, call the *Port Gibson-Claiborne County Chamber of Commerce* at (601) 437–4351.

Civil War buffs will want to stop by *Wintergreen Cemetery,* where Confederate General Earl Van Dorn is buried facing his beloved South and a section known as "Soldier's Row" is the final resting place for Union and Confederate soldiers. True Blue-and-Gray buffs can pick up a map of *General Grant's March Route* through the county, available at the visitors center on Church Street. Sections of the route have been left undisturbed for more than a century; the dirt road and steep ravines navigated by Grant's 20,000 troops remain largely untouched. The road is impassable during inclement weather, and explorers are advised to check in with the Grand Gulf Military Monument Park or Port Gibson-Claiborne County Chamber of Commerce before setting out.

The Port Gibson organization known as the **Mississippi Cultural Crossroads** was formed to preserve the southern African-American art form of quilting. Work by the Crossroads Quilters is displayed in galleries across the South. Colorful patchworks and vivid murals line the walls of the Cultural Crossroads' headquarters at 507 Market Street in downtown Port Gibson. Open weekdays 9:00 A.M.–5:00 P.M., the **Quilt Gallery** displays works of every size, color, and pattern, all made locally and all for sale. Of particular interest are "memory quilts," which depict scenes from the quilter's own life. Other folk art forms include "pants quilts," made from sturdy strips of work trousers, and "string quilts," which prove a good quilter can make something pretty out of almost nothing. Cultural Crossroads sponsors **Pieces and String,** an annual quilting exhibition and contest usually scheduled for the same weekend at the Port Gibson Spring Pilgrimage. For this year's dates, call the Port Gibson-Claiborne County Chamber of Commerce at (601) 437–4351 or the Cultural Crossroads at (601) 437–8905.

African-American history of a later era is preserved in the exhibit **No Easy Journey,** a permanent collection of photographs and artifacts commemorating the Civil Rights movement in Claiborne County. Haunting images of African-Americans facing billy clubs and guns, picketing local businesses, and marching the streets of a 1960s Port Gibson in search of equal rights remind visitors of the turbulence of the era and celebrate progress made over the past forty years. Housed in the Claiborne County administration building, this free exhibit is open Monday–Friday 8:00 A.M.–5:00 P.M.

No visit to the Port Gibson area is complete without a side trip to the **Windsor Ruins.** A dusty road winding through the quiet countryside leads to the crumbling remains of what was the largest antebellum mansion in Mississippi. Mark Twain wrote about the palatial Windsor in *Life on the Mississippi River,* noting that "the mansion high above the bluffs was visible for miles in every direction." Following the Battle of Port Gibson, Union troops claimed the house as a hospital, and the eloquent pleas of the mistress of Windsor saved the mansion from destruction at their hands on three separate occasions.

Windsor survived the war only to burn to the ground at the hands of a careless smoker in 1890. Twenty-three towering Corinthian columns are all that remain of the once-opulent mansion, and a sketch drawn by a Union soldier in May of 1863 is the only known image of the house in its heyday. The dramatic ruins have been featured in a number of movies, including *Raintree County,* which starred Elizabeth Taylor and Montgomery Clift. A map indicating the shortest route to the

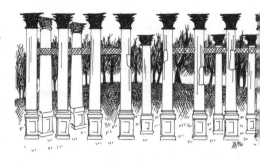

Windsor Ruins

Windsor Ruins is available from the visitors center on Church Street, or you can take Highway 61 South, then follow the signs to Mississippi 552 West and the ruins.

Heading back to Highway 61 on Mississippi 552, you'll pass **Alcorn State University,** the nation's first land-grant college for blacks. Alcorn's **Oakland Chapel** features the iron staircase that once led to the front doors of the Windsor mansion. This stretch of Mississippi 552 also winds past **Canemount Plantation,** a 6,000-acre working plantation and bed-and-breakfast inn built in 1855. Accommodations are in private cottages featuring wood-burning fireplaces or stoves. Call (800) 423–0684 for rates and reservations.

Just south of the intersection of Mississippi 552 and Highway 61 in **Lorman** is the **Old Country Store,** which first opened its doors to shoppers in 1875. Today the Old Country Store houses a craft mall and restaurant. Stop by between 9:00 A.M.–5:00 P.M. Monday–Saturday or noon–5:00 P.M. Sunday for a sandwich or ice-cream cone, or a taste of the "biggest, bestest burger around."

Just across Highway 61 from the Old Country Store is the turnoff to **Rosswood Plantation,** yet another of Mississippi's elegant antebellum bed and breakfasts. Nestled on a 100-acre Christmas tree farm, the 1857 mansion was built by David Shroder, the same architect who designed Windsor. Visitors may peruse the diary of Dr. Walter Ross Wade, Rosswood's original owner. His journal recounts the adventures of life on the plantation before and during the Civil War, including descriptions of parties and balls reminiscent of the opening scenes of *Gone With the Wind.* Rosswood is open for tours March–December 8:30 A.M.–5:00 P.M. Monday–Saturday and 12:30–5:00 P.M. Sunday. Admission is $6.50. Overnight rates begin at $100. Call (800) 533–5889 for reservations.

For an adventure way, way, way off the beaten path, take the first road to the right on the south side of the Old Country Store, turn left at the stop sign, bear right at the fork, and head for the *Rodney Ghost Town.* The road to Rodney alternates between gravel and pavement and will give your shock absorbers a workout they'll never forget. This rough passage winds past deserted country churches, junked cars, curious deer, and a number of trailer-and-shack complexes labeled as someone's "Huntin' Camp." Just when you think you're hopelessly lost, you'll pass an intersection identifying Rodney Road. The ghost town is just ahead.

Incorporated in 1828, Rodney was known for its high level of culture and business activity. The Mississippi River flowed past Rodney, rendering the town a bustling center of commerce and distribution. In its heyday, Rodney was home to two banks, two newspapers, thirty-five stores, a large hotel, an opera house, and several saloons. By 1860, with a population approaching 4,000, Rodney was one of Mississippi's most prosperous towns.

Travels With Frosty

*O*ne of the best research tools I've discovered for travel writing isn't a guide book, an Internet listing, or even a well-marked map.

It's my dog, Frosty.

An American Eskimo Spitz, Frosty is forty pounds of fluffy white fur, intelligent brown eyes, and adventurous spirit. The Eskimo Spitz is a striking dog and a rather uncommon breed for Mississippi—traits that turned out to be invaluable during the researching of Mississippi: Off the Beaten Path.

When I drove into small towns with Frosty hanging out the window, we caused quite a stir. People invariably wanted to pet him, offered him water, and, as an afterthought, talked to me, too.

I was made privy to local legends, received detailed directions to out-of-the-way attractions, and soaked up the local color, all from people who shared freely with me while petting my dog. I gathered critical information not because I was a skilled field researcher, but because I was Frosty's traveling companion.

As for Frosty himself, I'd like to believe he put up with all the attention as a favor to me and out of dedication to the project, not simply because he enjoyed being doted on by strangers all over Mississippi.

Since he worked so hard on this book, it's only fair that I tell you Frosty's favorite spot in Mississippi: Off the Beaten Path. It was the Windsor Ruins, paws down. It seems those twenty-three towering, Corinthian columns have a lot more doggy appeal than an ordinary fire hydrant.

Then the Civil War depleted Rodney's wealth, and the town was nearly wiped out by a series of disastrous fires. But it was Mother Nature who dealt the final blow. Around 1869 the Mississippi River changed its course, leaving Rodney high and dry. The population dwindled over the coming decades, and in 1930, Mississippi Governor Theodore Bilbo issued an executive proclamation abolishing the town.

From Slaves to Founders of a Nation

In 1834, Captain Issac Ross, a plantation owner in Lorman, freed his slaves and arranged for their passage back to their homeland on the west coast of Africa. Here, these freed slaves founded the nation of Liberia.

Years later, their descendants returned to Lorman and placed a commemorative stone at the captain's gravesite honoring his kindness and celebrating the magnanimous gesture that led not only to the freeing of their ancestors, but to the founding of their country.

Union gunboats shelled Rodney during the Civil War, and a cannonball is still embedded in the facade of the 1829 **Rodney Presbyterian Church,** the deserted town's most prominent building. Thick grass carpets the brick steps in front of the church, spreading all the way to the front doors. A separate entrance at the side of the building opens to a narrow flight of super-steep stairs leading to the old slave gallery. The ancient town cemetery is hidden behind the church up a steep hill, its overgrown grave sites surrounded by an ornate wrought-iron fence. A second old church, a Masonic lodge, and an old store are the only buildings still standing, and cotton grows in the old riverbed.

When the lonely feel of the ghost town begins to seem a bit unnerving, head back down that bumpy road to Highway 61 South. When you reach the intersection of Highway 61 and the **Natchez Trace Parkway,** you can take the Trace or continue on Highway 61 to **Fayette.** Either route will eventually lead you to Mississippi Highway 553 and **Springfield Plantation.**

Springfield boasts a legacy of intrigue and romance few historic homes can rival. In the spring of 1791, Andrew Jackson and Rachel Robards were married in the parlor of this beautiful mansion, touching off a scandal that would haunt the Jacksons for the rest of their lives. At the time of their marriage, both bride and groom mistakenly believed Rachel and her first husband had been granted a divorce. When word of their invalid marriage spread, political opponents began a vicious smear campaign, accusing Jackson of "sleeping under the blanket with another man's wife."

Like many homes with a romantic past, Springfield is rumored to be haunted. The strains of long-ago melodies are said to echo through the home's west wing, where a ballroom once occupied the second floor. Who knows—perhaps the restless spirits of the famous newlyweds still share a wedding day dance. Springfield Plantation is open year-round 9:30 A.M. until sunset Monday–Saturday and 10:30 A.M. until sunset Sunday. Hours vary November–March. Call (601) 786–3802 for specific hours and admission fees.

Highway 553 makes a scenic loop west of the Natchez Trace that includes the historic **Church Hill** community, home to a number of working plantations, historic homes, and churches. The 1830 **Cedars Plantation,** once owned by actor George Hamilton, is now a bed-and-breakfast inn. Call (601) 445–2203 for rates and reservations.

For a look at accommodations of a more rustic sort, rejoin the Natchez Trace from Highway 553 and head south to the **Mount Locust Inn,** a 1700s version of Howard Johnson's. Restored to its original 1780 appearance (complete with split rail fences and coonskin caps on the bedposts), Mount Locust offers a glimpse of the "luxury" accommodations of the day. Between 1785 and 1830, more than fifty of these frontier inns or "stands" existed along the Old Natchez Trace. For approximately 25 cents, weary travelers enjoyed a supper of "mush and milk" and the privilege of sleeping in a room packed with saddles, baggage, and other wayfarers. Located approximately a day's walk apart, these establishments offered not only a meal and a place to rest, but a spot of civilization in the vast wilderness surrounding the Trace. Mount Locust is the only inn left standing. The former sites of other frontier stands are marked along the parkway.

The next stop on the Trace is even older. Built around A.D. 1400 by ancestors of the Creek, Choctaw, and Natchez Indians, **Emerald Mound** is the second-largest Indian mound in the United States. The ceremonial earthen structure covers some 8 acres, measures 770 feet by 435 feet at its base, and stands 35 feet high.

The Natchez Trace ends at Highway 61, which runs into the heart of Natchez. But first you'll drive through the old territorial capital of **Washington,** once known as the "Versailles of the Mississippi Territory."

Turn right off Highway 61 at the sign pointing to historic **Jefferson College.** The first educational institution chartered in the Mississippi Territory, Jefferson College conducted its first classes in 1802. A young Jefferson Davis was a student here, and according to local lore, naturalist John James Audubon instructed drawing classes on campus, Andrew Jackson was entertained here following the Battle of New Orleans, and United States Vice President Aaron Burr was arraigned for treason under the campus's giant "Burr Oaks."

Classes were conducted here until the 1960s, when the buildings were restored to their 1800s appearance and the campus became a museum. If the college looks familiar, you may have seen it on television. Historic Jefferson College played West Point in the miniseries *North and South* and also appeared in *The Horse Soldiers* starring John Wayne and in Disney's *Huck Finn.* The grounds are open from sunup to sundown and the buildings are open 9:00 A.M.–5:00 P.M. Monday–Saturday and 1:00–5:00 P.M. Sunday.

Continue on Highway 61 South to **Natchez,** the oldest settlement on the Mississippi River. Prior to the Civil War, more than half the millionaires in America lived in Natchez, erecting palatial mansions with fortunes built on cotton. All told, Natchez boasts an incredible 500 antebellum structures, including breathtaking homes, ornate churches, and public buildings where history was made.

The grand southern tradition of the pilgrimage was born in Natchez way back in 1931. A late freeze wiped out the blooms scheduled for a

The Ghost of King's Tavern

*F*or a dining experience that's literally out of this world, stop by King's Tavern (619 Jefferson Street in Natchez), a steak and seafood house operating in the oldest building in the Natchez Territory. The fare at King's Tavern is quite delicious, but the restaurant's real attraction is Madeline, its resident ghost.

The exact origin of King's Tavern is lost to history, but the building was probably constructed somewhere around 1760. The first mail to the region was carried down the Natchez Trace by Indian runners and left in a small post office on the tavern's first floor. Bullet holes in the heavy doors speak of bandits who once stalked travelers along the Trace, the claw prints of bear and cougar are still visible in the floors, and in the 1930s three skeletons (accompanied by a

jeweled dagger) were unearthed in the tavern walls.

A young serving girl named Madeline—rumored to be the mistress of the tavern owner—worked in the midst of all this adventure. Apparently Madeline found King's Tavern so exciting, she just couldn't bear to leave—even 200 years after her death. Restaurant employees and patrons speak of lights switching on and off by themselves, footsteps that ring through the vacant upper floor, and water dripping in certain spots while everything else is dry. Apparently Madeline still tries to keep her customers happy—she operates the old dumbwaiter from time to time.

King's Tavern is open for dinner 5:00–10:00 P.M. and serves lunch during the pilgrimage. If you go, ask for a seat at one of Madeline's tables.

weekend garden tour, so the members of Natchez's garden clubs opened their antebellum homes for visitors instead. Many of these ladies were hesitant to participate in such a bold venture. Times had been tight in Natchez in the sixty years following the Civil War, they argued. Didn't the homes need remodeling to keep up with the times? Of course, it was the very fact that the homes *hadn't* been changed since the prewar days that made them such an attraction. This impromptu tour was such a fabulous success that in 1932 the ladies scheduled the first *official* Spring Pilgrimage, and the rest is tourism history.

During **Spring and Fall Pilgrimages** approximately thirty of Natchez's grand old buildings are open for tours. While most Mississippi pilgrimages are held over a week or weekend, the Natchez extravaganza lasts a full month, running from mid-March to mid-April and again in October. No experience on earth is as thoroughly southern. Costumed hostesses recite each magnificent home's history, punctuated by lots of curtseying, plenty of "y'alls," and frequent sips of that quintessential southern cocktail, the mint julep. Magnificent displays of antique roses, camellias, Japanese and saucer magnolias, dogwood trees, jasmine, daffodils, and azaleas remind guests that this spring spectacular began as a garden tour.

After so many years in the pilgrimage business, Natchez has home tours down to a science. Each morning or afternoon tour package buys admittance to four houses for $24; you'll need to stay several days in order to see all of the homes.

The festivities aren't limited to the home tours. During the spring pilgrimage, the most popular evening entertainment is the **Confederate Pageant,** a live performance featuring nearly 300 locals in period dress recalling the glory days of the Old South. Completely and unapologetically biased, the pageant is guaranteed to bring tears of pride to southern eyes and pangs of guilt to Yankee consciences.

Another side of the Old South is portrayed in the **Southern Road to Freedom,** a stirring musical celebration of the African-American experience in Natchez. Finally, Natchez pokes fun at its own traditions in **Southern Exposure,** a lighthearted satire of the pilgrimage itself performed at the Natchez Little Theatre. Pilgrims who visit during the fall can take in a vaudeville-style performance of the **Mississippi Medicine Show** or enjoy the music of **Amos Polk's Voices of Spiritual Hope.**

For pilgrimage dates, details on individual or group tours, reservations for bed-and-breakfast stays, and information and tickets to evening entertainment, call **Natchez Pilgrimage Tours** at (800) 647–6742.

The Roxie Gold Hole

*I*f a visit to Natchez leaves you longing for a mansion of your own, take a side trip 20 miles east of town down U.S. Highway 84 to the Roxie Gold Hole, a small pond dug one shovelful at a time by treasure hunters.

According to local legend, a gang of Natchez Trace bandits buried a treasure chest 7 feet wide and 3 feet deep in a sinkhole near Roxie. Treasure hunters dragged shovels around the woods in Roxie for years before finally unearthing a corner of what appeared to be the genuine treasure chest. The problem? All that gold was very heavy. Each time the hunters jarred the chest, it sank a little deeper into the sinkhole. Finally, in 1959, an enterprising group of diggers had the good sense to secure the chest with a thick chain, then brought in heavy equipment to hoist the treasure from its hiding place. Alas, the treasure still slipped away, and eventually people gave up the idea of ever retrieving it.

To the casual observer, the Roxie Gold Hole looks like nothing more than a small pond. But if you know what to look for, you'll soon spot a thick, taut cable, still firmly secured to a pine tree on one end and to something very, very heavy that lies underwater at the other.

Natchez Pilgrimage Tours can also provide information on **Christmas home tours and holiday events.**

About fifteen antebellum homes are open year-round, many of which double as bed and breakfasts. Each home has its own tale to tell, which may include unusual architecture, Civil War adventures, or a ghost story. Several of the mansions served as quarters for Union soldiers during the Civil War, and occasional tales of family treasure hidden behind paintings, buried on the grounds, or dropped down the cistern still surface. Many of the homes have appeared in movies and several were featured in the popular television miniseries *North and South.* The tour homes are located all over town, and admission prices and hours vary; stop by Natchez Pilgrimage Tours (located at the corner of Canal and State Streets in the Old Depot Building) for maps and up-to-the-minute information before embarking on a tour.

Tour homes of particular interest include **Rosalie,** which served as Union headquarters during the occupation; **Stanton Hall,** where the ghost of Colonel Stanton is said to greet overnight guests with a hearty, "Good morning"; and **Weymouth Hall,** where foundation reinforcements saved the house from toppling into the Mississippi and preserved one of the city's best views of Ole Man River. Established in 1988, the **Natchez National Historical Park** includes **Melrose,** the

1845 urban estate of a wealthy cotton planter, and the **William Johnson House,** the home of a prominent, free African-American whose diary reveals a different perspective of antebellum Natchez.

But the most haunting tour home by far is **Longwood,** the unrealized dream of Dr. Haller Nutt. The largest octagonal house in North America, Longwood was to be the wealthy Louisiana planter's town home—a 6-story, 32-room, 30,000-square-foot showplace. No expense was to be spared in the construction, furnishings, or workmanship; Dr. Nutt even arranged for the most skilled northern craftsmen to travel to Natchez to build his splendid palace. By early 1861, the exterior and basement of the home were complete. Then the Civil War swept through the South. The northern carpenters dropped their tools and returned home to join the fight, leaving Longwood unfinished. The war ruined Nutt financially, and he died in 1864, his glorious vision a mere shell. The craftsmen never returned to Longwood, and the mansion came to be known in Natchez as "Nutt's Folly."

Now the property of the Pilgrimage Garden Club of Natchez, Longwood remains exactly as it appeared in 1861, all the way down to the chisels and hammers dropped by the workmen, paintbrushes still in the original cans. Visitors wander through the oddly shaped, furnished rooms in the basement, then gaze up through level after level of scaffolding surrounding empty space. With such a tragic history, it's no surprise that Dr. Nutt's ghost is still spotted around Longwood, perhaps waiting for someone to complete his ill-fated masterpiece.

Natchez's rich history includes a strong African-American heritage, showcased in the **Natchez Museum of African-American History and Culture.** The museum houses more than 600 artifacts depicting African-American culture in Mississippi from the 1890s through the 1950s. Located at 307A Market Street, the museum is open Wednesday–Friday 1:00–5:00 P.M. and Saturday 11:00 A.M.–4:00 P.M. African-American art is the focus of the **Mostly African Market,** a collection of regional arts and crafts displayed and sold in the gallery at 125 St. Catherine Street. The market is open seasonally; call (601) 442–5448.

The rowdy riverboat landing at **Natchez Under-the-Hill** was once the notorious lair of gamblers, thieves, and ladies of the evening, a scandalous embarrassment to the decent citizens of Natchez. Many a boatman of the 1800s trekked up the Old Natchez Trace penniless and exhausted after a visit to the saloons and gambling houses Under-the-Hill, an area dubbed by an evangelist of the day as "the worst Hell hole on earth." Listed on the National Register of Historic Places, the landing is now a respectable, restored area of colorful shops, bars, and restaurants. More than a century after the last gaming house of the 1800s closed its doors, the landing is again home to a casino, *The Lady Luck.* Merry calliope music and steamboat whistles ring through the area when the luxury riverboats *Delta Queen* and *Mississippi Queen* make their regular stops in Natchez.

Natchez Under-the-Hill relives its days as a red-light district every June during the *Steamboat Jubilee.* The *Delta Queen* and *Mississippi Queen* dock in Natchez during their neck-and-neck race down the Mississippi River, and the city welcomes them with a wacky festival that includes the highly competitive *Best Floozie Contest.* The river is also the backdrop for another popular Natchez festival, the *Great Mississippi River Balloon Race.* This October event features dozens of colorful balloons racing across the Mississippi River (duck when you get to the bridge!) with arts, crafts, entertainment, and balloon rides for spectators. Expect a champagne dousing after your first flight. For event dates, call the *Natchez Convention and Visitors Bureau* at (800) 647–6724.

Natchez is home to a number of colorful shopping areas offering one-of-a-kind gifts, specialty foods, local artwork, "southern" souvenirs that border on the politically incorrect, and too many antiques shops to list. The *Canal Street Depot and Market, downtown Natchez,* and the *Franklin Street Marketplace* are all excellent places to begin a shopping expedition. If you're in the market for spirits, Natchez even boasts its own winery. Located just off Highway 61 at the northern outskirts of Natchez, the *Old South Winery* offers free tours and tastings of its muscadine wine from 10:00 A.M.–6:00 P.M. daily.

Natchez also offers several unique options for hungry visitors. Open for lunch year-round and lunch and dinner during the pilgrimage, the *Carriage House Restaurant* behind Stanton Hall serves up traditional southern dishes and is famous for its homemade biscuits. And yes, the restaurant is housed in the old plantation carriage house. Perched on a bluff above the Mississippi River, *Cock of the Walk* features the same Mississippi catfish and riverboat decor found in the restaurant's Jackson location.

If you need a reminder that Mississippi history didn't begin with the antebellum South, stop at the *Grand Village of the Natchez Indians* just south of Natchez off Highway 61 South on the banks of St. Catherine's Creek. The culture of the Natchez Indian tribe reached its peak in the mid-1500s, with the Grand Village serving as the center of activities for the sun worshippers from A.D. 1200–1729. The Natchez vanished as a nation following a hostile encounter with French settlers at the Grand Village in 1730. The Grand Village site was excavated in

1930, revealing a ceremonial plaza, burial mounds, and rare artifacts now housed in an on-site museum. The Grand Village is open 9:00 A.M.–5:00 P.M. Monday–Saturday and 1:30–5:00 P.M. Sunday.

The annual ***Pow-Wow at the Grand Village*** is two days of Native American dancing, music, and craft demonstrations. On-site camping is available. Call (601) 446–5117 for festival dates, which usually coincide with the Natchez Spring Pilgrimage.

As you head out of the area on Highway 61 South, you'll spot one last Old South icon just outside Natchez. In these days of political correctness, the sight of a 50-foot mammy smiling from the roadside is indeed a memorable one. Open the door in her bright red skirt and step into ***Mammy's Cupboard*** for a southern-style lunch. Be sure to snap a photo of the towering, smiling mammy, complete with kerchief and outstretched arms holding a serving tray. If you're from anywhere north of the Mason-Dixon line, your friends back home will never believe such a place still exists. Mammy's Cupboard is open for lunch and gift-shop browsing Tuesday–Saturday.

The Natchez Trace Parkway

The Lower Natchez Trace is actually the parkway's beginning. The original Natchez Trace was a one-way route that began in Natchez, then ran north to Nashville. In the late 1700s and early 1800s, flatboats floated merchandise downriver to Natchez and New Orleans, but the return trip north was along the Old Natchez Trace. By 1800, as many as 10,000 "Kaintucks"—the local lingo for boatman from anywhere north of Natchez—annually trekked the Trace, each armed with a rifle and a bottle of whiskey.

The terrain was rough, and a broken leg often spelled death for the lone traveler. Murderous

Mammy's Cupboard

bandits, savage Indians, ferocious wild animals, and other perils encountered along the way earned the Natchez Trace the nickname "Devil's Backbone."

The Lower Natchez Trace runs past a number of historic sites and nature trails, as well as many of the cities and towns listed earlier in this chapter. The nature trail at mile marker 122 in **Madison** winds through the deep green and heavy silence of the **Cypress Swamp,** where towering trees growing in an old riverbed form a lush canopy overhead. A short, boardwalked path through the swamp is easily explored in half an hour. Just north of Jackson, the Trace hugs the shoreline of the **Ross Barnett Reservoir** (see page 95) for 8 miles, with a scenic Reservoir Overlook located at mile marker 105. Beware of vengeful spirits as you explore a section of the **Old Trace** at mile marker 102. The dense wilderness surrounding the narrow trail is the perfect hiding spot for bandits or Indians. This section of the Parkway includes a stop at the **Mississippi Crafts Center** in **Ridgeland** (see page 94) before coming to a dead end just north of the capital city. To rejoin the Trace, take I–220 to I–20 West, which intersects the Parkway south of Jackson.

Little-Known Facts About the Heartland

- *The world's first human heart and lung transplants were performed in Jackson at the University of Mississippi Medical Center.*

- *Myrlie Evers-Williams, widow of assassinated NAACP field secretary Medgar Evers, went on to become the Chairman of the NAACP.*

- *Jackson's Malaco Records is the world's largest gospel music recording label.*

- *Neatniks worldwide owe a debt of gratitude to Harry Cole, Sr., of Jackson, the inventor of Pine-Sol.*

- *The Parent-Teacher Association (PTA) was founded in Crystal Springs in 1909.*

- *On May 11, 1887, a most unusual object plummeted from the skies above Bovina during a hail storm—a 6-inch by 8-inch gopher turtle, completely encased in ice.*

- *The Waterways Experiment Station in Vicksburg is the Army Corps of Engineers' largest research, testing, and development facility.*

- *Tipping the scales at more than eighteen pounds, the state record largemouth bass was reeled in from Natchez State Park Lake.*

This final leg of the Trace passes a number of picnic areas and historic sites, and a section of twisted, gnarled trees labeled "Tornado Damage." If you're traveling in the spring, you'll see a profusion of blooming dogwoods, redbuds, and an occasional patch of daffodils; the Trace's fall foliage display is equally impressive.

Any time of year, you're sure to notice the gray, gossamer substance dripping from the trees along this section of the parkway. That's *Spanish moss,* a native plant that looks dead, but keeps on growing, even if you move it indoors. Giant oaks laden with the stuff adorn the grounds of many of the area's antebellum homes, adding a gothic touch to the scenery. The farther south you travel, the more moss-draped trees you'll spot.

Forty miles south of Jackson, the *Rocky Springs National Park* offers a campground, picnic tables, and hiking and biking trails, all just a short walk from the forgotten settlement of Rocky Springs. A prosperous community of the 1800s, Rocky Springs was a center of agriculture and commerce, home to several businesses and large homes. The cotton that made the town rich, however, made the soil poor. Gradually the earth became depleted and eroded, and by 1930, Rocky Springs was a ghost town.

A stroll along the boardwalk through the preserved town site begins at a marker reading, THE TOWN OF ROCKY SPRINGS. POPULATION 1860—2,616. POPULATION TODAY—0. A church, cemetery, and rusting safe once filled with treasures are all that's left of the once-thriving community. The *Rocky Springs Methodist Church,* built in 1837, still overlooks the old town site and is open to the public. Visitors can also hike along a section of the original Old Trace thick with ferns and bamboo and wade in the shallow waters of Little Sand Creek. A marker at the entrance to the nature trail invites explorers to "Walk down the shaded trail and leave your prints in the dust, not for others to see, but for the road to remember."

Take a moment to explore a section of *sunken trace* south of Rocky Springs at mile marker 41. This deeply eroded tunnel through the wilderness is another portion of the original road. A canopy of trees stretches across the dirt bed of the trail—a route perhaps still trekked by the ghosts of earlier adventurers.

South of Rocky Springs the Trace parallels Highway 61 and offers exits to the towns, cities, and attractions described earlier in this chapter, including *Port Gibson, Lorman, Fayette, Washington,* and, of course, *Natchez,* where the fabled parkway was born.

PLACES TO STAY IN THE HEARTLAND

The following is a partial listing of the many hotels, motels, and bed-and-breakfast inns in the area.

CANTON
The Priestley House
(bed and breakfast),
138 East Fulton Street;
(601) 859–4449

JACKSON
Courtyard by Marriott,
6280 Ridgewood
Court Drive;
(601) 956–9991

The Edison Walthall Hotel,
225 East Capitol Street;
(601) 948–6161

French Quarter Inn,
1865 Lakeland Drive;
(601) 366–6661

Holiday Inn Express,
I–55 at High Street;
(601) 948–4466

The Fairview
(bed and breakfast),
734 Fairview;
(601) 948–3429

The Milsaps-Buie House
(bed and breakfast),
628 North State Street;
(601) 352–0221

The Old Capitol
Bed & Breakfast Inn,
226 North State Street;
(601) 956–2133

LINCOLN LTD. BED & BREAKFAST RESERVATIONS
Lincoln Ltd. is a full-time
reservation service for
bed-and-breakfast inns
statewide. For reservations
in any area of Mississippi,
call (800) 633–6477 or
(601) 482–5483.

NATCHEZ
Comfort Inn,
337 D'Evereaux Drive;
(601) 446–5500

Lady Luck Casino & Hotel,
645 South Canal Street;
(601) 446–6688

The Natchez Eola Hotel,
110 North Pearl Street;
(601) 445–6000

NATCHEZ PILGRIMAGE TOURS
Natchez Pilgrimage Tours
provides reservation ser-
vices for more than 30
antebellum and Victorian
mansions and bed-and-
breakfast inns in the area.
For information and
reservations, call
(800) 647–6742 or
(601) 446–6631.

PORT GIBSON/LORMAN
Canemount Plantation
(bed and breakfast),
Highway 552 West;
(601) 877–3784

The Cedars Plantation
(bed and breakfast),
Church Hill Community;
(601) 445–2203

China Grove Plantation
(bed and breakfast),
McDonald Road
off Highway 61;
(601) 437–5189

Oak Square Plantation
(bed and breakfast),
1207 Church Street;
(601) 437–4350

Rosswood Plantation
(bed and breakfast),
Highway 552 East;
(601) 437–4215

RIDGELAND
Homewood Suites,
853 Centre Street;
(601) 899–8611

Studio Plus,
800 Ridgewood Road;
(601) 956–0884

VICKSBURG
Anchuca
(bed and breakfast),
1010 First East Street;
(601) 631–6800

Cedar Grove Mansion Inn
(Mississippi's largest bed
and breakfast),
2200 Oak Street;
(601) 636–1000

Comfort Inn,
3959 East Clay Street;
(601) 634–8438

Duff Green Mansion
(bed and breakfast),
1114 First East Street;
(601) 636–6968

Hampton Inn,
3330 Clay Street;
(601) 636–6100

Harrah's Vicksburg
Casino Hotel,
1310 Mulberry Street;
(601) 636–3423

For a listing of additional bed-and-breakfast inns in Vicksburg, call the Vicksburg Convention and Visitors Bureau at (800) 221–3536.

PLACES TO EAT IN THE HEARTLAND

The following is a partial listing of the many restaurants in the area.

CANTON
Major fast-food chains

JACKSON
Bravo! (Italian),
Highland Village;
(601) 982–8111

Cups (sandwiches,
coffee house),
Lakeland Drive;
(601) 981–9088

Dennery's (seafood, steak),
330 Greymont Avenue;
(601) 354–2527

The Elite Restaurant
(steaks, chicken,
veal, seafood),
141 East Capitol Street;
(601) 352–5606

Hal 'n Mal's (sandwiches,
po' boys, seafood),
200 South
Commerce Street;
(601) 948–0888

Iron Horse Bar & Grill
(Tex-Mex),
320 West Pearl;
(601) 355–8419

Little Tokyo (sushi bar),
Lefleur's Gallery on the
Frontage Road;
(601) 982–3035

Mayflower Cafe (steak,
veal, chicken, seafood),
123 West Capitol Street;
(601) 355–4122

Nick's (fine dining),
1501 Lakeland Drive;
(601) 981–8017

Que Sera' (Cajun, Creole,
Sunday brunch),
North State Street;
(601) 981–2520

Times Change
(fresh game, fine dining),
Lefleur's Gallery;
(601) 366–8112

The Vineyard
(wine bar and tapas cafe),
2741 Old Canton Road;
(601) 984–3626

Major fast-food and dining
chains

LORMAN
Old Country Store
(sandwiches, plate lunches,
po' boys, ice cream),
Mississippi 552
and Highway 61;
(601) 437–3661

MADISON
Cock of the Walk (catfish),
141 Madison Landing at
the Ross Barnett Reservoir;
(601) 856–5500

Strawberry Cafe
(sandwiches),
Madison Depot Station/180
Main Street;
(601)–856–3822

Vasilios (Greek),
398 Highway 51;
(601) 853–0028

Major fast-food chains

MENDENHALL
The Revolving Tables
Restaurant (country-
cooking buffet),
100 William Gerald
Memorial Drive;
(601) 847–3113

NATCHEZ
Cock of the Walk (catfish),
200 North Broadway;
(601) 446–8920

King's Tavern
(steak, seafood),
619 Jefferson Street;
(601) 446–8845

Lady Luck Casino & Hotel
(three restaurants),
70 Silver Street;
(800) 722–5825

Mammy's Cupboard (sand-
wiches, country cooking),
Highway 61 South;
(601) 442–3492

Major fast-food chains

POCAHANTAS
Big D's Bar-be-cue
(barbecue),
1153 Main Street;
(601) 366–7489

RIDGELAND
Amerigo (Italian),
6592 Old Canton Road;
(601) 977–0563

The Brick Oven Cafe
(pasta, pizza),
The Promenade on County
Line Road;
(601) 956–2686

Deja Vu (Cajun, Creole, Sunday brunch), (look for my husband's wildlife photos on every wall), Lake Harbor Drive;
(601) 899–8690

The Dock (burgers, sandwiches, po' boys), Main Harbor Marina;
(601) 856–2168

Jubilees Patio Restaurant (fine dining),
565 Taylor;
(601) 981–7014

Keifer's (Greek, gyros), 705 Poplar Boulevard;
(601) 355–6825

Little Tokyo (sushi bar), The Promenade on County Line Road;
(601) 991–3800

McAlister's Gourmet Deli (salads, sandwiches),
731 Pear Orchard Road;
(601) 956–0030

Shapley's (steak),
868 Centre Street;
(601) 957–3753

The Parker House (fine dining),
Centre Park off County Line Road;
(601) 956–7352

Major fast-food and dining chains

VICKSBURG
Cedar Grove Mansion Inn (fine dining),
2200 Oak Street;
(601) 636–1000

Duff's Tavern & Grille (veal, beef, poultry, seafood),
1306 Washington Street;
(601) 638–0169

Goldie's Trail Bar-B-Que
4127 South Washington Street;
(601) 636–9839

Major fast-food chains

Vicksburg's casinos house several restaurants offering casual dining, fine dining, all-you-can-eat buffets, and fast foods.

OTHER ATTRACTIONS WORTH SEEING IN THE HEARTLAND

JACKSON
Highland Village (upscale shopping)

Jackson Zoological Park

LeFleur's Bluff State Park

Mississippi Sports Hall of Fame

Mississippi Museum of Art

Rapids on the Reservoir

Russell C. Davis Planetarium

State Capitol Building

NATCHEZ
Lady Luck Casino

Natchez State Park

PORT GIBSON
Energy Central Visitors Center, Grand Gulf Nuclear Reactor

VICKSBURG
Ameristar Casino

Harrah's Casino

Isle of Capri Casino

Rainbow Casino

Vicksburg Factory Outlets

Southern Mississippi and the Gulf Coast

Southern Mississippi is a contradictory blend of pioneer spirit and carefree coastal life, a region where rugged frontier land, thick forests, and tranquil beaches all lie within a couple of hours' drive.

Visitors to southern Mississippi can relive the adventures of early explorers, retreat to a quiet artists' colony, and roll the dice in a glitzy casino, all in the same day. This dynamic mix of cultures and lifestyles makes a single trip to southern Mississippi a multifaceted adventure.

The Old Southwest

The southwestern corner of the state is made up of towns and cities still proud of their frontier heritage and, for the most part, still living it today. Much of the area just south of Natchez remains undisturbed and unexplored, peppered with overgrown forts, old-fashioned mercantiles, and sturdy buildings largely unchanged since the first settlers erected them more than a century ago.

The 35-mile stretch of U.S. Highway 61 South between Natchez and Woodville is sprinkled with antiques shops, junk shops, and trailers labeled "Sister So-and-So, Spiritual Advisor." You'll pass establishments like *Relative Relics,* a combination grocery store/antiques shop/cafe where you can purchase a cold soft drink, depression-era glass, or a ventriloquist's dummy, rent a movie, and sample the blue plate special, all in one stop. Further shopping opportunities await a few miles down the road at *Panhandlers' Antique Store,* where the vast inventory of trash and treasures spills off the front porch and onto the lawn.

Don't browse too long—you'll need at least a day to explore *Woodville,*

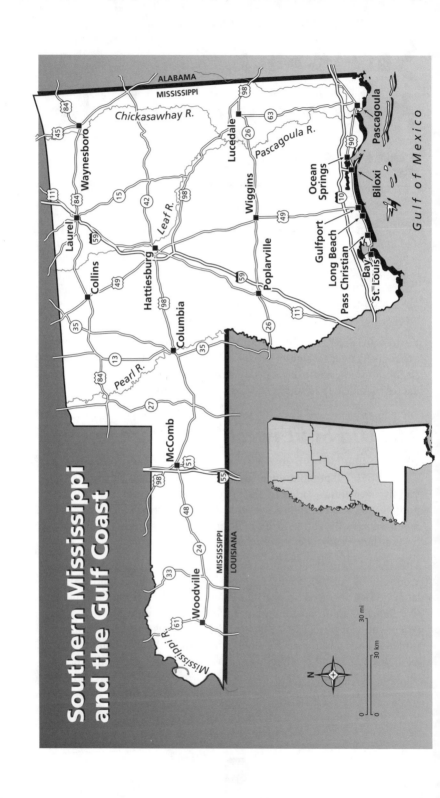

Southern Mississippi
and the Gulf Coast

SOUTHERN MISSISSIPPI AND THE GULF COAST

MARLO'S FAVORITE ATTRACTIONS IN SOUTHERN MISSISSIPPI AND THE GULF COAST

Rosemont, *Woodville*

Clark Creek Natural Area, *Pond*

Beautiful, Holy, Jewel Home of the Original Rhinestone Cowboy, *McComb*

Shopping in Old Town, *Bay St. Louis*

The shade of the Friendship Oak in July, *Long Beach*

The beaches of Ship Island, *accessible from Gulfport*

Beauvoir, *Biloxi*

The Ocean Springs Gallery District, *Ocean Springs*

Sunset over the water, *Mississippi Beach*

Fresh seafood, *Mississippi Beach*

Hitting blackjack in any casino,

the charming town Harvard University once described as "best typifying the Old South in appearance, customs, and traditions." That notoriety aside, Woodville remains for the most part an undiscovered treasure. Unlike Natchez, her tourist-oriented neighbor to the north, Woodville actually takes pleasure in remaining off the beaten path. At least for now, visitors can soak up the southern charm without calling for reservations, waiting in line, or catching a shuttle bus.

The town boasts a number of antebellum homes and churches, but Woodville's most famous link to the Old South is **Rosemont,** the childhood home of Jefferson Davis. As you come into town on U.S. Highway 61 South, follow the signs to the 300-acre plantation where the Confederate States of America's only president spent his boyhood. A sun-dappled gravel road winds through towering trees dripping with Spanish moss, ending at a shaded gazebo where visitors listen to a short recording before touring the main house.

Samuel and Jane Davis moved to this airy planter's cottage with their ten children in 1810. (It's interesting to note that Jefferson, the youngest child, was given the middle name "Finis.") Home to five generations of the Davis family over the next century, Rosemont remains much the same today as it appeared during Davis's childhood. Many of the furnishings and artwork are original Davis family pieces, including Jane Davis's spinning wheel, books inscribed with the family name, chandeliers fueled by whale oil, and champagne glasses once raised in presidential toasts.

A wall in the hallway bears the height charts of several Davis children, and Jefferson Davis's brother-in-law, Issac Stamps, scratched his name into one of the windows downstairs. Stamps was killed at the Battle of Gettysburg, and Davis's sister traveled all the way to Pennsylvania to bring his body home to Rosemont for burial. Davis issued a presidential pass allowing her to cross enemy lines.

Originally called "Poplar Grove," the plantation was renamed Rosemont in honor of Jane Davis's elaborate flower gardens. Many of the rose bushes still blooming on the grounds today were originally planted by

Jefferson Davis's mother in the early 1800s. The property also includes the Davis family cemetery where many members of Jefferson Davis's immediate family, including his mother and Issac Stamps, are buried. President Davis himself is buried in the old Confederate Capitol of Richmond, Virginia. Photos displayed at Rosemont capture the throngs of Confederate supporters who attended Davis's funeral in New Orleans. Some 200,000 mourners came to pay their last respects—the largest funeral attendance in history prior to services for President John F. Kennedy.

The $6.00 admission includes the house, outbuildings, cemetery, and lavishly landscaped grounds. Rosemont is open March 1–December 15 Monday–Friday 10:00 A.M.–5:00 P.M. and on weekends during the Natchez Spring and Fall Pilgrimages.

Head back to U.S. Highway 61 and go straight through the four-way stop to downtown Woodville, where you'll find the mandatory town square and courthouse. A block south of the courthouse, the **Wilkinson County Museum** features changing exhibits related to local history. For groups as small as four, the museum will put together a **Lost Architectural Treasures and Cemeteries Tour,** which includes a look at a number of centuries-old grave sites, crumbling columns, and other architectural relics around Wilkinson County. The tour can be as long, short, simple, or involved as the group would like and can include a picnic lunch. Call curator David Smith at (601) 888–3998 for details.

David can also point out a number of historic churches just off the town square. There's the 1809 **Woodville Baptist Church,** the oldest church in Mississippi; 1823 **St. Paul's Episcopal Church,** the oldest Episcopal church outside the original thirteen colonies; and 1824 **Woodville Methodist Church,** the oldest Methodist church in Mississippi. Woodville is also home to the state's oldest newspaper and continuously run business, *The Woodville Republican.*

Just around the corner from the museum on First South Street you'll spot the two modest graves that make up the infamous **Oswald Family Cemetery.** It seems that Lee Harvey Oswald had a number of relatives in the Woodville area, and history buffs still come in search of these right-off-the-sidewalk-but-still-hard-to-spot tombs. The tour guide at Rosemont recalls an encounter with one group who asked about the grave sites. "I told them I knew where they were because, unfortunately, I was distantly related to Oswald myself. They didn't appreciate that—apparently they were related to him too, and *didn't* find it unfortunate."

SOUTHERN MISSISSIPPI AND THE GULF COAST

If you're in Woodville around dinnertime, ask David Smith about his family's restaurant, *South of the Border.* Don't go in search of a taco—the border in question is the Mississippi–Louisiana state line, and the food is far from Mexican. Instead, you'll find a menu that David describes as "combination redneck, soul food, and coon-ass." He'll also explain that the restaurant is located in Louisiana because, "the idea was to create the last great southern roadhouse, and Mississippi was dry." South of the Border serves its varied and enticing menu in a cheerfully rowdy atmosphere Tuesday–Saturday 11:00 A.M.–10:00 P.M. and Sunday 11:00 A.M.–9:00 P.M.

History buffs and outdoor enthusiasts will find a side trip west of Woodville to the microscopic communities of *Pond, Pickneyville,* and *Fort Adams* a worthwhile adventure. Head west out of downtown Woodville to Mississippi Highway 24, then follow the Pond-Pickneyville Road 16 miles to the *Pond Store,* an old-fashioned general store in business since 1881. A mini-museum houses memorabilia from the store's early days. The proprietors live in back of the store and will give you a look at the traditional lifestyle of the merchant class for a small admission fee. The store sells sundries and provides information on the area seven days a week from 7:00 A.M.–7:00 P.M. Call (601) 888–4426 to arrange a tour of the proprietors' house.

The Pond Store is located near the entrance to the 1,400-acre *Clark Creek Natural Area.* The terrain at Clark Creek is wild and rugged, made up of steep ravines, water-sculpted rocks, and sheer loess bluffs crisscrossed with hiking trails. The area is home to seven breathtaking waterfalls, the highest of which tumbles some 50 feet down the bluff. This is not the place for a casual stroll. Reaching the waterfalls requires hiking boots, a healthy water supply, and most of all, stamina. Don't forget to pick up a trail map at the Pond Store—you'll need some help navigating this scenic but remote area. To avoid disappointment, call ahead to the Pond Store to be sure Clark Creek is open. Erosion problems occasionally present a safety hazard and cause the area to close for "repairs."

MARLO'S FAVORITE ANNUAL EVENTS IN SOUTHERN MISSISSIPPI AND THE GULF COAST

Biloxi

Confederate Memorial Day at Beauvoir,
April, (228) 388–9074

Blessing of the Fleet,
May, (228) 435–5578

Sun Herald *Sand Sculpture Contest,*
September, (228) 896–2434

Gulfport

Mississippi Deep Sea Fishing Rodeo,
July, (228) 388–2271

Hattiesburg

Hubfest, October,
(800) 238–4288

Mississippi Gulf Coast

Mardi Gras, February or March, (228) 432–8806

Ocean Springs

Landing of d'Iberville,
April, (228) 875–4424

Great Oaks Storytelling Festival,
October, (228) 875–4424

The Pond-Pickneyville Road continues into equally tiny Pickneyville, where you'll find the **grave of Oliver Pollack,** inventor of the dollar sign, and the **Desert Plantation,** a 1,000-acre plantation and bed-and-breakfast inn. The Desert Plantation is conveniently located 18 miles from both Woodville and **St. Francisville, Louisiana,** another town famous for its antebellum homes and pilgrimage tours. Call (601) 888–6188 for rates and reservations.

The neighboring community of Fort Adams is a virtual ghost town, home to little more than a handful of hunting and fishing camps. The 1700s fort that gave the town its name has long since been swallowed up by rampant vegetation.

Fort Adams's most famous resident was fictional. The town was immortalized in Edward Everett Hale's tale *The Man Without a Country* when character Philip Nolan, destined never again to set foot on American soil after denouncing the United States, did time in a Fort Adams prison. Fort Adams is just north of Pond at the end of Highway 24, but as one of the town's few residents puts it, "there's nothing much to do once you've gotten here except turn around and go back."

When you're ready to turn back, head east on Mississippi Highway 24, which turns into Mississippi Highway 48 just west of **Liberty** and the **Jerry Clower Museum.** The late Jerry Clower opened this small museum years ago to house an ever-expanding collection of memorabilia accumulated over his decades-long career as America's favorite country comedian. The collection includes the keys to forty-nine cities, an Indian headdress, numerous stuffed raccoons, and a plaque proclaiming Clower, "the World's Nicest Person." Call (601) 684–8130 for directions and to arrange a tour time.

When you've had all the country comedy you can stand, continue on Mississippi Highway 48 East to **McComb.** A bit of musical trivia—the McComb area has been home to a number of renowned musicians, including the legendary Bo Diddley, blues guitarist Vasti Johnson, and most recently, triple platinum R&B singer Brandy.

When you reach the junction of Highways 48/51, head south on 51, then turn left at Deer's Repair Shop. Across the street you'll spot a glittering cottage identified as the **"Beautiful, Holy, Jewel Home of the Original Rhinestone Cowboy."** The late Rhinestone Cowboy was a bit of a character, strolling around downtown McComb decked out in a vest, hat, and boots studded with "jewels," and fashioning original artwork from shiny rhinestones.

But the Cowboy's finest masterpiece is his house. The front door is encrusted with blue, pink, and purple rhinestones and draped with tinsel and Christmas lights; a portrait of the quirky cowboy in full dress smiles out from a front window. Inside, every room is plastered with glittering jewels arranged in endless mosaics—not a square inch is left unadorned, furniture included. From the orange and gold bedroom to the multicolored living room, bathroom, and hallway, the rainbow effect is overwhelming. The home has been closed since the Rhinestone Cowboy's death, but efforts are underway to preserve the house as a folk art attraction. In the meantime, a Rhinestone Cowboy relative who lives next door will occasionally open the house for curious visitors.

The best time to visit McComb is in late March or early April, during the *Lighted Azalea Festival.* Inspired by Japan's traditional lighting of the cherry blossoms, the first lighted azalea trail was staged in 1953. A drive through McComb provides a look at twinkling, decades-old azaleas of every size, shape, and color. For dates and a map of the *Azalea Trail,* call the *Pike County Chamber of Commerce* at (601) 684–2291.

Lunch in McComb means a trip to *The Dinner Bell,* a bastion of southern cooking located on Fifth Street off Highway 51 North. Diners are seated around lazy Susans loaded with squash, butterbeans, fried chicken, and other down-home delicacies. Lunch is served 11:00 A.M.–2:00 P.M. Tuesday–Sunday. The Dinner Bell also rings for an early supper 5:30–8:00 P.M. on Friday and Saturday nights from April to September.

If you're in the area in late April, take a side trip up I–55 North to Highway 84 East (about 40 miles total from McComb) and spend a day at the *Monticello Pioneer Pilgrimage.* Tours of rustic log cabins and live demonstrations of spinning, weaving, and blacksmithing take visitors back to a simpler, if not necessarily easier, time. A ticket for the weekend is $10; call (601) 886–7128 for specific dates.

From McComb, follow Highway 98 East into tiny *Foxworth* and *Leatha's Bar-B-Q Inn,* found across the railroad tracks under the Highway 98 overpass. Leatha's is way, way off the beaten path but well worth the trip, for owner Leatha Jackson is unquestionably the Mother of Mississippi barbecue. The food critic for Jackson's daily newspaper awarded Leatha's five stars—on a four-star scale. Ribs dripping with Leatha's secret sauce are the star attraction, far overshadowing the modest decor. If your nose doesn't lead you to Leatha's, just ask anyone in Foxworth for directions or call (601) 736–5163. Leatha serves lunch only Thursday–Saturday 11:30 A.M.–1:00 P.M.

Continue on Highway 98 East into downtown *Columbia,* where 100-foot-wide Main Street was designed to accommodate horse-and-wagon U-turns. Main Street's *Hill Hardware Company* stocks some 24,000 items, including plows, horse harnesses, and old-fashioned kitchen implements most modern homemakers would be at a loss to put to use. According to proprietor Leon Bohuslav, "If we don't have it, you probably don't need it." Tradition runs deep at Hill's; Bohuslav is only the third proprietor in the store's 100-year history.

Columbia's most famous son is former Mississippi Governor Hugh White. Built in 1925, the beautifully restored Spanish Colonial *Hugh Lawson White Mansion* features a sunken, walled garden and a formal dining room adorned with floor-to-ceiling murals created by an artist from Malta. For tour information, call Ann Simmons at (601) 736–1763.

Things in Columbia get a little squirrely the third Saturday in May when the town hosts its annual *Squirrel on the Pearl Festival.* Featuring live music, arts and crafts, amusement rides, games, and food, the festival is a tribute to former governor Hugh White's cherished white squirrels. The governor introduced the squirrels to his estate on Keys Hill more than sixty years ago. The frisky animals have since raised several generations of descendants in the Columbia area, and the city has adopted an ordinance protecting the squirrels.

Early exploration maps of the Columbia area include *Red Bluff,* also known as *"Mississippi's Little Grand Canyon."* Formed by the natural erosion of the west bank of the Pearl River near Morgan Town, Red Bluff is made up of colorful layers of sand, gravel, soil, and clay plunging 200 feet into a creek that empties into the river. The landscape around Red Bluff changes constantly; the road atop the bluff has been pushed back twice to accommodate the ever-widening canyon. Hikers will be disappointed to learn that Red Bluff is located on private property, but the unusual formation is easily visible from Mississippi Highway 587 about 15 miles northwest of Columbia.

If you're in the Columbia area on a Saturday or Sunday, take Mississippi Highway 35 South to *Sandy Hook* and the *John Ford House.* Built in 1809, this sturdy structure served as a frontier inn, fort, and territorial post office. The house has withstood not only the ravages of time but the fury of Hurricane Camille to become the oldest building in the Pearl River Valley. The inn was a center of activity in Mississippi's frontier days. Andrew Jackson slept here en route to the Battle of New Orleans, but he was given the best room in the house only after promising to watch his language. Tours take visitors back to the early 1800s, when the inn provided a safe haven from the dangers of the uncharted territory that later became the state of Mississippi. The house is open weekends 2:00–4:00 P.M. Admission is $2.00—a modest sum today, but probably a good deal more than the room rates of the early 1800s.

From Columbia, take Mississippi Highway 13 South to I–59 and head straight for the Mississippi Beach, or continue on Highway 98 East to Hattiesburg and the Piney Woods.

The Piney Woods

The Piney Woods begin at the northern tip of the DeSoto National Forest and stretch south to the Gulf Coast, forming a thick green canopy over the cities and towns in their path. Towering

The Unexpected Philanthropist: Oseola McCarty's Gift

Five years ago, the only people who had heard of Oseola McCarty were the Hattiesburg families whose laundry she washed and ironed.

But in July of 1995, her name became a household word when Ms. McCarty, an eighty-six-year-old laundress with a sixth grade education, donated $150,000 to the University of Southern Mississippi.

The gift represented more than half of Ms. McCarty's life savings, earned through seventy-five years of washing and ironing. In August of that year, eighteen-year-old Stephanie Bullock became the first recipient of the Oseola McCarty Scholarship. Through her generous gift, Ms. McCarty had provided for others the education she herself had been denied.

Ms. McCarty received countless honors in recognition of her selfless gift, including the Presidential Citizens Medal, the Wallenberg Humanitarian Award, and an honorary doctorate from Harvard University. The New York Times described Ms. McCarty as "living proof to impatient young people that dignity and reward in work is what you make of it." Newsweek called her, "a reminder that even the humblest among us can leave the world a better place for having walked on it."

But fame did not change Ms. McCarty. The now-retired laundress has remained humble and unaffected, despite glowing praise from admirers nationwide, constant demand for television interviews, even a meeting with the President. When asked to comment, Mississippi's most famous benefactress says simply, "People tell me now that I am a hero, but I don't feel that way. . . . I'm just proud I'm leaving something positive in this world. My only regret is that I didn't have more to give."

loblollies dominate most of this region's landscape, earning the area the nickname, "the pine belt."

The largest city in this region, **Hattiesburg** serves as a cultural dividing line. Towns north of Hattiesburg share the traditional southern personality of Jackson, while communities south of Hattiesburg lean toward the casual indulgence of the Gulf Coast. Life on the boundary line is a pleasant mix of both, with the spirited feel of a college town as an added bonus.

Highway 98 turns into Hardy Street in Hattiesburg, home of the **University of Southern Mississippi.** The campus is located at the intersection of U.S. Highway 98 and U.S. Highway 49, its main entrance marked by the multicolored, fragrant **All-American Rose Garden,** home to some 750 patented bushes.

From the campus main entrance, follow U.S. Highway 49 South to the old **Beverly Drive-In Theatre.** Built in 1948, the now-closed Beverly was once Mississippi's largest drive-in. Crowds flocked to the Beverly to take in the latest double feature under the stars and perhaps steal a kiss in the privacy of the family Ford. While the Beverly is no longer Hattiesburg's biggest attraction, it is Hattiesburg's most unusual residence. The Beverly's owner lives in the 4,000-square-foot area beneath the screen and gives tours by appointment. Call (800) 638–6877 for "show times."

Military buffs and veterans should continue on Highway 49 South about 12 miles past the Hattiesburg city limits to the **Armed Forces Museum at Camp Shelby.** The museum houses more than 6,000 artifacts representing every branch of the military and every war in which the United States has fought. The museum is open Tuesday–Saturday 9:00 A.M.–4:00 P.M. and Sunday 1:00–5:00 P.M. Follow signs on Highway 49 to the museum and a military surplus store.

Head back into Hattiesburg on Highway 49 North, then west on Highway 98/Hardy Street to Southern Avenue and the **Hattiesburg Historic Neighborhood District.** The 115-acre area includes a number of architectural marvels built between 1884 and 1930. The focal point of the historic neighborhood is the **Tally House,** a turn-of-the-century bed-and-breakfast inn. The 13,000-square-foot inn features an extensive collection of antiques, eleven fireplaces, and a two-story, wraparound porch. The grounds are planted with blooming plants and flowers, including more than 100 colorful species of daylilies. Rates begin at $65. Call (601) 582–3467 for reservations.

Hattiesburg offers two unique shopping opportunities for antiques buffs and flea market enthusiasts. *Old High School Antiques* (864 N. Main Street, 601–544–6644) showcases gifts, collectibles, furnishings, and other merchandise from over 60 dealers in more than 100,000 square feet of display space. Old High School Antiques is open Monday–Saturday 10:00 A.M.–6:00 P.M., Sunday 1:00–5:00 P.M. At 13,000 square feet with 53 shops, the *Calico Mall* is Mississippi's largest indoor daily flea market. Browse the glassware, clocks, clothing, furniture, jewelry, linens, and antiques Tuesday–Friday 10:00 A.M.–5:00 P.M., Saturday 9:00 A.M.–5:00 P.M., or Sunday 1:00 P.M.–5:00 P.M.

From Hattiesburg, take a short drive north on Mississippi Highway 11 to *Petal* and the *International Checker Hall of Fame.* Yes, the *Checker* Hall of Fame. This museum honoring the venerable board game is housed in the enormous (35,000 square feet) private residence of Robert Walker, the undisputed checkers world champion. The Hall of Fame also houses the Ripley's Believe-It-or-Not largest and second-largest checkerboards in the world. Checkerholics from around the globe travel to Petal to compete in nail-biting tournament play. Competitors make their moves on regulation-sized checkerboards, but large pillows positioned on the oversized, checkerboard floor allow visitors to observe every jump from the second-story viewing balcony.

In addition to checkers memorabilia, the Hall of Fame houses an eclectic collection of artifacts and displays related to everything and nothing at all. Exhibits include everything from stuffed game animals to a full suit of armor. The Hall of Fame is open during tournaments and for tours by appointment. Call (601) 582–7090 for directions and to schedule a friendly match with the checker master.

The section of U.S. Highway 49 north of Hattiesburg is punctuated with flea markets, fruit stands, and "outposts" offering canoe trips down *Okatoma Creek.* Billed as Mississippi's only "white water," the Okatoma runs through a series of small waterfalls and rapids as it flows through forests and farmlands. Canoe rentals are about $18 a day and include shuttle service to and from the water.

Tiny *Seminary* is home to acclaimed potter Claudia Ka Cartee, whose jewel-toned dinnerware and decorative pieces have been shown throughout the South. Cartee's downtown gallery, *Ka Pottery,* is open by appointment. The gallery is located on North Oak Avenue if you'd like to take a peek in the display window before calling (601) 722–4948 for a personal showing by the artist.

From Seminary, continue north on Highway 49 until you spot the bright yellow wall adorned with lions, tigers, and bears. The *Collins Exotic*

Animal Orphanage is exactly what its name implies—a refuge for exotics purchased as "pets," then abandoned when they became too large to manage. As the owner explains, "Foolish people buy a lion cub or a panther and expect to litter box train it. When it weighs several hundred pounds and starts eating their furniture and climbing the walls, they don't want it anymore. If the animals couldn't come here, they'd be destroyed." The $3.00 admission buys a look at lions, tigers, panthers, alligators, and other exotics housed in tiny cages. The view is more close-up-and-personal than in the average zoo, and it's hard to imagine anyone thinking of these powerful, enormous animals as "pets." This is one trip to the zoo that's almost as sad as it is educational.

Take the downtown **Collins** exit off Highway 49 North to Main Street and **Pope Company.** This grand old department store has survived the Great Depression, two World Wars, and the most serious threat of all—Wal-Mart. Pope Company opened for business in 1913 and has remained in the Pope family for three generations. Shoppers find modern-day merchandise from clothing to appliances displayed alongside horse collars, corn cutters, and mule feed. At one time, Pope Company even sold tractors. The hardwood floors, wooden display cabinets, and old-fashioned cash registers are reminders of a time when shopping was more a social event than a hassle and create a warm, folksy atmosphere that's not for sale at any price.

It's just a short drive from Collins to **Mt. Olive,** but a visit to the **Old Order German Baptist Community** feels more like a trip through time. Practicing a lifestyle similar to the Amish, the families who work these small farms live a simple life far removed from the hectic pace of the modern world. The German Baptists grow or raise virtually everything they eat, make their own clothing and furnishings, and rely on bicycles or horses for transportation.

It's in this tranquil community that Roger Jamison hand weaves his distinctive baskets. They come in all shapes and sizes, but in only two colors—natural or a reddish-brown that comes from homemade pecan shell dye. Finished baskets sell from $9.00 to $40.00; Roger will also custom-weave a basket in the pattern or shape you prefer. To get to **Roger's Basketry,** take Highway 49 North to Mississippi Highway 35 North, then go 1 mile to Mississippi Highway 532 East and watch for the signs.

The craftsmanship is equally impressive at **Diehl Bros. Furniture**, which specializes in hand-crafted, custom-made furniture and cabinetry. Owner Bill Diehl will sketch a one-of-a-kind design during your visit, then ship the finished piece home to you. Diehl Bros. also accepts orders by mail. For more information, write to Bill Diehl at 337 Highway 532, Mt. Olive, Mississippi 39119.

If you're traveling with a group of twelve or more, wrap up your visit to the Old Order German Baptist Community with a memorable lunch or dinner at **Martha's Kitchen**. Meals are served on the Diehl family farm and include fruits and vegetables grown on the property, home-made breads and pies, and freshly churned butter. To make reservations, write to Bill and Edith Diehl at 1462 Highway 532, Mount Olive, Mississippi 39119.

From Mt. Olive, continue east on Highway 532 to the tiny community of **Hot Coffee**. In the 1800s, weary travelers often parked their horse-drawn carriages at an inn in the area. The innkeeper's wife was known for her home-baked cakes and strong, piping hot coffee. The inn was referred to as "the Hot Coffee," and eventually, the surrounding area adopted the moniker as well.

Two old-fashioned general stores in Hot Coffee are worth a quick stop. **McDonald's Store** serves up hand-dipped ice cream, R. C. Cola, moon pies, hoop cheese by the slice, and plenty of—you guessed it—hot coffee. McDonald's is closed on Saturday. The **J&H Harper Grocery** in "downtown" Hot Coffee has served the area since the early 1900s and offers souvenir T-shirts, caps, and cups. J&H Harper is closed on Sunday. Both stores are located on Mississippi Highway 532.

Continue east on Highway 532 to U.S. Highway 84, then head east 20 miles to **Laurel**. Along the way you'll pass the Monroe Road turnoff to **Mitchell Farms,** a pick-your-own vegetable farm operated by Dennis and Nelda Mitchell. As many as 400 people show up a day to pick fresh veggies and watch Nelda create wood sculptures with a chain saw. Call (601) 765–8609 to find out what's in season.

Entering the elegant, oil-money town of Laurel, continue straight on Highway 84 East across 16th Avenue until it turns into 5th Street (streets and avenues are both numbered in Laurel; streets run east-west, avenues north-south). Veer left at 6th Avenue onto Carroll Gartin Boulevard, then take a left on 5th Avenue. At the end of the block you'll find the **Lauren Rogers Museum of Art,** Mississippi's oldest and arguably finest art museum. Permanent collections include eighteenth-century paintings and sculpture, an extensive collection of Georgian silver, eighteenth- and nineteenth-century Japanese Ukiyo-e wood block prints, and more than 800 baskets from around the world. The museum was founded as a tribute to Lauren Rogers, a twenty-three-year-old newlywed who died in 1922 following an appendectomy. His family chose his unfinished homesite as the location for a library and museum honoring his memory. The Lauren Rogers Museum of Art is open Tuesday–Saturday 10:00 A.M.–5:00 P.M. and Sunday 1:00–4:00 P.M. Incredibly, there's no admission fee.

The museum is located in the heart of Laurel's oak-shaded **historic district,** which features the largest collection of turn-of-the-century homes in the United States. Overnight accommodations are available in the historic district at the **5th Street Bed and Breakfast.** Rates begin at $70; call (601) 649–5197 for reservations.

Model train enthusiasts will enjoy a collection of a different kind at **Hobby Corner** (1534 North 1st Avenue), where more than fifty model trains travel some 400 feet of track. Hobby Corner stocks all gauges of model trains plus accessories; their motto is, "Railroading is our only business." The signal lights flash, engines clatter along the tracks, and the train whistles blow Tuesday, Wednesday, Friday, and Saturday 9:00 A.M.–6:00 P.M., Thursday 9:00 A.M.–10:00 P.M. All aboard!

From the museum, take 7th Street east to Mississippi Highway 15 South and **Landrum's Country Homestead and Village.** This old-fashioned "settlement" includes a water-powered gristmill, blacksmith shop, cabin, schoolhouse, and general store, all decorated with period

The Free State of Jones

*T*he small farm owners of 1860s Jones County resented the notion of fighting a "Planters' War" and sent a representative to the 1861 Mississippi state assembly to vote against secession from the Union. But once in Jackson, the representative was overwhelmed by the near-hysteria sweeping the capital city and instead cast his lot with the secessionists.

Back home, the good citizens of Jones County burned the representative in effigy, formed an independent government, and actually seceded from the Confederacy. Declaring Ellisville their capital and Confederate deserter Newt Knight their leader, renegades from "the

Free State of Jones" raided both Union and Confederate supply bases, supposedly practicing such atrocities that Union POWs quartered in Meridian were given arms to protect themselves.

When the city of Laurel dedicated a monument to the soldiers of the Confederacy decades later, most of the money was provided by a northern-born businessman. The benefactor noted the irony of the occasion, remarking, "You see here a handsome monument, erected with Yankee money to the Confederate dead of the Free State of Jones, which seceded from the Confederacy after the Confederacy seceded from the Union."

antiques. Tom Landrum and family are on hand to conduct personal tours of the village and talk you into sampling a sugary funnel cake or a slice of fresh bread slathered with homemade butter. The property includes a gift shop and RV park. Take a stroll through the past Monday–Saturday 9:00 A.M.–5:00 P.M. and Sunday 1:00–5:00 P.M. Admission is $3.00 for adults, $2.00 for children.

Continue on Highway 15 South to *Trapper's Gator Farm,* a menagerie of alligators, bobcats, raccoons, snakes, and other native species. Call (601) 428–4967 and ask owner "Trapper" Parker what time he'll be serving dinner at the gator pond—the sight of thirty hungry reptiles devouring whole chickens is one you won't soon forget. But Trapper's isn't all scary—there's a petting area where some of the tamer animals socialize with curious children. In fact, petting is allowed for most of the animals who reside at Trapper's—even some of the gators. Visit them weekends 10:00 A.M.–5:00 P.M. Admission is $2.00.

From Trapper's, take Highway 15 North back to Laurel and pick up I–59 South to the Gulf Coast. Just south of Laurel you'll see the exit to *Ellisville,* once the capital of the *Free State of Jones.* (See sidebar, page 144.)

Confederate deserter Newt Knight shot Major Amos McLemore, a Confederate soldier sent to capture him, in the living room of the *Deason House* in Ellisville. McLemore's blood seeped into the pine floors, staining them so badly the residents finally covered them with new boards. The ghost of the murdered major is still said to roam the halls of Deason House and the bloodstain occasionally reappears on the floor. Decide for yourself whether Deason House is truly haunted—call the *Ellisville City Hall* at (601) 477–3323 to arrange a visit to the murder scene.

Continue on I–59 South past Hattiesburg and through pastoral *Poplarville,* where actor Gerald McRaney and his actress wife Delta Burke own a ranch. When you reach the outskirts of *Picayune,* follow the signs to the *Crosby Arboretum,* home to 1,000 acres of native plants and trees. Walking trails wind through a savannah filled with carnivorous plants, a wetland thick with cypress trees, and shaded woodlands where azaleas bloom under loblolly pines. The arboretum's Pinecote Pavilion is the first—and so far the only—building in Mississippi to win the American Institute of Architecture's Honor Award for Design Excellence. Get back to nature at the Crosby Arboretum Wednesday–Sunday 10:00 A.M.–5:00 P.M. Admission is $3.00 for adults, $1.00 for children.

Before you leave Picayune for the Mississippi Beach, stop by *Paul's Pastry Shop* (Highway 43 North), the nation's largest shipper of king cakes. These cream cheese and fruit-filled pastries topped with green, gold, and purple frosting are a staple of Mardi Gras celebrations in New Orleans and throughout the South. Each cake is baked with a tiny plastic baby inside; whoever bites the baby has to host the next party, or at least buy the next king cake. Call (601) 798–7457, or to place an order after you've returned home, call (800) 669–5180.

The Mississippi Beach

rom Waveland to Ocean Springs, a chain of resorts, casinos, artists' colonies, and fishing villages is linked by 26 miles of sugar-white sand, the longest man-made beach in the world.

The French, Spanish, English, and Irish have all influenced the Gulf Coast area, resulting in a cheerful, vibrant mix of cultures that encourages and celebrates individuality. The coastal culture also borrows heavily from neighboring *New Orleans,* making an appreciation of food, festivals, and fun virtually mandatory.

Before you reach the beach, you'll have the opportunity to explore outer space with a trip to *NASA's John C. Stennis Space Center.* If you skip this adventure in favor of heading straight for the shore, you'll need to take an alternate route as travelers are not allowed to drive through the NASA complex. To get to the beach, take I–59 South from Picayune to Mississippi Highway 43 South, which intersects with Highway 90 at the beach.

If you opt for a visit to Stennis, follow I–59 south of Picayune and take Highway 607 South toward Bay St. Louis. Twelve miles north of this sleepy little hamlet by the bay, you'll find the NASA complex where all of America's space shuttle main engines are test fired.

Exhibits in the visitors center include a space suit, moon rocks, and a replica of the space shuttle, but the high point of the tour is heading out to the bleachers to experience the deafening roar and earthshaking force of a space shuttle main engine test firing. A single space shuttle engine weighs 7,000 pounds, stands 14 feet tall, and generates enough horsepower to fly two and a half 747 airliners. Prepare to get wet—the *one million gallons* of water used to cool things down turns to steam quickly, then showers onlookers with a fine, cool mist. The Stennis Center is open for free tours daily 9:00 A.M.–5:00 P.M. If it's the test firing you're really interested in, call (228) 688–2370 to be sure you schedule your visit for a testing time and day.

Following the noisy, high-tech excitement at Stennis, a visit to tiny *Waveland* is quite a contrast. From the space center, take Mississippi

Highway 607 South until it turns into U.S. Highway 90 at this pretty little fishing village, your first stop on the beach. Waveland was once a haven for pirates, and much of the local lore revolves around notorious swashbucklers complete with parrots, wooden legs, and buried treasure. It's this cutthroat legacy that gave Waveland's **Buccaneer State Park** its name. Summers find the Buccaneer **wave pool** packed with more children than treasure seekers. Buccaneer State Park is located 2 miles off U.S. Highway 90 on South Beach Boulevard. Call (228) 467–3822 for camping information.

It's little wonder that a favorite pastime on the Gulf Coast is cruising oak-studded U.S. Highway 90, the busy scenic route that parallels the beach. From Waveland, follow Highway 90 East, nicknamed "The Hospitality Highway," into **Bay St. Louis.** Take a right off Highway 90 at the Casino Magic sign, then take a right onto Main Street and into the heart of Bay St. Louis's **Old Town.**

"Quaint" may be an overused adjective, but there's simply no better word to describe this charming, 3-block area of galleries and shops that earned Bay St. Louis a listing in John Villani's book, *The 100 Best Small Art Towns in America.* The motto here is "Spend a Day in the Bay," and it's a more than welcome assignment. Park your car and enjoy a stroll along what is surely the only Main Street in Mississippi that's home to both a Methodist Church and a voodoo shop.

Perhaps the most unusual shop is **Cat Rock Corner** (124 Main Street). Owner/artisan S. Anne Lynch ships large, smooth river stones all the way to Bay St. Louis from Colorado, then transforms them into hand-painted, incredibly lifelike cats, dogs, and other animals. The shop's resident feline often poses in the window with its stone image, and it takes more than a glance to tell which is the real cat and which is the rock. Working from photographs, Ms. Lynch manages to capture not only each animal's likeness, but its very personality. Immortalize your kitty for $225, or invest $300 in a stone likeness of your favorite pooch. For more information or to see photo samples of Ms. Lynch's work, stop by the shop or call (228) 466–9944.

Cat Rock Corner isn't the only shop with a resident pet. Buddy the Dog is a fixture at **Paper Moon** (220 Main Street), where artist Vicki Lever makes one-of-a-kind paper sculptures, collages, and jewelry. Choose from tray after tray of vintage buttons, charms, and beads, then browse among the retro clothing and decorative items while Vicki makes you a pin, bracelet, or pair of earrings. And when she tells you, "It'll be 25," chances are good she means 25 cents, not $25. You'll want to stock up for yourself and do your Christmas shopping here—an original pair of delightfully quirky Paper Moon earrings, handmade while you wait, sells for as little as $3.00.

Other shops worth a visit include *Bay Crafts* (107 North Beach Boulevard), where you'll find upscale pottery, jewelry, and artwork created by more than 250 craftspeople; *Yesterday's Treasures* (209 Main Street), the town's oldest antiques shop and home to another resident cat; and *Summerland Magickal Shoppe* (128 Main Street), where the merchandise includes mojo bags and voodoo dolls, the staff performs psychic readings, and the motto is "Minds are like parachutes. They only function when open." Most of the shops open around 10:00 A.M. and close by 6:00 P.M., but the second Saturday of every month from May through August Old Town stays open into the evening, allowing for browsing under the stars.

A couple of blocks east of the main Old Town district you'll find the *home and studio of artist Alice Moseley.* Now in her eighties, Ms. Moseley was sixty-one when she began painting folksy, down-home scenes recalled

Praline Alley

*T*he stretch of Highway 90 between Bay St. Louis, Mississippi and New Orleans, Louisiana, is marked by countless roadside stands, souvenir shops, and country cafes all hawking one thing—pralines.

Sinfully caloric and sweet enough to make your teeth ache, the praline (repeat after me, "praw-lean") is a staple in every Southern cook's repertoire and a mandatory requirement of any visit to Mississippi. Whether your personal preference is gooey, crunchy, or somewhere in between, Mississippi has a praline that's just right for you—that perfect mating of sugar and nuts that will have you buying (and devouring) them by the bagful.

Of course, the best pralines are homemade. So after you've sampled a few of

the Mississippi-made variety, test the recipe below in your own kitchen.

Mississippi Pralines

2 cups sugar

1 cup buttermilk

½ teaspoon baking soda

2 tablespoons Karo syrup

2 tablespoons butter or margarine

2½ cups pecans (repeat after me, "puh-cahns")

Cream sugar, milk, soda, salt, and Karo. Boil five minutes, stirring often. Add butter and pecans. Stir for five minutes. Remove from heat. Cool one minute. Beat until creamy, then drop by teaspoon onto waxed paper. Let sit for five minutes before serving. Enjoy in moderation.

from her childhood. Her colorful paintings of life in the South have equally colorful titles; prints available include *Living High, Low, and Middle on the Hog, Three Sheets in the Wind,* and *Git Up to Snuff, You've Time Enough.* Located at 214 Bookter Street, Ms. Moseley's home and studio are open daily from 10:00 A.M.–5:00 P.M.

If the combination of sea air and shopping makes you hungry, Old Town is still the place to be. Sample the freshest of seafood and learn how the "Po' Boy" got its name at **Trapani's Eatery** on Beach Boulevard, or step across the street to **Dock of the Bay** and enjoy lunch or dinner on the breezy deck overlooking the water.

Located at the eastern edge of the Old Town district, the **Bay Town Inn** is the only area bed and breakfast boasting an unobscured view of the water. From the moment you step through the door of this elegant, turn-of-the-century inn, owner Ann Tidwell (aided by her toy poodle, Tudor) will go out of her way to make sure your stay is a pleasant one. Take a close look at the paper sculptures and collages on the walls downstairs—they're original pieces created by Ms. Tidwell's daughter Vicki, proprietor of the Paper Moon. The rooms are spacious and comfortable, but the inn's real attraction is a breezy front porch shaded by a centuries-old live oak tree that offers a soothing view of the bay. Rates at the Bay Town Inn are $75–85. Call (800) 467–8466 for reservations. If the Bay Town Inn is booked, try the **Palm House Bed and Breakfast** at (228) 467–1665. The Palm House is also within walking distance of the Old Town district; rates begin at $65.

Across the bridge east of Bay St. Louis, Highway 90 continues through the equally charming town of **Pass Christian.** (Don't give yourself away as a tourist—it's pronounced "Kris-chee-ann.") This section of Highway 90 is particularly picturesque, bordered by the beach on one side and stately mansions overlooking the water on the other. Many of these palatial homes were once mere summer retreats, built by wealthy southern planters and New Orleans aristocrats who fled to the Gulf Coast to escape the summer heat and the threat of malaria. Surrounded by ancient live oaks and generations-old camellias and azaleas, most of the homes feature open balconies and wide porches designed to catch the coastal breeze.

Watch for the left turn off Highway 90 onto Scenic Drive (the road gets a little tricky here—be careful not to wind up headed into traffic). The first building you'll spot is the **Harbour Oaks Inn,** a quaintly weather-beaten bed and breakfast that's stood watch over the Pass Christian Harbor since 1860. Rates begin at $78; call (800) 452–9399 for reservations. You'll pass a handful of upscale art, antiques, and gift shops before arriving in downtown Pass Christian, a tiny cluster of pastel-painted buildings. Just outside downtown you'll discover another bed and breakfast, the *Inn at the Pass.* Rates begin at $55, and a kennel is available for pets visiting the beach. Call (800) 217–2588 for reservations.

When you spot the MERMAID CROSSING sign you'll know you've arrived at *Hillyer House,* Pass Christian's most popular shopping spot. A favorite haunt of *Southern Living* magazine, Hillyer House showcases the work of 175 potters, jewelers, and painters from around the United States. The gallery/shop is open 10:00 A.M.–5:00 P.M. Monday–Saturday and noon–5:00 P.M. Sunday.

Back on Highway 90, you'll pass still more elegant old homes as you cross into *Long Beach,* another coastal community marked by blue sky, warm breezes, and sun-spangled waters. The beaches here are uncrowded and quiet, dotted with fishing piers stretching far into the Mississippi Sound. Take the exit to the University of Southern Mississippi-Gulf Coast, then drive straight ahead on campus to Hardy Hall and the *Friendship Oak.* According to legend, those who step into the shadow of this 500-year-old live oak tree must "remain friends through all their lifetime, no matter where fate may take them." At 50 feet tall with a 151-foot spread of foliage, the tree casts an enormous shadow indeed. The average length of the Friendship Oak's enormous limbs—which are supported by heavy cables and rest on blocks—is 66 feet from the trunk. A platform nestled high in its branches is a popular spot not only for photos, but for wedding ceremonies. If estimates of its age are accurate, the Friendship Oak was a sapling when Christopher Columbus set sail for the New World. The Friendship is the most famous of the many live oak trees found along the coast. Many of the trees bear names indicating age and wisdom ("Councilor" and "Patriarch," to name a couple) and are registered with the Live Oak Tree Society.

As Highway 90 crosses into *Gulfport,* the quiet artists' colonies and rustic fishing piers are replaced by the glitz and glitter of floating *casinos* and the hustle and bustle of the *Port of Gulfport.* Gift shops here sell more T-shirts and seashells than fine art, and the beaches are packed with sunbathers. Gulfport is home to a number of well-marked, modern beach pleasures, including helicopter tours, jet ski rentals, pleasure-boat rides, and deep-sea-fishing charters. Indulge in a banana split in honor of the Port of Gulfport—America's number one banana port. A navigational note—the section of Highway 90 that runs through Gulfport and neighboring Biloxi is also referred to as Beach Boulevard.

Follow the signs near the Port of Gulfport to the **Marine Life Oceanarium,** where you'll see the trained dolphins, sea lions, and tropical birds put through their paces. The Oceanarium also offers a half-hour train tour of the port, including a look at one of the largest banana terminals in the world. Call (228) 863–0651 for show times and admission prices.

Friendship Oak

Gulfport also offers **excursions to West Ship Island** 12 miles off the Mississippi mainland. The Mississippi Sound meets the Gulf of Mexico at Ship Island, one of four natural barrier islands that are part of the **Gulf Islands National Seashore.** Clear waters and constant surf make Ship Island the most popular spot for sunbathing and beach-combing on the coast; in fact *USA Today* named the beach at Ship Island one of the top ten in the United States. Snacks, beverages, and chair and umbrella rentals are available, and lifeguards are on duty in season. The boardwalk leading to the gulf side of the island is about one-third of a mile, so travel lightly. A word of warning—take *plenty* of sunscreen.

Ship Island is also home to **Fort Massachusetts,** which served as a Confederate POW camp during the Civil War. The fort even housed one female prisoner, a New Orleans housewife charged with teaching her children to spit on Union officers. Guided tours of the fort are available in summer, and history buffs can explore the structure anytime on their own.

Excursion boats bound for Ship Island leave the Gulfport Yacht Harbor daily March–October. Call (228) 864–3797 for the day's schedule. Round-trip excursions are $14.00 for adults and $7.00 for children. The hour-long ride to the island is an adventure in itself—playful dolphins usually accompany the ferry to its destination.

If you're back on the mainland by dinnertime, buzz on over to the **Blow Fly Inn,** "where people swarm for fine food." Don't let the name scare you—the Blow Fly is neat and tidy, nestled in a cove overlooking peaceful Bayou Bernard. The family-style restaurant's steaks, ribs, and seafood are indeed

Hurricane Camille

*T*hirty years later, the mere mention of her name still evokes images of death and destruction.

She was Camille, the most violent hurricane in United States history, a furious, howling hussy who tried—almost successfully—to wipe the entire Mississippi Gulf Coast off the map.

The night of Sunday, August 17, 1969, Camille slammed into the Mississippi Gulf Coast, packing 20-foot tides and 205-mile-an-hour winds—the highest in the history of the Western Hemisphere.

Though some 75,000 coastal residents evacuated, hundreds more stayed behind to ride out the storm. After all, the coast had weathered hurricanes before, and few could imagine just how monstrous Camille would be.

The stories of those who stayed behind to battle Camille have become Gulf Coast legend. There was the couple who remained at home "to put out pots and pans in case the skylights starting leaking." They wound up riding out the hurricane atop a 60-foot television antennae after Camille swept their entire house into the sea.

The residents of the Richelieu Manor Apartments in Pass Christian refused to evacuate, despite two visits from the chief of police. Instead they poured cocktails in anticipation of a "hurricane party." According to one of the survivors, there was more praying than drinking going on when Camille finally hit. The three-story Richelieu simply disintegrated; nothing was left but the cement foundation. Twenty-three party-goers joined the death toll.

In Hattiesburg, more than 70 miles north of the Gulf Coast, winds reached 140 miles per hour as Camille flattened most of the pinebelt. Two hundred miles from the storm's landfall, Jackson took gusts of up to 67 miles per hour. Camille tore through Tennessee, Kentucky, North Carolina, and into Virginia's Blue Ridge Mountains, where she dumped 27 inches of rain in eight hours—a deluge so heavy, people actually drowned trying to walk in it.

Monday morning, a shell-shocked Mississippi coast awoke to a level of destruction that defied imagination. Pass Christian, Gulfport, and Biloxi had been virtually erased. Four thousand homes had been simply wiped away, leaving nothing but their foundations and an occasional flight of stairs leading heavenward. Dozens of palatial southern mansions that had withstood not only centuries of storms, but the Civil War, were reduced to rubble. The luxury hotels that had looked out over the Mississippi Sound had vanished—1,600 rooms, gone in the blink of Camille's eye.

Shrimp boats rested in sand-filled front lawns up and down the coast. More than 5,000 cars and trucks were damaged beyond repair, including nearly all of the coastal police fleet. What hadn't been washed into the Sound was piled haphazardly in the middle of what was left of U.S. Highway 90. *(continued)*

The coast had been reduced to 260,000 tons of debris, and 129 Mississippians were dead.

But even amidst the terrible wreckage and chaos, there were signs of hope, indicators of a resilient people who would not be beaten by a mere hurricane. As early as one day after Camille's rampage, handwritten signs rose from the debris proclaiming, WE ARE COMING BACK and WE'LL RISE AGAIN.

And rise again the coast did. A decade later, the Biloxi Sun Herald issued a special Camille anniversary edition which juxtaposed photos of the 1969 devastation with shots of rebuilt, better-than-ever roads, homes, businesses, and hotels.

The headline? "Hurricane Camille. She won the battle, but we won the war."

tasty, but it's the name that attracts the most attention. The walls are adorned with crayon-colored blow fly cartoons, and each plate comes with a plastic blow fly garnish. You can even purchase a souvenir Blow Fly Inn T-shirt. The Blow Fly Inn is open Monday–Friday 3:00–11:00 P.M. and Saturday 10:00 A.M.–11:00 P.M. Take Highway 90 to Teagarden Street, turn right on Pass Road, then go left on Washington (watch carefully; it's hard to spot the street sign after dark), which dead-ends at the water and the restaurant.

You'll hardly notice you've left Gulfport and crossed into **Biloxi,** your next stop on Highway 90. Once a quiet community frequented by families in search of a budget beach vacation (and hung with the unfortunate nickname "Redneck Riviera"), Biloxi is now a hopping resort town offering twenty-four-hour **casino gaming.** Today Biloxi's beaches are packed towel-to-towel and lined with T-shirt shacks, hotels, eateries, miniature golf courses, and tattoo parlors. This is also the place to rent a jet ski, charter a deep-sea-fishing boat, or play golf year-round.

The beach takes on a new look in September when Biloxi hosts the **Sun Herald *Sand Sculpture Contest.*** The largest contest of its kind in the world, the Sand Sculpture Contest offers $4,000 in prize money to teams who create the most eye-catching artwork using only sand, water, and beach debris. Grab your shovel and pail and call (228) 896–2434 for dates and details.

Fortunately for nonbeach bums, everything in Biloxi doesn't involve sand. Just as you come into town from Gulfport, you'll spot a sign directing you to ***Beauvoir,*** the last home of Confederate President Jefferson Davis. Davis purchased this seaside estate from a family friend in 1879 for $5,500. Once you step onto the quiet grounds, it's easy to understand why the former president chose to spend the last years of

Hurricane Camille: The Worst Storm in U.S. History

- *Caused $1.4 billion of damage in Mississippi, Louisiana, Virginia, and West Virginia (in 1969 dollars)*

- *Caused $950 million of damage in Mississippi alone (in 1969 dollars)*

- *Killed 248 people, including 129 Mississippians*

- *Destroyed 6,022 homes, including 3,80 in Mississippi*

- *Damaged 48,016 homes, including 41,785 in Mississippi*

- *Destroyed 785 businesses, including 568 in Mississippi*

- *Left the Mississippi Gulf Coast with enough damaged timber to build 300,000 houses*

- *Split Ship Island, 12 miles off the mainland in the Mississippi Sound, in half*

his life writing his memoirs and enjoying the peace and solitude of the coast.

Davis was revered by southern patriots, and in the years following the war, Beauvoir ("beautiful view") hosted a constant parade of veterans and well-wishers—so many visitors, in fact, that neighbors had to lend the Davis family enough food to entertain them. Following Davis's death in 1889, his widow Varina rejected an offer of $100,000 for Beauvoir, instead selling the mansion to the Mississippi Division of the Sons of Confederate Veterans for $10,000 with the stipulation that Beauvoir be used as a home for Confederate veterans and their families. More than 2,000 residents signed the roster of the Beauvoir Confederate Soldiers' Home, including several former slaves who fought for the Confederacy. In 1941, the main house was opened as a shrine honoring Jefferson Davis. In 1957, the last two war widows were moved to a nursing home, and Beauvoir, its outbuildings, and grounds became a museum. The estate is still owned and managed by the Mississippi Division, United Sons of Confederate Veterans, who operate the attraction under the name Beauvoir, the Jefferson Davis Home and Presidential Library.

The Beauvoir tour begins in the old soldiers' home hospital, now the Confederate Museum. The building houses a tasteful presentation of artifacts related to the war and Beauvoir's years as a veterans' home. The mansion itself houses antique furnishings and memorabilia related to the Davis family, including Davis's personal copy of the book, *The Plantation Negro as a Freeman*. Displays include several family photos of Brierfield, Davis's plantation near Vicksburg. One photo shows the house under occupation by spiteful Union troops, who painted the words, "The house that Jeff built," over the front door.

The fifty-seven-acre property includes the only presidential library in Mississippi and a cemetery where nearly 800 soldiers who followed Davis in life are buried. Davis's father, Samuel Emory Davis, was re-interred in the Beauvoir cemetery in 1942. The ***Tomb of the Unknown Confederate Soldier*** stands just outside the cemetery. Located at 2244 Beach Boulevard, Beauvoir is open daily 9:00 A.M.–5:00 P.M. March 1–September1, 9:00 A.M.–4:00 P.M. September 1–March 1. Admission is $6.00. The troops march again each October during the Beauvoir ***Fall Muster,*** which features military drills and Confederate campsites. Call (228) 388–1313 for this year's reenactment date, or check the Beauvoir Web site at www.beauvoir.org.

As you continue east on Highway 90, you'll pass another Civil War–era landmark, the ***Father Ryan House.*** Now a bed-and-breakfast inn, the house is hard to miss—it's the one with a towering palm tree growing out of the front steps. Built in 1841, the house was the home of Father Abraham Ryan, poet laureate of the Confederacy. It was here that Father Ryan composed his best-known poems, *Sea Rest* and *Sea Reverie*. Rates at the bed and breakfast begin at $125; tours of the house are free. Call (228) 435–1189 for reservations.

Continuing on Highway 90 you'll spot the 65-foot ***Biloxi Lighthouse,*** the only lighthouse in the United States beaming from smack in the middle of a four-lane highway. Built in 1848, the lighthouse was painted black following the assassination of President Abraham Lincoln. Take a

Father Ryan House

left at the lighthouse and follow the signs to the **Biloxi Visitors Center,** operating in the 100-year-old Brielmaier House. Leave your car at the visitors center, pick up a free **walking tour brochure** inside, and enjoy a stroll through the city's historic district.

Begin your tour at the **George E. Ohr Arts and Cultural Center** located on the second floor of the Biloxi Public Library. The building is easy to spot—it's the angular, thoroughly modern structure in the middle of the historic district, and its entrance is marked by a giant, mustachioed archway labeled "Mr. Ohr's Neighborhood." Ohr was a colorful Biloxi folk artist of the 1890s whose eccentric behavior and two-foot-long mustache earned him the nickname "the Mad Potter of Biloxi." His contemporaries described Ohr as "one fork short of a place setting," a reputation he cultivated in order to draw attention to his art. Photos of Ohr indicate his talent for facial contortioning was on par with his gift for throwing pots.

Ohr was frustrated by critics who didn't appreciate his "mud babies," and at one time even buried a cache of pots in hopes a more "enlightened" generation would unearth them. That future generation has arrived. Ohr's pottery is now critically acclaimed and has been collected by a number of celebrities, including Andy Warhol.

The Ohr Cultural Center houses a permanent exhibit of the Mad Potter's work. A gift shop—appropriately known as Ohriginals—sells pottery and art. Join the madness at the Ohr Center Monday–Saturday 9:00 A.M.–5:00 P.M. Admission is $2.00. On an interesting side note, Ohr's grandson, artist Joe Moran, operates **Moran's Art Gallery** in Biloxi near the visitors center. Moran's work has been displayed at the Smithsonian.

From the Ohr Cultural Center, stroll through the **Rue Magnolia Walking Mall.** The oak-shaded complex is home to **Mary Mahoney's Old French House,** the coast's legendary courtyard restaurant. The building and old slave quarters remain much the same as when they were originally constructed in 1737; the towering **Patriarch Oak** in the courtyard is estimated at 2,000 years old. And if the ambience isn't enough to inspire a visit, the food at Mary Mahoney's is nothing short of delicious. Ms. Mahoney once catered a party for President Ronald Reagan on the White House lawn; an autographed photo of Mary with the President still hangs in the restaurant. In 1985, the city of Biloxi even hosted a "Mary Mahoney Day" in honor of its most famous restaurateur. The restaurant complex includes several dining rooms in the main house, open-air dining in the brick-walled courtyard, two lounges (one in the old slave quarters), a sidewalk cafe open twenty-four hours a day, and the Magnolia Memories gift shop.

Across the mall from Mary Mahoney's you'll spot the **Magnolia Hotel,** a fashionable coastal retreat built in 1847. The hotel no longer rents rooms but does house the **Mardi Gras Museum,** a collection of colorful costumes and memorabilia donated by royalty of the coast's Mardi Gras krewes. The museum is open irregularly; call (228) 432–8806 before planning a visit. You can see the krewes in action each February, when **Mardi Gras** parades roll through Biloxi and other coastal communities. Mardi Gras on the Gulf Coast is equally colorful but a little more family-oriented (read "tame") than the same celebration in neighboring New Orleans. For dates and parade routes, contact the Gulf Coast Carnival Association at (228) 432–8806.

If you'd like to see more of Biloxi's architecture, pick up the "Mississippi Beach Historic Homes Driving Tour" brochure back at the visitors center. This guide includes directions to several historic sites and architectural marvels, including the **Church of the Redeemer,** where Jefferson Davis's pew is still preserved and **St. Michael's Catholic Church,** where the roof is made of sea shells and stained glass windows depict the apostles as fishermen.

Back on Highway 90 you'll spot one of the coast's antebellum summer homes, **Tullis-Toledano Manor.** Built in 1856 by a wealthy New Orleans cotton broker, the manor is now open for tours Monday–Friday 10:00 A.M.–noon and 1:00.–5:00 P.M. Admission is $1.50 for adults, $1.00 for seniors, and 50 cents for children. The house shares the two-and-a-half-acre property with the 600-year-old **Councilor Oak,** which once provided shade for Indians and early explorers.

Continue on Highway 90 to Point Cadet Plaza and the **J. L. Scott Marine Education Center.** The $3.00 admission buys a look at some forty aquariums, including the 42,000-gallon Gulf of Mexico tank. Point Cadet is also home to the **Maritime and Seafood Industry Museum,** where exhibits depict not only the history and growth of the seafood business along the coast, but how the industry influenced the culture and lifestyle of its people. Admission is $2.50 for adults, $1.50 for seniors and children. The museum is open Monday–Saturday 9:00 A.M.–4:30 P.M. and Sunday noon–4:00 P.M. The museum is also home to two replica sailing schooners, the *Glenn L. Swetman* and the *Mike Sekul,* both of which are available for day long, half-day, or sunset **cruises on the Mississippi Sound.** Call (228) 435–6320 for cruise information and reservations.

Seafood is still big business in Biloxi, and its contribution to the local economy is celebrated each spring during the **Biloxi Shrimp Festival**

and Blessing of the Fleet. The festivities begin with a mass at St. Michael's Catholic Church, followed by a huge shrimp festival at Point Cadet Plaza. Following the crowning of the Shrimp King and Queen, activities move to the Biloxi Harbor, where commercial vessels and pleasure boats parade past a "blessing boat." The Catholic priest sprinkles each gaily decorated craft with holy water to ensure a safe and plentiful fishing season. Call (228) 435–5578 for this year's blessing and festival dates.

Cross the bridge east of Biloxi and you'll find yourself in ***Ocean Springs,*** a tranquil artists' colony so peaceful and so serene it's as if the crowded resorts just 3 miles to the west don't even exist.

Little-Known Facts About Southern Mississippi and the Gulf Coast

- *The world's first can of condensed milk was produced in Liberty, Mississippi by inventor Gail Borden.*

- *A plane carrying the rock group Lynyrd Skynyrd crashed just south of McComb on October 20, 1977, killing six.*

- *The Pioneer Aerospace Corporation of Columbia is the world's largest manufacturer of parachutes.*

- *Columbia's Walter Payton was the first football player ever featured on a Wheaties cereal box.*

- *Hattiesburg's Camp Shelby is the largest National Guard Training facility in the United States.*

- *Leontyne Price of Laurel was the first African-American to achieve international stardom in the world of opera, performing with the New York Metropolitan Opera.*

- *Astronaut Fred Haise of Biloxi was aboard the ill-fated flight to the moon immortalized in director Ron Howard's Apollo 13.*

- *Confederate President Jefferson Davis was restored to U.S. citizenship in 1978—during the presidency of Jimmy Carter.*

- *Barq's Root Beer was invented in 1898 by Edward Barq of Biloxi.*

- *New Orleans may have made it famous, but Mardi Gras was first celebrated in the New World in Mississippi. The original "Fat Tuesday" was observed in 1699 by explorer Pierre LeMoyne d'Iberville and his crew at Fort Maurepas in Ocean Springs.*

- *The rarest of North American cranes, the Mississippi Sandhill Crane lives in a protected area in the grassy savannahs of Jackson County.*

Take a right off Highway 90 (known within the Ocean Springs city limits as Bienville Boulevard) onto Washington Avenue and you'll find yourself in Ocean Springs's charming business district. Washington Avenue crosses Robinson Avenue and Government Street, then runs 4 more blocks before dead-ending at the beach. On these three easily walked streets, you'll discover a number of quaint shops, restaurants, galleries, and artists' studios.

Choose an original piece of metalwork or jewelry from the *Gayle Clark Gallery* (1000 Washington Avenue), admire the glazes at *Mississippi Mud Works* (1009 Government Street), watch as pewter smiths meld original tableware and sculptures at *Ballard Pewter Ltd.* (1110 Government Street), or enjoy the paintings and prints at the *Local Color Gallery* or *Local Color Too* (1111 and 1141 Robinson Avenue).

Kids and grown-ups alike will enjoy a fun-filled visit to *Miner's Toy Stores* (927 Washington Avenue), five-time winner of the Playthings National Award, the highest honor in the toy industry. In addition to virtually every game, toy, and doll imaginable, Miner's sells collectible Civil War toy soldiers, hand-crafted of pewter by local artist and historian Ron Wall. According to owner Maryalice Miner, "We can't keep enough of Robert E. Lee, but we've got plenty of Grants." If all that shopping leaves you hungry, be sure to stop by the *Tatonut Shop* (1114 Government Street) to sample a rare treat—doughnuts made from potatoes.

Washington Avenue is also home to Ocean Springs's most conveniently located and most unusual bed and breakfast, *Who's Inn?* Owned by botanical sculptor Trailer McQuilkin and his wife Sharon, the two-room inn is housed in back of an art gallery called *Art Who?* The gallery's name was inspired by Andy Warhol. It seems Warhol once attended an opening and was driven to distraction by a dowager who kept telling him how much she loved art. An exasperated Warhol finally asked, "Art who?"

Rooms at Who's Inn? are elegantly decorated with contemporary paintings and sculpture, all of which are for sale. Guests are within walking distance of all the downtown attractions and have access to a pair of bicycles perfect for exploring the beaches. Rooms at Who's Inn? are $85 weekdays, $95 weekends and $500 per week. Call (228) 875–3251 from 10:00 A.M.–5:00 P.M. Monday–Saturday when the Art Who? gallery is open, or (228) 875–2900 after 5:00 P.M. and on Sunday.

Breakfast is served across the street at *Le Croissant French Bakery Cafe.* This is an authentic French pastry shop, where an owner whose accent will make you think you've awakened at the Eiffel Tower serves up the biggest, freshest, tastiest pastries you will ever put in your mouth.

You'll appreciate Ocean Springs's artistic legacy even more after a visit to the **Walter Anderson Museum of Art** (510 Washington Avenue). Creative types have been drawn to Ocean Springs for centuries, but the town's most famous son was eccentric painter Walter Inglis Anderson. Anderson was known for his vivid paintings and block prints depicting the rich plant and animal life of the Gulf Coast, its marshes, and wetlands. To describe Anderson as obsessed by his work is an understatement—his efforts to capture nature in all her majesty once included lashing himself to a tree during a hurricane. In the early 1950s, Anderson began retreating for weeks at a time to a tiny cottage to work in solitude. When his family opened the cottage after his death in 1965, they discovered brilliant murals painted on every inch of the walls and ceiling. The entire "little room" mural, which depicts a coastal day from sunrise to sunset crowned with a brilliant zinnia on the ceiling, has been moved to the museum. The museum adjoins the **Ocean Springs Community Center,** the interior walls of which Anderson adorned with brilliant murals for the fee of $1.00. The murals are appraised today at more than $1 million. The Walter Anderson Museum of Art is open Monday–Saturday 10:00 A.M.–5:00 P.M. and Sunday 1:00–5:00 P.M. Admission is $4.00 for adults and $1.50 for children. Call (228) 872–3164 or visit www.motif.org.

If you'd like to take a piece of Anderson's genius home, choose a print from the museum gift shop, the **Local Color Gallery,** or **Realizations, the Walter Anderson Shop** (1000 Washington Avenue), which also carries clothing featuring Anderson's work. **Threadneedle Street** (619 Washington Avenue) carries Anderson designs for cross-stitch kits and needlepoint.

Walter Anderson is the most famous member of an entire family of gifted artists. Walter's talented brother Peter established **Shearwater Pottery** in 1928. Shearwater is still a family affair, now run by Peter's son James. The very picture of an artists' colony, the twenty-four-acre Shearwater compound includes a studio and gallery housed in rustic cabins and surrounded by thick green woods. The pottery collection includes dinnerware, vases, and sculpture. Pieces and table settings can be custom ordered, but don't expect to receive your shipment in the usual four to six weeks. Each piece is an individual work of art, and Shearwater Pottery doesn't do rush orders. Art lovers from around the world have sought out the remote colony in this tiny seaside village. Comments in the guest book include, "I loved the woods," "I could have stayed all day," "Dazzled," and "Expensive, but worth it."

Follow the signs from Washington Avenue past the Ocean Springs harbor and across the bridge to the Shearwater complex. The showroom is open Monday–Saturday 9:00 A.M.–5:30 P.M. and Sunday 1:00–5:30 P.M.

The Heat Is On

*M*ississippi is hot.

Oh, forecasters may try to soften the blow with euphemisms like "sultry," "balmy," or the highly understated "very warm," but take my word for it, the best description for Mississippi in the summertime is "sweltering."

Temperatures reach the upper nineties before noon. The sun is relentless, the breeze, nonexistent. And humid? You almost need scuba gear just to breathe.

A few summers ago, my family spent July in New England, where the high reached a mere 82 degrees—a refreshing reading our thermometer at home hadn't seen since April. After three months of stifling Mississippi heat, the five of us reveled in the simple pleasure of taking a noon-day stroll without sweating. We ate virtually every meal al fresco, always landing the best patio tables because the locals found it "too warm to eat outdoors." My husband's children were amazed to learn that there were actually cars and houses that did not come equipped with air conditioning.

We were all most amazed, however, by the New Englanders themselves, who were positively wilting in what was, to us, a cold snap. When we described summer conditions in Mississippi, they invariably asked (with a look of horror), "How on earth can you live there?"

So, how do Mississippians cope with a summer heat index that seems perpetually stuck at 110? Well, from June through September we pretty much stay indoors and give thanks for air conditioning and iced tea.

But when October rolls around, we breathe a sigh of relief and celebrate the crisp days and brilliant colors of fall. Come January, we marvel at the plight of northerners up to their eyeballs in snow and wonder if we'll really need to take a jacket with us on our daily stroll. And in early March, when most of the country is still looking forward to another six weeks of snow and ice and slush, we see the first of our spring flowers in bloom.

Truth is, while we may complain about it, Mississippians have long since made peace with the heat. It's a small inconvenience that's simply part of life here in the Deep South—a life most of us would never trade for existence in a winter wonderland.

Let a little heat and humidity run us die-hard southerners out?

When Mississippi freezes over.

The workshop is open weekdays from 9:00 A.M.–noon and 1:00–4:00 P.M. Ocean Springs honors Shearwater's founder the first weekend of November during the annual *Peter Anderson Arts and Crafts Festival.* Fine artists from around the Southeast display and sell paintings, pottery, woodcrafts, jewelry, and furniture in downtown Ocean Springs. For more information call the Ocean Springs Chamber of Commerce at (228) 875–4424.

No trip to Ocean Springs would be complete without a visit to *Crooked Feather.* In 1976, Hungarian sculptor Peter Toth presented the city of Ocean Springs with a massive carving of an Indian head christened "Crooked Feather." Toth spent four months in Davidson Park on Highway 90 carving the 30-foot tall monument out of a 2,000-year-old cypress log.

Crooked Feather is one of a family of sixty-seven Indian sculptures carved by Toth throughout North America. The artist traveled the continent from 1982 to 1988, carving at least one statue in every state in the nation and two in Canada. Toth refers to the sculptures collectively as the "Trail of the Whispering Giants." Each statue was a gift to the community in which it was carved; Toth expected no pay for his work.

"I hope my work opens people's eyes to the plight of the American Indians and the contributions they have given us," Toth said. "It might be arrogant of me to think so, but I hope my work has helped improve relations between Americans and Native Americans."

Founded in 1699, Ocean Springs is one of the oldest cities in the United States. Three centuries ago, Pierre LeMoyne d'Iberville stepped ashore at Ocean Springs and claimed the area for France. The annual *Landing of d'Iberville* celebrates this historic event with a weekend-long spring festival that includes a children's pet parade, a historical ball and pageant, and a full-scale reenactment of the landing at a replica of the French *Fort Maurepas* located on the beach at the foot of Jackson Avenue (1 block west of Washington Avenue).

Ocean Springs also hosts two popular fall festivals. The highly original *Scarecrow Contest* finds the town populated by themed straw men while the *Great Oaks Storytelling Festival* attracts renowned tale-spinners from around the country. Call the *Ocean Springs Chamber of Commerce* (228–875–4424) for this year's festival dates.

Ocean Springs is home to a number of restaurants welcoming hungry travelers, most specializing in—you guessed it—fresh seafood. Enjoy lunch or dinner with a view at *Anthony's Under the Oaks,* an elegant eatery nestled among 400-year-old oaks overlooking Fort Bayou. The upscale menu includes steak, seafood, and veal. Anthony's serves lunch Tuesday through Friday and dinner Tuesday through Saturday and kicks off the week with a Sunday champagne brunch—the corks start popping at 11:30 A.M. Anthony's is located at 1217 Washington Avenue north of Highway 90.

Another local favorite is *Jocelyn's,* housed in the hard-to-miss, bright fuchsia cottage on Highway 90. When the popular Ocean Springs restaurant known as Trilby's changed hands some years ago, cook Jocelyn Mayfield decided to take her recipes and strike out on her own. She transformed her in-laws' small house into a restaurant, painted it pink, and opened her doors to diners hungry for her sophisticated approach to seafood, beef, and chicken. Jocelyn's is open for dinner 5:00–10:00 P.M. Tuesday–Saturday.

Continue on Highway 90 East to the well-marked entrance to the Mississippi headquarters of the *Gulf Islands National Seashore.* The entire seashore includes some 150 miles in Mississippi and Florida. The Mississippi portion of this national park begins at *Davis Bayou* on the mainland, then stretches into the Mississippi Sound to include the *barrier islands of West Ship, East Ship, Horn,* and *Petit Bois.* West Ship and East Ship Islands were originally one; Hurricane Camille split the island in two in 1969. Horn Island—a favorite inspiration of artist Walter Anderson—and Petit Bois Island have been designated wilderness areas by the U.S. Congress. Protected from development and human interference, these islands provide habitats for uncommon species of birds, animals, and marine and plant life.

The headquarters at Davis Bayou includes miles of secluded marshlands brimming with wildlife, a campground, picnic shelters, nature trails, and boat launches. Misty mornings are prime time for birdwatchers, photographers, and fishermen. The marsh provides a home for creatures representing every level of the food chain. From industrious fiddler crabs to stately Great Blue Herons to inquisitive alligators, you're sure to spot something scurrying, splashing, or flying in every corner of the bayou at every hour of the day. On summer weekends a park naturalist takes visitors by the boatload on free tours. Schedules are available at the visitors center, which also houses exhibits describing the flora and fauna of the mainland marshes and the islands.

There's no beach at Davis Bayou, but excursion boats departing from Gulfport transport visitors to the swimming and recreational beaches at West Ship Island daily during spring, summer, and fall (see page 151).

Information about charter boats licensed to ferry adventurous explorers and campers to the wilderness islands is available at the visitors center.

From Ocean Springs, continue on Highway 90 East through the quiet community of **Gautier** (Go-shay). When you spot the giant shipyards lining the beach, you'll know you've arrived in **Pascagoula.** Follow the signs to the **Scranton Floating Museum,** a retired shrimp boat docked in the Pascagoula River Park. The free tour includes a look at the tiny galley, cramped crews' quarters, and aquariums and dioramas displayed in the hull. The entire tour takes less than ten minutes. Visitors who find themselves feeling a bit claustrophobic are sure to leave with a new respect for the shrimpers who worked the boat—not many people would volunteer to spend two weeks at sea in such spartan quarters. The museum is open 10:00 A.M.–5:00 P.M. Tuesday–Saturday. From the river park, head back toward Highway 90 East. Pay close attention to where you're going; the area around the river park is in need of directional signs and includes several unmarked roads leading to industrial sites.

Back on Highway 90 you'll cross the **Pascagoula River,** also known as the **"Singing River"** (see sidebar, page 165). The river has apparently been musically inclined for centuries; French explorer d'Iberville referenced the "Singing River" in journal entries dated 1699. A young member of d'Iberville's crew, Joseph Simon de la Pointe, became the master of Pascagoula a few years following d'Iberville's landing. In 1718, de la Pointe built what is now known as the **Old Spanish Fort** on the original town site. The oldest building in the Mississippi Valley, the fort features 18-inch-thick walls made of oyster shells, moss, and mud. A museum on the grounds displays artifacts from Pascagoula's Indian era as well as relics from the eighteenth century. Follow the signs from Highway 90 East to the Old Spanish Fort at 4602 Fort Drive. The fort and museum are open Monday–Saturday 9:30 A.M.–4:30 P.M. and Sunday noon–5:00 P.M.

Continuing east on Highway 90 you'll reach the Mississippi Highway 63 junction. Take Highway 63 North to Lucedale, or continue a few miles farther on Highway 90 to the **Gulf Coast Gator Ranch.** The self-proclaimed "fastest, most furious, fun-filled extravaganza in Mississippi," the Gator Ranch offers airboat tours of a marshland area populated by alligators, beavers, and other creatures at home in the swamp. The tall marsh grasses provide camouflage for hundreds of the scaly gators— keep your fingers out of the water! Airboat tours and a stroll through the gator farm are $10.00 for adults and $5.00 for children. Walking tours of the gator farm only are $2.00 for adults and $1.00 for children. A gift shop sells gator skulls, teeth, rubber impostors, and other gator memorabilia. Call (228) 475–6026 or stop by for tour schedules.

From the Gator Ranch, double back toward Pascagoula on Highway 90 West to Mississippi Highway 63 North, the shortest route to the Holy Land. You'll find the cities and geography of the Bible duplicated in miniature 12 miles north of **Lucedale** at the **Palestine Gardens.** Built by a Presbyterian minister who believed people had to understand the Bible's geography in order to understand its stories, the gardens re-create the Holy Land on twenty wooded acres. The scale in relation to the real Holy Land is about 1 yard per mile. Signs identify major cities and landmarks, including Bethlehem, Nazareth, Joseph's carpentry shop, and Golgatha, site of the crucifixion. The gardens are open Monday–Saturday 8:00 A.M.–6:00 P.M. and Sunday 1:00–6:00 P.M. Admission is $2.00 for adults, $1.00 for children. The gardens are located 6.5 miles east of U.S. Highway 98. Follow the signs from Lucedale or from Highway 98 or call (601) 947–8422 for directions to this out-of-the-way inspiration.

Head back into downtown Lucedale for a visit to **Bailey's Scratching Post.** No one seems to remember how or why a back-scratching post ended up in the middle of downtown, but when you've got an itch, it really doesn't seem to matter. Celebrities from Ronald Reagan to Dizzy Dean have unabashedly scratched their backs right there on Main Street.

From Lucedale, take Mississippi Highway 26 West to **Wiggins** and **Archie Batson's aquaculture, blueberry, and fish farm.** Batson's offers a genuine, down-home country experience guaranteed to

The Legend of the Singing River

*L*egend has it that centuries ago, a young princess of the Biloxi Indian tribe was betrothed to a hot-tempered Biloxi warrior. The princess, however, fell in love with a young chieftain of the peaceful Pascagoula tribe, and the two ran away together.

The spurned Biloxi warrior then led his braves in an attack on the Pascagoula. Rather than face death or slavery at the hands of the enemy, the entire Pascagoula tribe linked hands and walked into the Pascagoula River, singing a traditional tribal death chant as they surrendered their souls to the waters.

How much of the legend is true will forever remain a mystery, but whether the source is Indian ghosts or scientific phenomena, the Pascagoula River does sing. The music has been likened to everything from buzzing bees to the strains of a harp, and it usually reaches its highest volume on late summer and early autumn evenings. In fact, the river's song has been so loud it's actually stopped traffic on the bridge.

Is it a trick of the sand and silt, or the last sad song of a people long extinct? Spend a summer evening listening to the concert firsthand, then decide for yourself.

charm and relax harried city folk. In addition to acres of ponds used to grow catfish, crawfish, and freshwater shrimp, Batson's offers an open-air petting zoo, home to the largest assortment of domestic livestock since Noah.

Batson's aquaculture products are sold by the pound; for a small fee, visitors can pick their own blueberries or try their luck in the fish ponds, which are home to monster catfish, bass, and rainbow trout. Archie Batson also gives guided tours of his parents' cabin, which overlooks the property. Surrounded by carefully arranged pieces of petrified wood, the rustic cabin is packed to the rafters with antique farm tools and Indian artifacts collected at nearby Arrowhead Springs. A waterwheel below the cabin provides the home with fresh spring water.

Batson's is located off Highway 26, about three miles west of the Highway 49 intersection. To make reservations for group tours or check on the availability of aquaculture products, call (601) 928–5271.

PLACES TO STAY IN SOUTHERN MISSISSIPPI AND THE GULF COAST

The following is a partial listing of the many hotels, motels, and bed-and-breakfast inns in the area.

BAY ST. LOUIS

Bay Town Inn
(bed and breakfast),
208 North Beach
Boulevard;
(228) 466–5870

Casino Magic Inn,
711 Casino Magic Drive;
(228) 466–0891

Palm House
(bed and breakfast),
217 Union Street;
(228) 467–1665

BILOXI

Broadwater Beach Resort,
2110 Beach Boulevard;
(228) 388–2211

Comfort Inn Beach Resort,
1648 Beach Boulevard;
(228) 432–1993

The Father Ryan House
(bed and breakfast),
1196 Beach Boulevard;
(228) 435–1189

Grand Casino Biloxi Hotel,
245 Beach Boulevard;
(228) 432–2500

Isle of Capri Casino Crowne
Plaza Resort,
151 Beach Boulevard;
(228) 435–5400

Treasure Bay Casino Resort,
1980 Beach Boulevard;
(228) 385–6000

GULFPORT

Grand Casino
Gulfport Hotel,
Highway 90;
(228) 870–7777

Hampton Inn,
9445 Highway 49;
(228) 868–3300

HATTIESBURG

Comfort Inn,
6595 Highway 49;
(601) 268–2170

Dunhopen Inn
(bed and breakfast),
Highway 11;
(601) 543–0707

Fairfield Inn by Marriott,
173 Thorn Hill Drive;
(601) 296–7777

Hampton Inn,
6563 Highway 49 North;
(601) 264–8080

Tally House
(bed and breakfast),
402 Rebecca Avenue;
(601) 582–3467

LAUREL
The Fifth Street
Bed and Breakfast,
808 West Fifth Street;
(601) 649–5197

The Mourning Dove
(bed and breakfast),
556 North Sixth Avenue;
(601) 425–2561

LINCOLN LTD. BED & BREAKFAST RESERVATIONS
Lincoln Ltd. is a full-time reservation service for bed-and-breakfast inns statewide. For reservations in any area of Mississippi, call (800) 633–6477 or (601) 482–5483.

LONG BEACH
Red Creek Inn
(bed and breakfast),
7416 Red Creek Road;
(228) 452–3080

MAGNOLIA
The Coney House
(bed and breakfast),
204 South Clark Avenue;
(601) 783–3000

McCOMB
Comfort Inn,
107 Scott Drive;
(601) 249–0080

OCEAN SPRINGS
Shadowlawn
(bed and breakfast),
112A Shearwater Drive;
(228) 875–6945

Who's Inn?
(bed and breakfast),
623 Washington Avenue;
(228) 875–3251

PASS CHRISTIAN
Harbour Oaks Inn
(bed and breakfast),
126 West Scenic Drive;
(228) 452–9399

Inn at the Pass
(bed and breakfast),
125 East Scenic Drive;
(228) 452–0333

WOODVILLE
Desert Plantation
(bed and breakfast),
Pickneyville-Pond Road;
(601) 888–6188

Rosemont Plantation
(bed and breakfast),
Highway 24 East;
(601) 888–6809

Southern Gallery Inn
(bed and breakfast),
540 Highway 61 North;
(601) 888–6301

PLACES TO EAT IN SOUTHERN MISSISSIPPI AND THE GULF COAST

The following is a partial listing of the many restaurants in the area.

BAY ST. LOUIS
Casino Magic
(three restaurants),
711 Casino Magic Drive;
(800) 562–4425

Trapani's Eatery
(seafood, steak),
116 North Beach Boulevard;
(228) 467–8570

BILOXI
Mary Mahoney's Old
French House
(French, seafood),
138 Rue Magnolia;
(228) 374–0163

Biloxi's many casinos house dozens of restaurants offering casual dining, fine dining, all-you-can-eat buffets, and fast foods.

Major fast-food and dining chains.

COLLINS
Covington House Restaurant (steak, seafood),
Highway 49 North;
(601) 765–1684

Martha's Kitchen
(home cooking; groups of twelve or more only),
1462 Highway 532; (write to 1462 Highway 532, Mt. Olive 39119 for information and reservations.)

FOXWORTH
Leatha's Bar-B-Q-Inn,
Highway 98
East Underpass;
(601) 736–5163

GULFPORT
Copa Casino
(two restaurants),
777 Copa Boulevard;
(800) 946–2672

Grand Casino Gulfport
(seven restaurants),
3215 West Beach Boulevard;
(800) 946–7777

Blow Fly Inn
(steaks, seafood),
Washington Street;
(228) 896–9812

Vrazel's
(French, Italian, Cajun),
3206 West Beach Boulevard;
(228) 863–2229

Major fast-food and dining
chains

HATTIESBURG
Nanny's Country Kitchen
(country cooking,
plate specials),
907 Edwards Street;
(601) 583–1117

The Purple Parrot
(pasta, steak, seafood),
4640 Hardy Street;
(601) 264–0656

California Sandwich Shop
(deli sandwiches,
po' boys, chili),
217 East Front Street;
(601) 582–0726

Coney Island Lunch Stand
(po' boys, burgers),
400 Main Street;
(601) 582–8513

McAlister's Deli (specialty
sandwiches and salads),
2300 Hardy Street;
(601) 545–1876

Shelby's Coffee Company
(coffees, pastries),
631 North Main Street;
(601) 583–9600

Major fast-food and dining
chains

McCOMB
The Dinner Bell
(country cooking),
229 Fifth Avenue;
(601) 684–4883

OCEAN SPRINGS
Que' Pasa Coffee & More
(coffee, pastries),
1599 Bienville Boulevard
(Highway 90);
(228) 818–0440

The Bayview Gourmet
(breakfast, gourmet
sandwiches, coffee),
1210 Government Street;
(228) 875–4252

The Porter House
(seafood, steaks),
604 Porter Avenue;
(228) 875–3663

Fisherman's Wharf
(seafood),
1409 Bienville Boulevard
(Highway 90);
(228) 872–6111

Salvetti's Family
Italian Restaurant,
708 Washington Avenue;
(228) 875–0120

Anthony's Under the Oaks
(seafood, steak),
1217 Washington Avenue;
(228) 872–4564

Jocelyn's (seafood, steaks),
1608 Bienville Boulevard
(Highway 90);
(228) 875–1925

PICAYUNE
Paul's Pastry Shop
(Mardi Gras king cakes),
Highway 43 North;
(601) 798–7457

**OTHER ATTRACTIONS
WORTH SEEING IN
SOUTHERN MISSISSIPPI
AND THE GULF COAST**

BAY ST. LOUIS
Casino Magic

BILOXI
Boomtown Casino

Casino Magic

Grand Casino Biloxi

Imperial Palace Casino

Isle of Capri Casino

Lady Luck Casino

Palace Casino

President Casino

Treasure Bay Casino

GULFPORT
Copa Casino

Grand Casino Gulfport

Gulfport Factory Stores

HATTIESBURG
Hattiesburg Zoo

Index

INDEX

INDEX

INDEX

INDEX

About the Author

Marlo Carter Kirkpatrick is a freelance writer and resident of Madison, Mississippi, where she lives with her husband, photographer Stephen Kirkpatrick, and their dogs, Frosty and Icy.

Marlo writes travel and lifestyle articles promoting destinations throughout North and South America, as well as advertising and promotional materials for corporate clients in Mississippi and the southeastern United States. She has received more than seventy-five local, regional, and national awards for creative excellence.

Marlo was a contributing writer for *Jackson: The Good Life*. She and her husband are currently collaborating on a pictorial coffee-table book, a journey into the Peruvian Amazon entitled *Romancing the Rain*.

To Orlando —
Thank you for coming to the
book signing. It was a pleasure
meeting you.
Antoine Gnintedem

Doom, Gloom, and the Pursuit of the Sun

Antoine F. Gnintedem

ISBN: 1983421278

ISBN 13: 9781983421273

Library of Congress Control Number: 2018900115

CreateSpace Independent Publishing Platform

North Charleston, South Carolina